LANGUAGE AND STYLE SERIES

General Editor: STEPHEN ULLMANN

13

NORMAN PAGE

THE LANGUAGE
OF
JANE AUSTEN

BARNES & NOBLE BOOKS · NEW YORK
(a division of Harper & Row Publishers, Inc.)

Published in the U.S.A. 1972 by HARPER & ROW PUBLISHERS,
INC. BARNES & NOBLE IMPORT DIVISION

© Basil Blackwell, 1972

ISBN 06 4954501

TO MY FATHER AND MOTHER

Printed in Great Britain

REF
LIT

CONTENTS

	Author's Note	vii
	Introduction	1
1.	Style in Jane Austen's Novels	7
2.	'The Best Chosen Language'	54
3.	'Vision in Action': a Note on Syntax	90
4.	'Frequent Conversations'	114
5.	The Epistolary Art	168
6.	Conclusion	187
	Bibliography	198
	Index	205

P 18.50

AUTHOR'S NOTE

Part of Chapter 1 was originally published, in a slightly different form, in *Ariel*, and parts of Chapter 2 in *A Review of English Literature* and *Wascana Review*. I am grateful to the editors of these journals for permission to reprint material which appeared in their pages. The section on *Persuasion* in Chapter 4 was first published in the *Modern Language Review*, and is here reprinted by permission of the Modern Humanities Research Association and of the Editors.

All references to Jane Austen's novels and letters are to the editions of R. W. Chapman cited in the Bibliography. These editions, as Johnson says of Gray's *Elegy*, it is 'useless to praise', and everyone who studies Jane Austen seriously must be heavily indebted to them. In quoting from the fiction, the following abbreviations are used, followed by a figure or figures indicating the page number(s):

NA	*Northanger Abbey*
SS	*Sense and Sensibility*
PP	*Pride and Prejudice*
MP	*Mansfield Park*
E	*Emma*
P	*Persuasion*
MW	*Minor Works*

Similarly, *L* indicates Chapman's complete edition of the *Letters*. Four of the six novels (from *Sense and Sensibility* to *Emma* inclusive on the above list) were originally published in three-volume form, and Chapman retains the original chapter-numbering in his edition of these novels. To avoid the clumsiness of

frequent references by volume and chapter, and also for the sake
of readers who may have some other edition at hand, I have
preferred a consecutive system of chapter-numbering as in most
other editions; so that (for instance) Volume 2, Chapter 1 of
Pride and Prejudice is cited simply as Chapter 24. The following
conversion table may be useful: Roman figures refer to the
original volume-numbers, figures in square brackets to the continuous chapter-numbering found in most modern editions.

Sense and Sensibility
   (Chapman, Vol. 1)   I, Chs. 1–22
                                II, Chs. 1–14 [23–36]
                                III, Chs. 1–14 [37–50]

Pride and Prejudice
   (Chapman, Vol. 2)   I, Chs. 1–23
                                II, Chs. 1–19 [24–42]
                                III, Chs. 1–19 [43–61]

Mansfield Park
   (Chapman, Vol. 3)   I, Chs. 1–18
                                II, Chs. 1–13 [19–31]
                                III, Chs. 1–17 [32–48]

Emma
   (Chapman, Vol. 4)   I, Chs. 1–18
                                II, Chs. 1–18 [19–36]
                                III, Chs. 1–19 [37–55]

The remaining two novels, *Northanger Abbey* and *Persuasion*,
were published together, posthumously in 1818, in a four-volume
edition. The two volumes devoted to the former novel contain
respectively fifteen and sixteen chapters; the remaining two each
contain twelve chapters of *Persuasion*.

My many references to that indispensable tool of all writers on
language, the *Oxford English Dictionary*, are by the initials OED.
In references to books in the footnotes and bibliography, the place
of publication is London unless otherwise stated.

INTRODUCTION

Jane Austen's six short novels, with a volume of letters and a handful of juvenilia and fragments, have given rise to a stream of critical commentary which, starting quietly enough in her own lifetime and hardly increasing in the course of the nineteenth century, has in our own generation swollen to a mighty torrent. At times, indeed, its rushing and roaring threatens to drown the author's own voice; and it may well be wondered whether there is just cause for yet another full-length study of the modest *oeuvre* of this novelist, whom Ian Watt has aptly described as 'the most lucid and the least recondite of authors'.[1] The justification of the present study must be that, rather than offering an 'interpretation' of the novels which claims to find new answers to familiar questions, it sets out to explore an area of her work that seems to be of indubitable importance and interest, yet which has, with only a very few exceptions, been generally neglected. This neglect has, of course, been only one example of an indifference, until very recently almost total, to the language of fiction. Or, when the attitude in question has not been one of indifference, there has been a basic uncertainty about the susceptibility of the material to analysis. The last few years, however, have seen a welcome and long overdue enlargement of stylistic horizons to include the English novel, and it is now more widely accepted that the language of a novelist is an aspect of his work that may reward serious and close attention. More than this, style-study, so far from being (in Graham Hough's phrase) merely concerned with 'the icing on the cake',[2] is capable of taking us quickly to the

[1] I. Watt (ed.), *Jane Austen: a Collection of Critical Essays* (Englewood Cliffs, New Jersey, 1963) 1.

[2] G. Hough, *Style and Stylistics* (1969) 39.

heart of some of the fundamental issues raised by a great writer's work. Nevertheless, it remains true that, even without going beyond the major English novelists, much remains to be done in this field.[3]

This book has originated in the conviction that style is a component of exceptional importance in Jane Austen's work, and that it is only through an unremitting alertness to her language in action that her meaning can be fully understood—both, that is, the local meaning of the text, and the wider meaning of the novels as statements about human experience. Such an approach is not offered, it is perhaps necessary to say, as a substitute for others which may be more familiar; but it can be argued to be an essential complement to other scholarly and critical procedures. At best, stylistic stud; provides a fresh means of access to well-known texts, and at many points brings the reader directly into contact with the author's intentions as conveyed by his language, with a sense of discovery and of closeness to the original purpose that other approaches do not always provide.

My debts to other writers on Jane Austen are recorded in the footnotes and the bibliography, but two previous studies call for special mention. Mary Lascelles' *Jane Austen and her Art*, first published in 1939, is one of the earliest and still one of the best of the full-length discussions; I have found her short chapter on 'Style' unusually fertile in suggestions and insights. Howard S. Babb's *Jane Austen's Novels: The Fabric of Dialogue* (1962) is, at the time of writing, the only attempt to examine Jane Austen's language at length.[4] Although the scope and methods of his study

[3] For details of some examples of the stylistic analysis of English fiction, see L. Milic, *Style and Stylistics: an Analytical Bibliography* (New York, 1967); R. W. Bailey and D. M. Burton, *English Stylistics: a Bibliography* (Cambridge, Mass., 1968). There are also useful bibliographies in H. C. Martin (ed.), *Style in Prose Fiction* (New York, 1959), and W. C. Booth, *The Rhetoric of Fiction* (Chicago, 1961).

[4] K. C. Phillipps' *Jane Austen's English* (1970) appeared after the completion of the present book. An even more recent stylistic study, based upon an elaborate computer analysis of her work, is contained in Karl Kroeber's *Styles in Fictional Structure: the Art of Jane Austen. Charlotte Brontë, George Eliot* (Princeton, 1971).

are different from my own, I have often found myself reaching similar conclusions to Professor Babb in spite of travelling by another route. In particular, I am indebted to the penetrating observations on the general characteristics of Jane Austen's style in his opening chapter.

A word should be added on the chronology of the novels—an important matter for the student of a style, but a very vexed question in Jane Austen's case, greatly complicated both by the virtually complete absence of manuscript material and by her apparent practice of having more than one piece of work in hand at a time, and of returning to an earlier draft after a long interval, and sometimes more than once, to make often radical revisions. Speculation about her methods and her artistic development must, in these circumstances, be necessarily somewhat tentative. Since her career as a published author covers less than six years, whereas she was writing for more like thirty, dates of publications are of little significance. It would be rash to suggest that the following chronological table has any claim to be other than approximate in some of its details, but although there is plenty of room for argument (notably over some of the datings) the broad pattern is perhaps generally accepted. Much of the information is given in Cassandra Austen's memorandum, probably written soon after her sister's death, and reproduced in Chapman's edition of the *Minor Works* (facing p. 242; but see also the article by C. S. Emden listed in my bibliography). There is a useful discussion of chronological problems in B. C. Southam's *Jane Austen's Literary Manuscripts*, which rejects Q. D. Leavis's influential theory that *Mansfield Park* and *Emma* represent later reworkings of, respectively, *Lady Susan* and *The Watsons*.[5]

[5] The relevant articles by Q. D. Leavis appeared in *Scrutiny* in 1941. (See bibliography.) Their conclusions are cogently refuted by Southam in 'Mrs Leavis and Miss Austen: the "Critical Theory" Reconsidered', *Nineteenth Century Fiction*, 17 (1962) 21–32.

CHRONOLOGY OF JANE AUSTEN'S WORKING LIFE

1775   Jane Austen born at Steventon, Hampshire on 16 December.

c. 1787–93   Juvenilia written. (Later published as *Volume the First*, *Volume the Second*, *Volume the Third*; the second of these has also been published under the title *Love and Freindship*).

? 1793 or 1794   *Lady Susan* written.

1796 (or earlier)   *Elinor and Marianne*, an epistolary novel, written and read to the Austen family; later rewritten and published as *Sense and Sensibility* (see below).

1797   *First Impressions* completed. (This was revised between 1809 and 1812, probably very extensively, and eventually published as *Pride and Prejudice*; see below). Revision of *Elinor and Marianne* begun.

1798–9   *Susan* written (later revised, under the new title *Catherine*, and eventually published as *Northanger Abbey*; see below).

1801   Jane Austen and her family move to Bath.

1803   A rewritten version of *Susan* is sold to a publisher, but not published.

1804   *The Watsons* begun (remained uncompleted).

1806   Jane Austen moves to Clifton, then to Southampton.

1808   Jane Austen moves to Chawton Cottage, Hampshire.

1809–10   *Sense and Sensibility* revised. Revision of *First Impressions* begun.

1811   *Mansfield Park* begun, 'somewhere about February' according to Cassandra Austen. *Sense and Sensibility* published in

November (all Jane Austen novels were published anonymously).

1812   *Pride and Prejudice* sold to a publisher in November.

1813   *Pride and Prejudice* published in January; a second edition followed in November. *Mansfield Park* completed in June.

1814   *Emma* begun, on 21 January, according to Cassandra Austen. *Mansfield Park* published in May.

1815   *Emma* completed in March, and published in December (the title page is dated 1816). *Persuasion* begun on 8 August, according to Cassandra Austen.

1816   Original ending to *Persuasion* (the cancelled chapters) written in July; the novel completed in August. Revision of *Susan* (as *Catherine*) begun. *Plan of a Novel* written.

1817   Between January and March, fragment of *Sanditon* written. Jane Austen dies in Winchester on 18 July. *Northanger Abbey* and *Persuasion* published in December (dated 1818).

CHAPTER ONE

STYLE IN JANE AUSTEN'S NOVELS

Confronted with Jane Austen's novels, the reader is made repeatedly and perhaps disconcertingly aware of a disparity between subject-matter and significance. A heroine is involved, it may be, in committing herself to a line of conduct in relation to some issue trivial enough in itself—or so, at least, it is apt to seem. Catherine Morland declines an invitation to join the Thorpes on a pleasure jaunt; Elizabeth Bennet gets her feet wet in visiting her sick sister; Fanny Price resists her cousins' attempts to involve her in amateur theatricals. Examples might be multiplied many times; and, on each occasion, the sense of momentous implications, of profound moral overtones, is unmistakable. One feels that crucial revelations hang upon these trifling matters. Saintsbury recognized this nearly sixty years ago when he observed, of *Emma*, that whilst the novel represents 'the absolute triumph of that reliance on the strictly ordinary', at the same time 'every event, every circumstance, every detail, is put *sub specie eternitatis* by the sorcery of art'.[1] Now a preoccupation with 'the strictly ordinary' is perhaps no more than might be expected of a realistic novelist who was also a woman with a strong affection for family life, and who could write, in the same novel, of 'all those little matters on which the daily happiness of private life depends'. All this may sound like putting an argument into the hands of the depreciators. The individual and the local may seem to impose severe, even fatal, limitations, and the 'strictly ordinary' can quickly become synonymous with the unimportant.

[1] G. Saintsbury, *The English Novel* (1913) 198.

(One recalls that J. H. Newman complained of *Emma* that 'The action is frittered away in over-little things'.[2]) Saintsbury's phrase 'the sorcery of art' provides a retort without taking us very far.

This disparity between surface and content, between apparent narrowness and shallowness and actual comprehensiveness and profundity, is of course a commonplace of Jane Austen criticism. It is paralleled by an exceptional range of evaluations of her status as a novelist, from those who find in her only a snobbish parochialism (and this group includes her fellow-novelists Mark Twain and D. H. Lawrence) to those who regard her as a major writer and a profound moralist. Her critics, and particularly her recent critics, have sought to account for the contradictory natures of the appearance and the reality in a variety of ways. One of the most familiar resolutions of the problem is in terms of her ironic sense, discussed by critics from Richard Simpson (1870) to D. W. Harding (1940) and Marvin Mudrick (1952). Other attempts to reconcile the contradiction have stressed the psychological or mythopoeic dimensions of her work, the way in which her domestic stories acquire deeper meaning through the suggestion of basic or archetypal situations. In the technique of the novel, she has been claimed as a precursor of James (a critical position curiously anticipated by the Cockney in Kipling's *The Janeites*), and, in her use of symbolism, has been compared to Kafka. Nor has the fact that she died before either Marx or Freud was born deterred others from detecting Marxist and Freudian elements in her work.[3]

[2] Quoted by C. B. Hogan, 'Jane Austen and her Early Public', *Review of English Studies*, 1 (1950) 51. The comment occurs in a letter of Newman's written in 1837.

[3] On the history of Jane Austen's reputation, see J. Cady and I. Watt, 'Jane Austen's Critics', *The Critical Quarterly*, 5 (1963) 49–63; Ian Watt's editorial introduction to *Jane Austen: a Collection of Critical Essays* (New Jersey, 1963) 1–14; N. Page, 'A Short Guide to Jane Austen Studies', *The Critical Survey*, 3 (1968) 230–34. B. C. Southam, *Jane Austen: the Critical Heritage* (1968) is a useful collection of material covering the period 1812–70.

The emphasis of the present study, however, is placed some-what differently. It will be argued that the 'triumph' of the novels is to a large extent a triumph of style, and that the fact that they constantly transcend the level of cultivated gossip or conventional story-telling is to be explained partly in terms of certain qualities of language. The achievement was not only one of individual genius, of course. Short of pastiche, a writer can use only the resources made available to him by the language of his day; and part of Jane Austen's greatness lay in exploiting the distinctive strengths of the English language as she found it, and in resisting some of the influences which were at work to change it even as she wrote. At the same time she was an innovator too, notably in prose syntax and in narrative modes. If we take into account the difference between her subject-matter (that is, her apparent field of interest) and the inner meaning of her novels as signalled, very largely, by the particular features of their language, we can begin to understand the contradictory judgments which have been passed upon them. For those who see only the surface—the morning visit and the ball, the dinner party and the picnic—her work suffers from damaging limitations; on the other hand, her power to suggest, through her style, the major issues inherent in minor incidents justifies F. R. Leavis's claim to find in her an 'intense moral preoccupation'.[4]

To return to the point from which this chapter started: how is this sense of the far-reaching importance of the local and the ephemeral conveyed? Largely, it will be suggested, by stylistic means: it is Jane Austen's finely-controlled use of language which brings to the reader's attention the true import of episodes and conversations apparently slight in themselves. Not that the task of recovering her meaning fully and accurately is always an easy one, involving as it does a willingness to accept her linguistic resources—resources both narrower in range and more sharp-edged in quality than our own—at her valuation. Certainly her achievement as a stylist has not been generally recognized,

[4] F. R. Leavis, *The Great Tradition* (1948) 7.

B

perhaps because individuality of style has often been equated with eccentricity. To some extent this has been part of a widespread indifference to the language of fiction, a neglect to which there were until very recently only a few exceptions. Even that arch-Austenite R. W. Chapman doubted whether she 'was conscious of having a style of her own. Outside her dialogue it is not highly individual; it is just the ordinary correct English that, as Johnson had said, "everyone now writes".'[5] There is a half-truth in this statement, for admittedly Jane Austen is not a stylist in the not yet extinct sense of being highly idiosyncratic, as are (to give instances at random) Lamb and Carlyle and even her favourite Dr Johnson. Her language does not habitually draw attention to itself: her attitude to style is too critical to permit 'fine writing', and her satirical sense too strong to permit elaborate effects. What is in question often involves no more than the use of an unexpected word or phrase, or a temporary departure from normal syntax. But a concept of style which permits us even to observe of a writer that 'he has no style' is excessively narrow and takes into account only the most insistent features. The proper retort to Chapman's comment is that Jane Austen's English was in fact written not by everyone but by none but herself. Reading her predecessors and contemporaries in the novel—Fanny Burney and Mrs Radcliffe, Maria Edgeworth and Mrs Inchbald—one is struck first by the stylistic elements they have in common with Jane Austen, and next by the subtle but important differences. There is a sense in which they share a common idiom, and especially a common vocabulary; but it remains equally true that a passage from any other writer could not be attributed to her. For her prose is generally of unusual distinction, an instrument both firm and flexible; and the variety of her effects is much wider than is often assumed. Many comments on her style, indeed, seem to be based on a recollection that leaves many passages of her prose out of account.

To take a single example: she is traditionally regarded as an

5 R. W. Chapman, *Jane Austen: Facts and Problems* (Oxford, 1948) 209.

anti-Romantic, a chronological anomaly standing perhaps somewhat timidly aside from the mainstream of the literary move-
ments of her time. Such a verdict ignores many short but striking
passages in her novels which reveal both a sensitive response to the
beauty of landscape and a skill in conveying such feelings in
language. It is true that, although she was a contemporary of
Wordsworth, Coleridge and Scott, when she uses the word
romantic it is most often in the eighteenth-century sense of
'extravagant' or 'foolishly unrealistic'. Yet what could be
more romantic, in the Wordsworthian sense, than her description of the coastal scenery of the Lyme Regis district in *Persuasion*?

. . . a very strange stranger it must be, who does not see charms in
the immediate environs of Lyme, to make him wish to know it
better. The scenes in its neighbourhood, Charmouth, with its high
grounds and extensive sweeps of country, and still more its sweet
retired bay, backed by dark cliffs, where fragments of low rock
among the sands make it the happiest spot for watching the flow
of the tide, for sitting in unwearied contemplation;—the woody
varieties of the cheerful village of Up Lyme, and, above all, Pinny,
with its green chasms between romantic rocks, where the scattered
forest trees and orchards of luxuriant growth declare that many a
generation must have passed away since the first partial falling of
the cliff prepared the ground for such a state, where a scene so
wonderful and so lovely is exhibited, as may more than equal any
of the resembling scenes of the far-famed Isle of Wight: these
places must be visited, and visited again, to make the worth of
Lyme understood. (*P*, 95–6)

Some of the ideas of this passage are remarkably similar to those
of the earlier Romantic poets: the sense of the passing of time,
the taste for seclusion and for 'sitting in unwearied contemplation',
the stress on first-hand experience and on the value of revisiting
a scene, are essentially Wordsworthian. Furthermore, the language is in places close to that of Romantic poetry: not only the
phrase 'unwearied contemplation', which might have come
straight from the *Lyrical Ballads*, but the epithets *sweet*,

wonderful, lovely, and the description of 'green chasms between romantic rocks' with its striking echo of Coleridge's *Kubla Khan.*[6] A novelist who can write like this, as well as with cool analysis and epigrammatic wit, can hardly be justly accused of narrowness of style or sensibility.

All of which seems sufficient justification for embarking on a detailed exploration of certain aspects of her language. The present study does not pretend to say the last word about Jane Austen's style: since, like all great writers, she has not one style but many, this would in any case be hardly possible. But it sets out to investigate the words she uses, particularly the staple items of her vocabulary through which she assesses character and motive—those nouns and epithets which indicate some basic aspects of human nature and human behaviour, and of which many recur so strikingly both within a given novel and within her work as a whole. After a brief consideration of the syntax of her prose, it turns to her use of dialogue: both the linguistic techniques of its presentation and the use of speech to reveal character. A short chapter on letter-writing is followed by a conclusion which attempts to define the peculiar quality of her style by setting it in relationship to some of her predecessors and successors in the English novel. My aim has been not so much to use the novels as a quarry for linguistic or philological material, however intrinsically fascinating, as to endeavour to reach a deeper understanding of their meaning and artistry as works of literature, and to suggest that it may be not only appropriate but also often illuminating to approach them through a study of their style, as a complement to more traditional methods. It goes without saying that there are other novelists for whom a similar approach is possible and rewarding.

Not only are the novels of Jane Austen written *in* language of conscious precision and exceptional subtlety: the early novels in particular are to a striking extent *about* language, in that the use

[6] Cf. A Hayter, 'Xanadu at Lyme Regis', *Ariel*, 1 (1970) 61–4; A. W. Litz, *Jane Austen: a Study of her Artistic Development* (New York, 1965) 153.

and abuse of words is a frequently recurring theme. Style looks inward upon itself: not only does the authorial voice draw the reader's attention to linguistic issues, but some of the characters observe themselves, and each other, in the act of using language. In the later novels the interest is less overt—the concern with language now being implicit in the variety and originality of the methods through which character and situation are presented— but Jane Austen is still in the habit of stressing the attitudes to language held by Mr Knightley or Mary Crawford. An account of some aspects of the role of language in the juvenile writings and the six major novels will, therefore, form an appropriate introduction to the more detailed and specialized discussion of the chapters that follow. What is offered in the rest of this chapter is in no sense an attempt at full-dress appreciations or interpretations of these works: a task that is beyond the scope of this book, and also one that has often been undertaken at length, and will no doubt be returned to by fresh generations of critics. My concern at this stage must be to single out, and briefly to identify and illustrate, some leading features of the language of Jane Austen's fiction, and to suggest in the process that each book possesses certain distinctive linguistic qualities which help to determine its particular nature and effects. Inevitably many questions will be raised at this point for which fuller consideration must be deferred to a later chapter.

The juvenilia occupy a substantial portion of the volume in Chapman's fine edition which is devoted to her minor writings: the Brontës apart, probably no other major English novelist provides us with a similar opportunity to study the early development of attitudes which find fuller expression in the work intended for publication. They are, in the main, more openly satirical and parodic in intention than the later writings; although the latter certainly retain something of the same spirit, it is not manifested with the exuberance and the delighted exaggeration of *Love and Freindship* or the short tales in *Volume the First*. There is, as might be expected, a difference in stylistic qualities which corresponds to this, the early writings showing a marked fondness for devices which become much more infrequent in the later work. Some of these devices are:

(a) *puns*, as when a domestically-minded character in *Lesley Castle* observes, of a more artistically-minded sister, ' "She loved drawing Pictures, and I drawing Pullets." ' (*MW*, 129)

(b) *zeugma*: in the same work an erring wife is described as departing 'in company with Danvers and dishonour'. (*MW*, 111)

(c) comic *alliteration*, already illustrated twice. Elsewhere, a heroine speaks of being 'celebrated both in Public, in Private, in Papers, and in Printshops' (*MW*, 136), and a more extreme example is the dedication of *A Collection of Letters* (*MW*, 150).

(d) comic *similes*: one character is 'as White as a Whipt syllabub), another 'as cool as a cream-cheese'. (*MW*, 113, 130)

(e) the use of *French words and phrases* current in fashionable society: *bon-mot, éclaircissement, éclat, entrée*, etc.

(f) parody of Johnsonian *syntax*, in such balanced sentences as ' "Beware of the unmeaning Luxuries of Bath and of the stinking fish of Southampton." ' (*MW*, 79)

(g) the frequent use of *colloquial words and idioms*: two tall girls are described as 'such tremendous knock-me-down figures', one young lady tells another to 'set her cap at' a young man; a dance is a 'hop', and so on. (*MW*, 127, 122, 158)

The author's keen sense of the absurd encourages a linguistic adventurousness that was to be very largely suppressed in the more fundamentally serious productions of later years, in which her awareness of the comic possibilities of language finds an outlet mainly in the speech of the foolish and the vulgar. An important consideration is that these early stories and sketches were written not for publication but for private consumption within the family circle; in later years, the letters were to retain many traces of the linguistic high spirits that could not be admitted into the fiction except upon special conditions. The normal decorum of her novelistic style permits departures from accepted standards to serve well-defined purposes: to indicate a particular kind of speaker, for example, or sometimes to mark a moment of special intensity. Thus, remembering Johnson's dictum that 'good prose should be native in character', Jane Austen reserves continental importations for the speech of the vulgar and the pretentious: they are fit for a Mrs Elton but not for an Emma Woodhouse.

In *Northanger Abbey*, the parodic spirit persists in the burlesque of the Gothic novel. Indeed, according to F. W. Bradbrook, all the first three novels 'tend towards parody, burlesque and antithesis'.[7] (In the spirit of this comment, the treatment here is in the likely order of composition, not of publication.) One might observe that parody is an activity in which a high degree of verbal self-consciousness is generally present. Recalling this, one feels that it is surely no accident that *Northanger Abbey* begins and ends with statements that are deliberately ambiguous:

No one who had ever seen Catherine Morland in her infancy, would have supposed her born to be an heroine . . . (*NA*, 13)
. . . I leave it to be settled by whomsoever it may concern, whether the tendency of this work be altogether to recommend parental tyranny, or reward filial disobedience. (*NA*, 252)

At the outset, Catherine's status as heroine is equivocal: does that opening sentence mean that she proved a heroine in spite of early appearances to the contrary, or that of course there was never any question of her becoming a heroine? And, at the conclusion, the moral of the story is presented as a joke upon fictional didacticism, the two alternatives offered being equally absurd. Even the novelist's attitude to the reader is ambiguous: is the latter the sharer in, or the victim of, this gentle mockery? Conventional expectations are skilfully disappointed: the appearance of a familiar word such as 'heroine', or of a novelistic cliché such as 'the tendency of this work . . . to recommend . . .' first arouses certain assumptions and then calls for reinterpretation, since they clearly cannot be taken at their face value.

[7] F. W. Bradbrook, 'Style and Judgement in Jane Austen's Novels', *Cambridge Journal*, 4 (1951) 535.

Between this opening and close there occur many instances of ambiguity of various kinds. Sometimes the confusion is lexical, turning on the intrinsic capacity of words to mislead. There is a good example of this in Chapter 14, when the naïve Catherine observes to Henry Tilney and his sister, 'in rather a solemn tone of voice', ' "I have heard that something very shocking indeed, will soon come out in London." ' (*NA*, 112.) Miss Tilney and Catherine talk at some length, each in ignorance of the other's meaning, until Henry Tilney, who has grasped the nature of the misunderstanding, intervenes:

Miss Tilney . . . hastily replied, 'Indeed!—and of what nature?'
'That I do not know, nor who is the author. I have only heard that it is to be more horrible than any thing we have met with yet.'
'Good heaven!—Where could you hear of such a thing?'
'A particular friend of mine had an account of it in a letter from London yesterday. It is to be uncommonly dreadful. I shall expect murder and every thing of the kind.'
'You speak with astonishing composure! But I hope your friend's accounts have been exaggerated;—and if such a design is known beforehand, proper measures will undoubtedly be taken by government to prevent its coming to effect.'
'Government', said Henry, endeavouring not to smile, 'neither desires nor dares to interfere in such matters. There must be murder; and government cares not how much.'

The key-words in this dialogue are each capable of more than one interpretation: *come out* (be perpetrated, be published), *author* (perpetrator, writer), *murder* (in fact and in fiction); and the words which Catherine readily applies to her favourite reading—*shocking, horrible, dreadful*—are given a different valuation by Miss Tilney. Tilney contrives to continue the conversation in calculatedly ambiguous terms (' "There must be murder . . ." '),and it is not until his sister exclaims ' ". . . have the goodness to satisfy me as to this dreadful riot" ', that the misunderstanding becomes generally evident. *Riot*, which collocates naturally enough with *murder* in reference to a real life outrage, refuses to fit into the pattern of allusions to Gothic fiction which Catherine has had in mind, and with this word the line of ambiguity is broken—though Tilney characteristically continues by punning on *riot*: ' "My dear Eleanor, the riot is only in your own brain. The confusion there is scandalous." ' Such a passage is, of course, no mere verbal *tour de force* but an illustration, very pertinent to the central theme of the novel, of the confusions arising when the make-believe of fiction is mistaken for reality. It is, indeed, a foreshadowing of the more extensive misinterpretations of Catherine when she visits Northanger Abbey.

An earlier example occurs at the beginning of the second chapter, when the agitation of the heroine's mother of popular fiction is ironically contrasted with the placid commonsense of Mrs Morland in bidding her daughter farewell: the paragraph in question arouses expectations only in order to disappoint them, but when the precise wording of the earlier part is examined, it is again seen to be ambiguous:

When the hour of departure drew near, the maternal anxiety of Mrs Morland will be naturally supposed to be most severe. A thousand alarming presentiments of evil to her beloved Catherine from this terrific separation must oppress her heart with sadness, and drown her in tears for the last day or two of their being together; and advice of the most important and applicable nature must of course flow from her wise lips in their parting conference in her closet . . . (*NA*, 18–19)

In the event, Mrs Morland's actual behaviour is bathetic—she warns her daughter against catching cold, and advises her to keep a note of what she spends—and the reader conversant with Jane Austen's methods has already been alerted to her ironic intent by the inflated language ('alarming presentiments of evil', 'terrific separation'). A good deal of the ambiguity stems from the verb-forms: *will be . . . supposed, must oppress, must . . . flow*. These seem, but only seem, to carry the force of inevitability; yet *must* can mean 'will be conventionally expected to' as well as 'actually is compelled to': for the moment the ambiguity remains open. Here the deception is not between one character and another, but between author and reader, as it is again when Catherine penetrates to the forbidden regions of the Abbey:

On tip-toe she entered; the room was before her; but it was some minutes before she could advance another step. She beheld what fixed her to the spot and agitated every feature.—

This sounds like a reasonable account of a maiden's emotions on entering Bluebeard's chamber; but astonishment and agitation are ambiguous emotions, as the words which follow plainly show:

She saw a large, well-proportioned apartment, an handsome dimity bed, arranged as unoccupied with an housemaid's care, a bright Bath stove, mahogany wardrobes and neatly-painted chairs, on which the warm beams of a western sun gaily poured through two sash windows! (*NA*, 193)

We now understand that Catherine's emotion has been caused not by the horror of what she sees before her (a horror that the previous pages have encouraged the reader to expect) but by its extreme ordinariness, and her consequent shame at her error. The point is underlined a moment later: 'Catherine had expected to have her feelings worked, and worked they were'. Here, the deception and enlightenment of the reader parallel the experience of the heroine.

A somewhat different kind of effect is produced by passages in which reason is shown to be unreason: what appears to Catherine, in her immaturity, to be logic is in fact highly illogical. At the opening of the second volume, she reflects on General Tilney: 'That he was perfectly agreeable and good-natured, and altogether a very charming man, did not admit of a doubt, for he was tall and handsome, and Henry's father.' (*NA*, 129) Later, her suspicions of the General lead her to distrust the truth of his language as publicly displayed on a church monument to his dead wife: '. . . the perusal of the highly-strained epitaph, in which every virtue was ascribed to her by the inconsolable husband, who must have been in some way or other her destroyer, affected her even to tears'. (*NA*, 190) As it happens, Catherine

is still wrong, though the language of the epitaph (which recalls
Dr Johnson's pronouncement on lapidary inscriptions) probably
justifies her distrust. Once again, words are shown as not always
meaning what they say.

The use of ambiguity in different forms, then, is a marked
feature of the style of *Northanger Abbey*—not surprisingly, in a
novel which sets out to show that things are not necessarily what
they seem. A related stylistic feature is the use, already illustrated
and particularly notable when the satire on the Gothic novel is
most prominent, of language which is of a strength strikingly in
excess of the subject treated. Thus, when Catherine is let down
by her dancing-partner, the author comments:

> To be *disgraced* in the eye of the world, to wear the appearance of
> *infamy* while her heart is all *purity*, her actions all *innocence*, and
> the *misconduct* of another the true source of her *debasement*, is one
> of those circumstances which peculiarly belong to the heroine's
> life, and her *fortitude* under it what particularly *dignifies* her
> character. (*NA*, 53; my italics)

The irony here derives from the disparity between the words used
(some of the stock terms of eighteenth-century reflective prose)
and their referents; its target is the scale of values which belongs
to the heroine's inexperience. Elsewhere, the ironic intention may
be signalled by repetition. When Catherine asks Maria Thorpe
'for some particulars of their yesterday's party', she learns 'that
it had been altogether the most delightful scheme in the world;
that nobody could imagine how charming it had been, and that
it had been more delightful than anybody could conceive'. (*NA*,
116) 'Such', is the ensuing comment, 'was the information of the
first five minutes'; and clearly Maria's epithets are no more to be
taken at their face value than the ironic *information*. The linguistic device serves as a completely adequate comment on
Maria Thorpe's character.

Other aspects of the style of *Northanger Abbey* will be touched
upon in later chapters. This general discussion should not be
concluded, however, without reference to the value placed upon

verbal precision by the novel's hero. Henry Tilney shares his
creator's serious concern for keeping up the language as well as
her delight in linguistic folly: his sister says of him that 'He is
for ever finding fault with me, for some incorrectness of language',
and he is prompt to react to the thoughtless exaggerations and
imprecisions of female conversation. Apart from his well-known
strictures on Catherine's use of the word *nice*, he also takes her
up on *amazingly* and *faithfully*. (*NA*, 107–8, 195–6) Catherine,
as many passages show, is easily deceived not least because
she is unaware of the normal insincerities of polite speech. One of
the key-passages of the novel expresses her puzzlement over
General Tilney's inconsistency: '. . . why he should say one thing
so positively, and mean another all the while, was most un-
accountable! How were people, at that rate, to be understood?'
(*NA*, 211) Henry Tilney represents verbal maturity and awareness as Catherine does immaturity.

Precision, and the lack of it, in using language are also among
the recurring themes of *Sense and Sensibility*, which evinces an
alert interest in language as an aspect of social behaviour and,
more particularly, as a clue to the strengths and frailties of human
character. The recording of the use and abuse of language by the
various characters in that novel resembles the line traced by a
sensitive instrument: even minor deviations from the norm of
what is deemed acceptable serve to betray the presence of disturb-
ing elements. In the third chapter, Elinor and her mother dis-
cuss Edward Ferrars:

'It is enough,' said she; 'to say that he is unlike Fanny is
enough. It implies everything amiable. I love him already.'
'I think you will like him,' said Elinor, 'when you know more
of him.'
'Like him!' replied her mother, with a smile. 'I can feel no senti-
ment of approbation inferior to love.'
'You may esteem him.'
'I have never yet known what it was to separate esteem and love.'
(*SS*, 16)

What Mrs Dashwood, in the last remark quoted, boasts as a virtue, her creator plainly regards as evidence of moral confusion. Mrs Dashwood is not prepared to make a distinction between terms (*like, love, esteem*) that for her daughter (as for the novelist) represent important differences of feeling and imply appropriate differences of behaviour. The conversation is echoed a few pages later, when Elinor uses similar terms in discussing Edward with her sister:

'I do not attempt to deny,' said she, 'that I think very highly of him—that I greatly esteem, that I like him.'
Marianne here burst forth with indignation—
'Esteem him! Like him! Cold-hearted Elinor! Oh! worse than cold-hearted! Ashamed of being otherwise. Use those words again and I will leave the room this moment!' (*SS*, 21)

This, Jane Austen seems to imply, is the very ecstasy of misplaced enthusiasm. Marianne is evidently her mother's daughter, and her passionate rejection of words suggesting anything less than intense emotion prepares us for the misjudgments that she makes later in the novel. Indifference to verbal discriminations is a token of disregard for other, non-verbal conventions that is to have far-reaching consequences.

Another kind of linguistic shortcoming is illustrated when Sir John Middleton tells Marianne what he knows of Willoughby:

'And what sort of a young man is he?'
'As good a kind of fellow as ever lived, I assure you. A very decent shot, and there is not a bolder rider in England.'
'And is *that* all you can say for him?' cried Marianne indignantly. 'But what are his manners on more intimate acquaintance? What his pursuits, his talents and genius?'
Sir John was rather puzzled.
'Upon my soul,' said he, 'I do not know much about him as to all *that*. But he is a pleasant, good humoured fellow, and has got the nicest little black bitch of a pointer I ever saw. Was she out with him to-day?' (*SS*, 43–4)

In an almost literal sense, Sir John and Marianne do not speak the same language: the former sees Willoughby not in the abstract terms of *manners*, *talents* and *genius*—his practical man's contempt for 'all *that*' is obvious—but in the physical terms of his shooting, his riding, and his gun-dog. His language reflects the limited nature of his perceptions, and his initial use of the epithet *good* is quickly devalued by what follows: the reader is made aware that Sir John is no judge of any kind of goodness that really matters. When he does attempt to describe character rather than behaviour, he slips into the ready-made phrases of gossip, as when he describes the Miss Steeles as 'the sweetest girls in the world', and a few lines later tells the Miss Dashwoods that they are 'the most beautiful creatures in the world'—praise that cuts no ice with Elinor, who 'well knew that the sweetest girls in the world were to be met with in every part of England, under every possible variation of form, face, temper, and under-standing'. (*SS*, 119)

Such careless use of language is more than a linguistic offence: it is a deeply-rooted sign of moral confusion, just as the vul-garisms of a Lucy Steele are an offence against decorum and civilized behaviour. Against these is set the author's own con-cern with defining and refining the ethical vocabulary through which her judgments are conveyed. We may take as an example the key-concepts of the neatly antithetical title. Marianne's early reactions to Willoughby are presented in a manner which stresses their disproportionate quality, and which recalls the satire of *Northanger Abbey*: when he leaves unexpectedly, we read of 'that violent sorrow which Marianne was in all probability not merely giving way to as a relief, but feeding and encouraging as a duty', and the absurdity of the word *duty* in this context brings home to us the folly of her conduct. Later we read of her 'in-dulgence of feeling', and again of her 'excessive affliction', and such phrases serve to give substance to the abstraction *sensibility* as Jane Austen understands it. It is also, of course, defined by its opposite: Elinor's behaviour translates *sense* from a concept to a living reality. It is put to the test when she tells her sister of her disappointment over Edward Ferrars: the emotional ordeal is now Elinor's, but the violent emotions are still displayed by Marianne:

Her narration was clear and simple; and though it could not be given without emotion, it was not accompanied by violent agitation, nor impetuous grief.—*That* belonged rather to the hearer, for Marianne listened with horror, and cried excessively. Elinor was to be the comforter of others in her own distresses, no less than in theirs . . . (*SS*, 261)

Edward himself, though his role as the true hero of the novel is not at first made clear, has an authentic Austen hero's concern with the purity of the language, and in at least one speech he can claim kinship with Henry Tilney. In Chapter 18, he discusses the beauty of a landscape with Marianne, and repudiates all knowledge of 'the picturesque' (the word, thus used, is dated 1794 by the *OED*, and must have had much of the gloss of newness upon it when this passage was written): he tells her ' "I shall call hills steep, which ought to be bold; surfaces strange and uncouth, which ought to be irregular and rugged; and distant objects out of sight, which ought only to be indistinct through the soft medium of a hazy atmosphere . . ." ' And a few lines later, he adds: ' "I like a fine prospect, but not on picturesque principles. I do not like crooked, twisted, blasted trees. I admire them much more if they are tall, straight, and flourishing. I do not like ruined, tattered cottages. I am not fond of nettles, or thistles, or heath blossoms . . ." ' The specific satire of this passage is less important than its general bearing, which is unmistakably in the direction of plain, unaffected, unexaggerated language. In this novel, then, we see prudence ranged against folly, and each revealed to a large extent by the use and abuse of language: Elinor and Edward provide models of restraint and decorum, whilst a more numerous group of characters—Marianne, Mrs Dashwood, Willoughby, Sir John, Lucy Steele, Mrs Palmer—represent different varieties of linguistic irresponsibility. A final example refers to another minor character, Lady Middleton, who suspects the sisters of being 'satirical': 'perhaps without exactly knowing what it was to be satirical; but *that* did not signify. It was censure in common use, and easily given'. For Jane Austen, 'common use' is not enough, and uncommon precision can only be secured at the price of constant vigilance.

The final title of *Pride and Prejudice* resembles that of *Sense and Sensibility* (both were, of course, second thoughts), but the similarity is only superficial. Whereas the earlier novel presents a study in contrasted temperaments, its successor permits no easy matching of character with abstraction. Reading the novel, we may reasonably begin by attributing 'pride' to Darcy and 'prejudice', largely created by that same pride, to Elizabeth; but we quickly learn that each has a share of both qualities. Elizabeth's pride is not of the same kind as Darcy's, though she is capable of reminding Lady Catherine de Bourgh that she is the daughter of a gentleman: she is an exceptional individual confident in the knowledge of her own powers of mind and personality, in contrast to the external sources of pride—rank, wealth, land, general esteem—associated with the owner of Pemberley. And the proud Darcy is also prejudiced: his objection to her family is one of the principal obstacles in the way of his love for her. In an important passage in Chapter 36, the two words occur in the same context (they occur also at other points in the novel), when Elizabeth comes to realize her double failure of judgment in underestimating Darcy and overestimating Wickham:

She grew absolutely ashamed of herself. Of neither Darcy nor Wickham could she think, without feeling that she had been blind, partial, prejudiced, absurd.

'How despicably have I acted!' she cried. 'I, who have prided myself on my discernment! I, who have valued myself on my abilities!'

(*PP*, 208)

For Elizabeth, to be forced to acknowledge to herself her own intellectual fallibility is a deeper source of humiliation than the social snubs she receives from Lady Catherine and Miss Bingley. The title, then, offers for the reader's consideration not two sharply defined and contrasting terms, but a pair of qualities whose precise nature we are compelled to scrutinize in a particular instance. More especially, we are invited to contemplate different kinds of pride and their relative worth. The abstractions are thus brought vividly to life, and their functioning in specific human situations is dramatically exemplified.

This has often, indeed, been regarded as the most dramatic of Jane Austen's novels; and certainly dialogue, and various substitutes for dialogue, play a very important part in its narrative technique. *Pride and Prejudice* is full of conversations and of references to conversation: R. A. Brower observes that the dialogue is 'dramatic in the sense of defining characters through the way they speak and are spoken about',[8] and speech plays a major role in character-presentation, both for those who (like the heroine) are brilliant talkers and for those who, though far from brilliant, consistently reveal themselves through an individual mode of speech. In the social world of this novel, where the characters belong to a leisured class, talk is a major occupation, often seeming to fill a place in their lives which for the less privileged would be taken up by earning their bread. Where the members of a society, and especially its female members, are virtually without prescribed duties—there are some scornful references to 'female accomplishments', and 'work' for Jane Austen's women characters usually means decorative needlework—conversation takes on a significance that it can hardly afford to possess in a working community; and the ability to talk—to anyone, about anything, or nothing—becomes highly prized. For not all talk is equally valuable. The Bingley sisters are characteristically endowed with the gift of speech as a social asset: 'They could describe an entertainment with accuracy, relate an anecdote with humour, and laugh at their acquaintance with spirit', and their malicious discussion of Elizabeth includes the damning observation that 'she has no conversation'—which is perhaps not as wide of the mark as it appears, since her notion of 'conversation' is very different from theirs. Again, Elizabeth's favourable first impressions of Wickham owe something to his skill as a conversationalist: his conversation, 'though it was only on its being a wet night and

[8] R. A. Brower, *The Fields of Light* (New York, 1951) 168.

C

on the probability of a rainy season, made her feel that the commonest, dullest, most threadbare topic might be rendered interesting by the skill of the speaker'. Lady Catherine talks 'without any intermission', as does her social inferior Mrs Bennet; and even Mr Collins can boast 'a happy readiness of conversation'. In such a society, the appearance of a fresh topic, such as the arrival of a letter or a stranger, tends to assume an importance that may strike us as exaggerated. Its value lies in the nourishment it provides for daily discourse, and this novel may be said to be, to an appreciable extent, not so much about what is done as about what is said. Furthermore, the society described is one in which relationships, particularly those between men and women, can have little opportunity for development save in the setting of the formal or semi-formal social occasion—the ball, the dinner-party or the morning visit. On such occasions talk becomes a major social activity, only temporarily interrupted by dancing or listening to a song or a pianoforte solo: it is through conversation that relationships come into existence, grow and flourish or decline. At many points in the novel, social groups are described by reference to the speech, or the silence, of the various members. At the end of the visit to Netherfield, in Chapter 18, for instance, those who remain are enumerated as follows:

Mrs Hurst and her sister scarcely opened their mouths except to complain of fatigue, and were evidently impatient to have the house to themselves. They repulsed every attempt of Mrs Bennet at conversation, and by so doing, threw a languor over the whole party, which was very little relieved by the long speeches of Mr Collins, who was complimenting Mr Bingley and his sisters on the elegance of their entertainment, and the hospitality and politeness which had marked the behaviour to their guests. Darcy said nothing at all. Mr Bennet, in equal silence, was enjoying the scene. Mr Bingley and Jane were standing together, a little detached from the rest, and talked only to each other. Elizabeth preserved as steady a silence as either Mrs Hurst or Miss Bingley; and even Lydia was too much fatigued to utter more than the occasional exclamation of 'Lord, how tired I am!' accompanied by a violent yawn. (*PP*, 102–3)

This has something of the quality of stage-directions (in, for instance, the reference to Mr Bingley and Jane 'standing together, a little detached from the rest'); but its most striking feature is the use of speech, or silence, to delineate the characters and attitudes of the various members of the group. And at such times silence can be as expressive as speech: Darcy and Mr Bennet reveal themselves no less than Mr Collins or Mrs Bennet.

The novel is 'dramatic', then, in the sense that talk is very important for most of its characters, and most of them talk a great deal. Substantial stretches of the text consist of dialogue (the first two chapters, for example, contain little else). This is normally presented as direct speech: as a later chapter will suggest, there is in this novel relatively little use of the indirect forms. But even when direct speech is not presented, there are very frequent references to conversations taking place. It is dramatic, too, in the further sense that scenes seem often to be conceived and conducted in stage terms: not only the use of dialogue but the collecting of characters in appropriate groups, and the contriving of exits and entrances, suggest a debt to the theatre.[9] The episode of Jane Bennet's engagement to Bingley (Chapter 55) will serve as an illustration. Elizabeth, unaware of what is afoot, enters the drawing-room and discovers the striking tableau of 'her sister and Bingley standing together over the hearth as if engaged in earnest conversation'. Bingley, whispering briefly to Jane, runs from the room, leaving her to impart the joyful news to her sister. We learn in the course of the ensuing dialogue that Bingley has in fact gone to ask Mr Bennet for his daughter's hand; and Jane then sets off to tell her mother—both

---

[9] This theatrical influence may have been derived not only from Jane Austen's playgoing and reading of dramatic literature but, more indirectly, from her reading of Richardson's novels. On the theatrical element in Richardson, see G. Sherburn, 'Samuel Richardson's Novels and the Theatre: a Theory Sketched', *Philological Quarterly*, 41 (1962) 325–9; and essays by G. Sherburn and L. Hughes in *Restoration and Eighteenth Century Literature: Essays in Honor of Alan Dugald McKillop* (Chicago, 1963) 201–9 and 239–50.

these subordinate dialogues taking place off-stage, as it were, leaving Elizabeth for a short time alone on the stage to contemplate the satisfactory outcome of events and the gratifying discomfiture of Miss Bingley, until Bingley re-enters and greets her as a sister. The single setting is retained throughout. The elements of difference from stage-presentation are as important as the similarity, however: the novelist is at liberty to present as fully or as briefly as she wishes the various phases of a scene or episode, making possible a flexibility of pace and, in this instance, a speed and economy that would hardly be possible in the theatre, since all that has just been summarized occupies no more than a couple of pages of the novel text. To call *Pride and Prejudice* dramatic, therefore, is only to suggest that it adopts some of the distinctive virtues of the stage-play without renouncing the peculiar advantages of fiction.

The dialogue itself has a wit, polish and vivacity that makes it outstanding in the Jane Austen canon—qualities which the author herself obviously recognized, when she described it as perhaps too 'light, and bright, and sparkling' for some tastes. For the heroine, speech is the chief means of self-assertion, of demonstrating her qualities of mind and character, and of insisting upon her right to independent judgments. Like her creator, she is bound by the conventions of the society to which she, and those she loves, belongs, though she does not lack courage to defy those conventions (in walking alone, in bad weather, to visit her sick sister, for instance) when the need arises. But the splendid gesture of a Jeanie Deans or a Lizzie Hexam is not open to her: Jane Austen is not writing the kind of novel that can accommodate heroic action on this scale, nor is she writing about a social class in which it would be thinkable for a young woman to walk from Scotland to London to save her sister's life, or jump into the Thames to rescue her drowning lover. It is through speech, used in the situations of everyday social life, that Elizabeth Bennet must make upon the world the mark of her own unique personality. Accordingly, her language is markedly more vigorous, and employs a wider range of verbal resources, than that of most of

Jane Austen's heroines. She is capable not only of walking through
the mud but of venturing on acts of *linguistic* boldness and unconventionality, in words that can elsewhere carry the stigma
of ignorance or vulgarity. She can quote a proverb to Darcy's
face (telling him to ' "Keep your breath to cool your porridge" '),
and she is the only one of the heroines capable of the magni-
ficently colloquial response to the news of the de Bourghs'
arrival:

'And is this all?' cried Elizabeth. 'I expected at least that the
pigs were got into the garden, and here is nothing but Lady
Catherine and her daughter!' (*PP*, 158)

The pertness of many of her replies recalls the conversational
style of the letters, and there is an affinity too between her speech
and the narrative style of the novel, which reveals at many points
a sense of language as both a delightful plaything and an instrument of devastating comment. None of the later novels makes
such extensive use of comic devices such as zeugma and oxymoron: Mary Bennet is reported to be 'deep in the study of
thorough bass and human nature'; for Elizabeth walking with
the Gardiners in the grounds of Pemberley, 'time and her aunt
moved slowly'; and we read of Mrs Bennet's 'querulous serenity'
and of Elizabeth's indulgence in 'all the delight of unpleasant
recollections'. The tone of the narrative voice often bears a strong
resemblance to that of the heroine.

Linguistically, Elizabeth is undoubtedly her father's child, but
the wit and relish of folly in his speech is tinged with a cynicism
and even callousness, produced by an unwise marriage, from
which hers is free. The incisiveness of his repartee, and the ruthless
logic which he applies to his wife's intellectual confusion, can be
seen in a passage which suggests the extent of Ivy Compton-
Burnett's debt to Jane Austen. The subject is the entail which will
leave Mrs Bennet and her daughters homeless at her husband's
death:

'Indeed, Mr Bennet,' said she, 'it is very hard to think that
Charlotte Lucas should ever be mistress of this house, that *I* should

be forced to make way for *her* and live to see her take my place in
it!'

'My dear, do not give way to such gloomy thoughts. Let us hope
for better things. Let us flatter ourselves that *I* may be the sur-
vivor.' . . .

'I cannot bear to think that they should have all this estate. If it
was not for the entail I should not mind it.'

'What should you not mind?'

'I should not mind anything at all.'

'Let us be thankful that you are preserved from a state of such
insensibility.'. . .(*PP*, 130)

Just as Mr Bennet has bestowed his intellectual powers upon
Elizabeth, Mrs Bennet finds her counterpart in the foolish and
'noisy' Lydia, whose garrulity comes close to rivalling her
mother's, and whose irresponsibility, at first mere girlish thought-
fulness, reveals itself as grave moral confusion when she elopes
with Wickham.

Darcy's speech presents a less straightforward case. He quickly
earns a reputation for taciturnity, even moroseness: he spends
long periods in silence (when he calls on the Bennets he is liable
to sit 'ten minutes together without opening his lips'), and admits
to Elizabeth:

'I certainly have not the talent which some people possess . . . of
conversing easily with those I have never seen before. I cannot
catch their tone of conversation, or appear interested in their con-
cerns, as I often see done.' (*PP*, 175)

Since 'ease', the happy knack of being at home in any company,
is a quality often singled out for commendation, this sounds like
a shortcoming; and it certainly counts as a failure by the standards of the society already described. Yet the evidence of the
housekeeper at Pemberley, who has known him from boyhood,
contradicts the notion of a haughty indifference to others: ' "Some
people call him proud, but I am sure I never saw anything of it.
To my fancy, it is only because he does not rattle away like other
young men." ' One recalls a notably fluent speaker, John Thorpe
of *Northanger Abbey*, in connection with whom that useful

eighteenth-century term 'a rattle' is invoked: readiness of discourse is a social virtue—but mere glibness is to be distrusted, as a symptom of superficiality or worse. For Darcy, there is no place in life for talk that exists only to kill time. He speaks when he has something to say, and is prepared to remain silent in defiance of conventional expectations. This brings him in line with Jane Austen's other heroes—Mr Knightley, for instance, is given to speaking briefly and to the point—and his gravity also acts as a foil to Elizabeth's irreverence.

Other characters are similarly individualized by their mode of speech, at times moving close to eccentricity. With Mr Collins, for instance, dialogue comes close to caricature, and a fuller examination of his speech (and of Lady Catherine's) will be undertaken in Chapter 4. The tendency of many speakers to throw off epigrams also calls for comment: here again is a feature common to dialogue and narrative style alike. Not only the sententious Mary Bennet but Darcy, Elizabeth, Charlotte Lucas and others all employ a device which recalls the comedy of manners as well as the copybook and, more seriously, the impressive example of Dr Johnson. The four examples which follow are from the characters named, in that order:

'Pride relates more to our opinion of ourselves, vanity to what we would have others think of us.'

'We all love to instruct, though we can teach only what is not worth knowing.'

'The power of doing anything with quickness is always much prized by the possessor, and often without any attention to the imperfection of the performance.'

'Happiness in marriage is entirely a matter of chance.'

Dialogues are important throughout the novel, but there is another element occurring throughout, and particularly important in the second half, which should be briefly mentioned here. I refer to the letters which, quoted in whole or in part, summarized, or simply alluded to, play such a significant role in the narrative.

None of the other novels exhibits such physical mobility in its characters. Whereas the world of *Emma*, for instance, is relatively static, here we find journeys a commonplace. Bingley and his sisters and Darcy come and go, as do Mr Collins and the Gardiners; Elizabeth goes to Kent and later to Derbyshire; Lydia and Wickham go to Brighton and then to London, followed there by Mr Bennet; and so forth. At moments the arrivals and departures come thick and fast. At the opening of Chapter 53, Lydia and Wickham have no sooner departed for Newcastle than Bingley returns to Netherfield to provide a fresh infusion of interest. Given the frequent separations, letter-writing assumes a major role in the development of relationships and the transmission of news, and material which would otherwise have been conveyed through dialogue is presented in letter-form. A letter can thus be seen as a form of 'speech to the absent', and a correspondence as a prolonged conversation or debate. Since the presence of the heroine normally determines at any given point the setting of the action, news of the absent comes largely through the post, the importance of which is made clear after Lydia's disgrace:

Every day at Longbourn was now a day of anxiety; but the most anxious part of each was when the post was expected. The arrival of letters was the first grand object of every morning's impatience. Through letters, whatever of good or bad was to be told would be communicated, and every succeeding day was expected to bring some news of importance. (*PP*, 296)

At such a time, the postman's knock is the most dramatic event. Appropriately, the novel draws to a conclusion with a burst of epistolary energy, in various styles, in the penultimate chapter. Elizabeth writes to the Gardiners, Darcy to Lady Catherine, Mr Bennet to Mr Collins, Miss Bingley to her brother, and to Jane, and Miss Darcy to *her* brother. It would seem that the happy outcome of the Elizabeth–Darcy relationship is incomplete until news of it has been transmitted to all absent but interested parties. And, as a comparison of the letters quoted readily shows, letters bear the imprint of their writers' individuality at least as much as dialogue; indeed, as a later chapter will suggest more fully, such qualities as Mr Collins's pomposity and Lydia's irresponsibility appear more blatant in the kind of sustained monologue that a letter represents.

Dialogue, then, and correspondence as a substitute for dialogue, carry much of the narrative load in *Pride and Prejudice*. At certain points, however, Jane Austen avoids dialogue where it might reasonably have been anticipated. Some examples are: Elizabeth's unexpected meeting with Darcy in the grounds of Pemberley (Chapter 43), Lydia's return home after her marriage (Chapter 51), Elizabeth's acceptance of Darcy (Chapter 58), and her 'important communication' to her mother that she is to marry him (Chapter 59). In the first example cited, the chapter begins with a long passage of direct speech in which Elizabeth finds new light shed on Darcy's character by the testimony of his housekeeper; after his sudden appearance, however, the scene is presented so consistently through Elizabeth's consciousness that the objectivity of direct speech would seem out of place. Instead, we are given only the sketchiest indications of the ensuing dialogue (Darcy speaks with 'perfect civility', and makes 'civil inquiries after her family'): in its place is a kind of inner speech, a presentation of Elizabeth's unspoken thoughts:

Her coming there was the most unfortunate, the most ill-judged thing in the world! How strange must it appear to him! In what a disgraceful light might it not strike so vain a man! It might seem as if she had purposely thrown herself in his way again! Oh! why did she come? or why did he thus come a day before he was expected? . . . And his behaviour, so strikingly altered—what could it mean? That he should even speak to her was amazing!—but to speak with such civility, to enquire after her family! . . . (*PP*, 252)

The absence of quotation marks involves no ambiguity about the status of this passage: its exclamatory manner, quite unlike that of the narrative style, suggests the heroine's violent emotions, and its questions show the self-searching that she must carry out in the process of adjusting to the changed situation.

The second example referred to also calls for further comment. At the beginning of Chapter 51, the scene is set in the Bennet's breakfast-room for Lydia's return with her husband. What follows is certainly conceived in dramatic terms to the extent that the disposition of those present, and the arrival of the newcomers, are carefully indicated. The narrative is reminiscent at one point of stage-directions:

Lydia's voice was heard in the vestibule; the door was thrown open, and she ran into the room. Her mother stepped forwards, embraced her . . . gave her hand with an affectionate smile to Wickham, who followed his lady . . . (*PP*, 315)

But for a time at least there is no dialogue. Lydia's insensitively effusive arrival, her mother's rapturous welcome, the cooler reception she receives from her father, the 'easy address' of Wickham, are all narrated; it is evident that 'there was no want of discourse', but (with the exception of two speeches by Lydia) the author chooses not to present this painful scene through dialogue. (The reasons for the deliberate shunning of direct speech where it might seem an appropriate technique will be examined in Chapter 4.) Such instances, however, only constitute exceptions, though significant and interesting exceptions, to the prevailing dramatic method of the novel: a method which Jane Austen uses to some degree, and with various modifications, throughout her work, but nowhere more brilliantly and memorably.

Mansfield Park is generally agreed to possess fundamental and puzzling differences from the other novels, differences affecting both its individual elements and its general tone. Jane Austen said that its theme was 'ordination'[10]—an unpromising enough starting-point, one might suppose, for the author of *Pride and Prejudice*. None of the novels has been more highly praised: Lionel Trilling has claimed that 'No other book can tell us more specifically how the modern world as we know it came into being

[10] *L*, 298 (dated 29 January 1813).

than this novel';[11] yet none has caused so much uneasiness among
Jane Austen's critics. No heroine has so often been found unsatisfactory as Fanny Price, and no single episode has stimulated
such discussion, and prompted such defensive exegetical fervour,
as those ill-fated theatricals. The mood of the novel seems to have
little in common with that of the books which preceded and
followed it: where *Pride and Prejudice* and *Emma* are gay,
Mansfield Park is serious and even humourless. It seems worth
inquiring, therefore, what there is in the language of the novel
which corresponds to, and perhaps contributes to, this basically
different impression received by the reader. Most notable, perhaps, is the absence of witty dialogue and ironic commentary, of
humour and parody, repartee and epigrammatism. To a very
large extent this must be explained by the nature of the heroine
and the particular ideal of womanhood that she represents. Fanny
Price has none of the pert vivacity of Elizabeth Bennet or the
optimistic self-assurance of Emma Woodhouse: she is shy, meek
(she has 'habits of ready submission'), withdrawn, nervous,
serious-minded, often tearful, and physically weak. Whereas they
habitually initiate conversation or action, or at least play an equal
part with others, she is frequently the passive recipient of others'
confidences—she has a willing ear rather than a ready tongue.
Much of all this is owed to her background and her chronic
(and in the circumstances not unreasonable) sense of inferior
status, which the equivocal position she holds in the Bertram
family does nothing to cure. She lacks confidence in her own
judgment; yet she is more often right than anyone else, even
Edmund. Jane Austen thus offers us the apparent paradox of this
timid and often naïve girl perceiving the truth unerringly,
whereas Elizabeth Bennet and Emma Woodhouse, for all their

[11] L. Trilling, 'A Portrait of Western Man', *The Listener*, 49 (1953) 970.
Cf. Q. D. Leavis's claim that '*Mansfield Park*, in technique and subject
and prose style and in its thoughtful inquiries into human relationships,
looks forward to George Eliot and Henry James; so *Mansfield Park* is the
first modern novel in England' (Introduction to the MacDonald Illustrated Classics edition of *Mansfield Park* (1957) xiv).

sophistication and articulateness, are both capable of serious misjudgments. One has only to look at Fanny's interviews (the word seems called for) with Sir Thomas, and to set beside them Elizabeth's handling of Lady Catherine, to feel that, in respect of personality, the two heroines occupy different worlds. Yet Fanny is not less right than Elizabeth, and her moral victory is in no way inferior. At the same time, it is of Elizabeth's sister, the tedious blue-stocking Mary Bennet, that we are at moments reminded in Fanny's conversation. There is, for instance, something very unyouthful in her reflections on mutability in Chapter 22 (' "How wonderful, how very wonderful the operations of time, and the changes of the human mind!" '): one suspects that no girl in her teens has a right to sound quite so much like an eighteenth-century essayist. It is perhaps significant that Johnson's *Idler* is among Fanny's reading.

Fanny's language, then, has almost nothing in common with that of her sister-heroines. For one thing, it is a much scarcer commodity. Although there is a good deal of dialogue in the novel, she contributes little to it: perhaps no heroine of a great novel has quite such a fondness for silence. Her 'favourite indulgence' is 'being suffered to sit silent and unattended to', and much of her time spent in her beloved Edmund's company is devoted to what he calls on one occasion 'the luxury of silence'. ' "I suppose I am graver than other people" ', she confesses; and this gravity makes for a somewhat monochrome effect in the accounts of Fanny's outward behaviour. Her inner life is a different matter, however; and it is through the passages which convey her unspoken feelings rather than through what she says that we learn to know her. This means that some of the most important passages in the novel are of 'inner speech' or 'interior monologue', stylistically distinguishable in various respects from the narrative into which it merges. Thus, when Henry Crawford makes his unwelcome proposal to Fanny,

She was feeling, thinking, trembling, about every thing;—agitated, happy, miserable, infinitely obliged, absolutely angry. It was all beyond belief! He was inexcusable, incomprehensible!—But such were his habits, that he could do nothing without a mixture of evil. He had previously made her the happiest of human beings, and now he had insulted—she knew not what to say—how to class or how to regard it. She would not have him be serious, and yet what could excuse the use of such words and offers, if they meant but to trifle? (*MP*, 302)

Characteristically, Fanny's strongest feelings do not find utterance: we read elsewhere that 'she was always more inclined to silence when feeling most strongly'. These 'soliloquies', as they are later called (the word is not to be taken literally, but suggests the relationship of such passages to speech), serve an important function in the presentation of the heroine's emotional life. Their style, and particularly their syntax, is distinctive. In the passage quoted, the first sentence acts as a bridge between narrative and inner speech by its dramatic and calculatedly confused listing of epithets: since the confusion is, obviously, Fanny's rather than the author's, the former's state of mind is already colouring the apparently objective prose. What follows, with its mingling of reflection, exclamation and question, and its hesitations and uncertainties (particularly in the sentence beginning 'He had previously made . . .'), without being formally presented as either speech or thought, takes us straight into Fanny's consciousness.

The liveliness that one associates with Jane Austen's heroines, and which Fanny so conspicuously lacks, is possessed in full measure by another character in the novel, Mary Crawford. The irreverent wit which, in Elizabeth Bennet, testified to independence of mind is now produced as evidence of grave moral irresponsibility. ' "Your lively mind" ', Edmund tells Mary, ' "can hardly be serious even on serious subjects" '; later he refers to her 'playfulness' and 'high spirits', and again to 'her too lively mind'. More pervasively, liveliness (often called 'animation') is seen in the later novel as a quality to be distrusted. Any display of high spirits is liable to constitute evidence of impropriety, most obviously in the episode of the amateur theatricals; when Sir Thomas returns and the acting is abruptly terminated, and decency and decorum have reasserted themselves, 'it was all sameness and gloom, compared with the past'—and yet the past has achieved gaiety only at the expense of moral offence. This is one of the crucial difficulties of the novel, that the characters held up for disapprobation are often more attractive, and more like the heroines and heroes of Jane Austen's other novels, than those we are asked to admire. In *Pride and Prejudice* seriousness, so far from being a prime virtue, was reserved for the pedantic Mary Bennet; in *Mansfield Park* the qualities for which Elizabeth Bennet is praised have become the grounds of Mary Crawford's moral inadequacy. And since the latter is witty and gay, there is no alternative but for Fanny, as her antithesis, to be grave and even dull. Mary's easy acceptance of Mrs Rushworth's adultery is intended to shock us by its casualness; but, in the process, Fanny is compelled to exhibit a moral reaction that may seem to many readers excessive. She feels the event as a 'horrible evil', and is physically ill with shock. (*Horrible* and *horror*, though not used very widely elsewhere by Jane Austen with serious intent, are often invoked to describe Fanny's response to situations of varying import; and *evil* also makes very frequent appearances in this novel.) Furthermore, since readiness of speech is associated with the vicious, and taciturnity with the virtuous, any fluency becomes suspect, whether it is Mary Crawford's brilliant and entertaining gossip, Sir Thomas's orotund periods, or the volubility of Mrs Norris. Significantly, when Tom Bertram learns wisdom through suffering, he becomes 'steady and quiet'. Noise, indeed, is regarded as an unmitigated evil, and *noisy* is a common term of reproach applied to an individual or a group (Fanny is 'almost stunned' by the noise of her Portsmouth home). The wished-for opposite is often identified as *tranquillity*, another recurring word, and it is the 'peace and tranquillity of Mansfield' which Fanny longs for during her Portsmouth sojourn. Whether we interpret such observations as a reflection of the author's own mental and spiritual state during the period of composition is a matter for the biographical critic. Q. D. Leavis has suggested that 'the language of a religious change of heart' may be traced in *Mansfield Park*,[12] and it is worth noting that a contemporary writer on language, illustrating the use of the word *tranquillity*, places it in a religious context: 'What a state of tranquillity does the religious man enjoy; no outward things have the power to ruffle or discompose him!'[13]

These examples also suggest the importance in this novel, as in all Jane Austen's work, of key-words: recurring terms which, properly scrutinized, afford an insight into the dominant attitudes and values of the novel. David Lodge has shown the existence of 'a vocabulary of discrimination' in *Mansfield Park*, a whole range of words which appear and reappear and which are closely related to social and moral standards.[14] He has pointed out, for example, that *judgment* and its associated words occur more than a hundred times. Jane Austen's use of key-words is more fully discussed in the next chapter, but it will be worth examining at this point a single instance which recurs with surprising frequency and has, it can be argued, an important bearing on Fanny Price's role. *Comfort* is not on Lodge's list of words indicating 'the finest shades of social and moral value', though it occurs much more frequently than many which are. If we count such closely related words as *comfortable*, *comfortably*, and *uncomfortable*, it appears some seventy or eighty times, sometimes making three or four appearances on a single page, especially in the last quarter of the novel, where moral issues and moral verdicts become most emphatic.

At first sight, *comfort*, at least in its most familiar present-day uses, seems to have little to do with 'social and moral value'; yet the word is endowed with wider and deeper meanings by Jane Austen, and to fail to grasp these is surely to have an incomplete understanding of many important passages. Let us look more closely at Jane Austen's use of the epithet *comfortable*. Only a

[12] Q. D. Leavis, 'A Critical Theory of Jane Austen's Writings', *Scrutiny*, 10 (1942) 276.
[13] J. Trusler, *The Difference between Words Esteemed Synonymous in the English Language* ... (1766) I, 82.
[14] D. Lodge, *Language of Fiction* (1966) 94–113.

minority of instances relate to physical or material comfort ('a comfortable home') or social ease ('shy and uncomfortable'), the normal twentieth-century usages. The majority, as the context usually makes clear, refer to emotional needs and satisfactions, and the fact that the word is employed in relation to the heroine far more often than to anyone else suggests that a scrutiny of its range of meanings may contribute to an understanding of a character otherwise puzzling in many ways. To the modern reader, there is an unfamiliar ring about such phrases as 'comfortable hopes . . . that he would find Mr Crawford at home', or 'so comfortable a talk with him about William'. We would probably use *comforting*, or some quite different word such as *pleasant* or *reassuring*, with these nouns. (We also find in the novel a 'comfortable conclusion' and 'a comfortable walk': the latter phrase, which today brings to mind the walker's footwear rather than his feelings, emphasizes sharply the nature of the shift of meaning involved.) Our sense of the changed role of the adjective *comfortable* may be expressed by saying that the number of nouns with which it may normally and appropriately be linked has diminished considerably. We apply it to chairs, beds, rooms, houses and journeys, but scarcely to hopes, talks or (except in the physical sense) walks. For this reason, such statements as that 'Fanny had not felt so comfortable for days and days', and Edmund's remark (in his letter to Fanny in Chapter 44) that 'I am not comfortable enough to be fit for any body', require an adjustment on the reader's part to an unfamiliar meaning. To be comfortable, it is now becoming clear, is to possess that 'tranquillity' which has already been indicated as a highly desirable state of mind and spirit. It is the attribute that Fanny has sought from the beginning of her life at Mansfield Park, and which she eventually shows herself capable of bestowing upon others. For the word, and its related noun, have a knack of occurring at important moments in her history. When, near the beginning of the novel, Edmund befriends the miserable child, we are told 'From this day Fanny grew more comfortable'. Later, Mary Crawford is shown to be 'the chief bane of Fanny's comfort';

William, on the other hand, is a great source of 'comfort' to his sister: when Mrs Norris threatens to accompany them on their journey together to Portsmouth, Fanny sadly reflects that 'All the comfort of their comfortable journey would be destroyed at once', and it is clearly emotional satisfaction rather than physical well-being that is in question. After Mrs Rushworth's adultery and Julia's elopement, Fanny is 'sent for as a comfort', Edmund greets her with the words ' "My Fanny—my only sister—my only comfort now" ', and even Lady Bertram manages a burst of eloquence: ' "Dear Fanny! now I shall be comfortable." ' In the closing pages of the novel, the author states her intention of restoring 'every body, not greatly in fault themselves, to tolerable comfort', Sir Thomas at last comes to realize that, in Fanny, 'His charitable kindness had been rearing a prime comfort for himself', and, in the final glimpse of the wedded happiness of Fanny and Edmund, we learn that 'their home was the home of affection and comfort'. (There are nine other appearances of this key-word, not quoted here, in the same final chapter.)

Such recurrences of a single word or a group of related words, appearing not only frequently but at important points of the story, can hardly be without significance. Without anticipating the later discussion of key-words in Jane Austen, it can be claimed that *comfort* and *comfortable* provide a clue to the essential nature and role of Fanny Price. Fanny is not concerned to challenge society or to shape the destinies of others. She is above all anxious to achieve a state of emotional security where, within circumscribed limits, she may feel at ease. For a large part of the novel, she feels desperately the need for love and reassurance; her self-discovery (that process which falls within the experience of all Jane Austen's heroines) is that she is capable of providing these for others; and the final portion shows her giving needed comfort to Sir Thomas and Lady Bertram as well as to Edmund. In this way, a single item of vocabulary can be seen to be carrying, inconspicuously but persistently, a share of the meaning of a major element in the novel; and scrutiny of the word, its range of

D

meanings and associations, is rewarded by a fuller understanding of the central character.

Emma is, like *Northanger Abbey*, a comedy of errors; the difference is that the later novel presents a variety of comedy which has serious if not tragic implications. Catherine Morland's errors are of a kind that is likely to produce temporary embarrassment, but Emma's come near to ruining the happiness, first of Harriet Smith, and later (as she supposes) of herself. Again, Catherine's mistakes result from her tendency to see life in terms learned from the circulating library, but Emma's take their source more profoundly from the faults of her character and upbringing. The first page of the novel stresses Emma's precocious self-assurance: she has 'a most affectionate, indulgent father', her mother-substitute Miss Taylor has scarcely been able to bring herself 'to impose any restraint', and this spoilt child has 'a disposition to think a little too well of herself'. What follows serves to confirm this initial generalization: Emma's social pride makes her too sure of herself, and too confident that she knows what is best for everyone else. This leads her to hold fast to her first impressions, instead of reviewing them in the light of experience: she lacks impartiality, in Jane Austen's sense of the word—that coolness of judgment which makes possible a detached and unprejudiced assessment of a character or situation. She is too often dogged by her previous convictions, so to speak: with Mr Elton, for example, she is 'too eager and busy in her own previous conceptions and views to hear him impartially, or see him with clear vision'. Such an attitude is likely to be a rich source of misunderstandings, and Emma, like Catherine, contributes her own preconceptions to the ambiguity often inherent in everyday speech and behaviour. The confusions which thus arise are, at the simplest level, similar to those of *Northanger Abbey*, though the tone of mockery is absent, and in place of the somewhat contrived ambiguities of the earlier novel we find in *Emma* a reliance on the normal susceptibility of the commonplace remark or action to be open to more than one interpretation.

Much of Mr Elton's conduct in the Harriet Smith affair, for instance, is genuinely though unwittingly ambiguous. His initial modesty over writing a charade is typical: ' "He was afraid not even Miss Woodhouse"—he stopped a moment—"or Miss Smith could inspire him" '. Quite unconsciously, Mr Elton here establishes some kind of record for the most pregnant and most equivocal pause in the novel. His hesitation might be taken (as Emma takes it) as evidence of the natural bashfulness of a lover in uttering his lady's name, with Miss Woodhouse taking precedence on the grounds of rank but not in his affections; or, it might equally well be what in fact it is: a sign that 'Miss Smith' is very much an afterthought, added to prevent the compliment from appearing too fulsome and too presumptuous but in no way implying that Emma comes anywhere but first in his thoughts. Emma's unshakable belief in his passion for her friend, however —a belief in which the wish has been father to the thought— prevents her from detecting any alternative meaning, and she sees his words as merely confirming her hopes and plans. She never admits the doubts which a more open mind might have entertained. When, the next day, Elton produces a charade and hands it to Emma, she again has no trouble in interpreting the evidence to fit her pet theory: 'There was deep consciousness about him, and he found it easier to meet her eye than her friend's.' The observed 'consciousness' or embarrassment of Elton's manner is a fact, but the second part of the sentence (after the comma) conveys Emma's unspoken thoughts; the ambiguity thus stands before the reader, untouched by any authorial intervention. A look or a pause can give rise to radical misunderstanding, and language itself is shown to be a highly equivocal medium. It is perhaps no accident that the whole episode turns on a charade, the essence of which is a hidden and therefore enigmatical meaning. Poor Harriet's puzzlement over the charade Elton produces is an apt comment on the prevailing linguistic situation: ' "Do help me. I never saw anything so hard . . . Can it be Neptune? . . . Or a trident? or a mermaid? or a shark?" ' Another similar situation arises when Elton heaps praise on Emma's portrait of Harriet: whether his 'raptures' are prompted by the sitter's beauty or the artist's skill is again a fertile source of misunderstanding; and again, when Emma's remarks on Frank Churchill are taken by Harriet to refer to Mr Knightley.

Ambiguity and its close relation irony also operate more pervasively in this novel, informing the verbal texture in passages of exposition as well as, more obviously, in the dialogue. The following account of the wooing and winning of Mr Elton's bride is characteristic:

The charming Augusta Hawkins, in addition to all the usual advantages of perfect beauty and merit, was in possession of an independent fortune, of so many thousands as would always be called ten; a point of some dignity, as well as some convenience: the story told well; he had not thrown himself away—he had gained a woman of 10,000*l.* or thereabouts; and he had gained her with such delightful rapidity—the first hour of introduction had been so very soon followed by distinguishing notice; the history which he had to give Mrs Coles of the rise and progress of the affair was so glorious — the steps so quick, from the accidental rencontre, to the dinner at Mr Green's, and the party at Mrs Brown's—smiles and blushes rising in importance—with consciousness and agitation richly scattered—the lady had been so easily impressed—so sweetly disposed—had in short, to use a most intelligible phrase, been so very ready to have him, that vanity and prudence were equally contented. (*E*, 181–2)

This sentence (it runs to over 160 words) shows an impressive control of tone and syntax. (For a fuller discussion of its syntactical features, see pp. 107–8 below.) The brutal truth that the marriage was one of mutual wordly advantage is kept at a distance until the last dozen words. Yet the ironic signals, mainly communicated by ambiguity of word and phrase, are unmistakable from the first line. 'The usual advantages' immediately suggests the hollowness of the judgments made by the voice of society, thus casting doubt before and after on the other terms used: it quickly becomes apparent that *charming*, *beauty* and

merit cannot be taken at their face-value in a context in which
they consort with the ironical phrase quoted. Sham and reality
are set side by side: 'perfect beauty and merit' are seen to be
merely an embellishment to, or an artifice created by the more
solid virtues of 'an independent fortune', and the pattern thus
established is repeated in the bathos of 'dignity . . . convenience'.
Another phrase, 'The story told well', suggests the romantic
fiction of a whirlwind love-affair, which is the public version of
the cruder and mercenary private truth; since *story* means 'in-
vention' as well as 'history', the phrase suggests that it is indeed
no more than a polite fiction. 'Delightful rapidity' is, likewise,
ambiguous: the speed of events is as delightful as a romantic
idyll, with the almost allegorically-named Mrs Brown and Mr
Green reinforcing the impression of remoteness from realism;
but it is even more literally delightful to the ambitious and im-
pecunious Elton, whose values are sufficiently indicated by the
repeated verb 'gained', with its associations of commercial
profit-making. The climactic 'glorious' has, to the reader attuned
to the controlled discriminations of Jane Austen's vocabulary,
a strong mock-heroic flavour; and the harshly colloquial quality
of the 'most intelligible phrase' which follows has the effect of a
cold-water douche of truth and realism after the glib phrases
(lifted, it might almost seem, from a sentimental novel) of the
previous lines. Instantly, however, colloquialism and ambiguity
are alike dismissed, decorum reasserts itself in the solid and literal
abstractions of 'vanity' and 'prudence', and we are back again
in the world of real values. All of this, the analysis of which is
more lengthy and less subtle than the performance, is accomplished in the course of a single sentence of varying yet carefully
regulated tone. Beginning in frosty detachment, it gathers
momentum (round about 'delightful rapidity') and moves
through parody to a destructive anti-climax, after which judicial
detachment again resumes its reign. At such times, ambiguity,
often manifested as irony and parody, becomes more than a local
device for humorous or dramatic effect: it becomes, rather, a key
to the values for which the novel stands and a means of stressing

the importance of right judgments in situations where appearances can often be mistaken for realities.

Towards the end of the novel, the vivacious and confident Emma is plunged in gloom by the thought that her manoeuvrings as a match-maker have caused her to lose Mr Knightley. This is the heroine's mental and emotional crisis, for in seeming to lose him she finds herself; and this section of the novel, and the joyful reversal that ensues, are characterized by several devices not often met with elsewhere in this author's work, at least not in passage of indubitable seriousness. Emma's realization of the truth about her own feelings is marked by an image, remarkable not in itself but for the rarity with which such figures are used: 'It darted through her, with the speed of an arrow, that Mr Knightley must marry no one but herself!'[15] Her state of mind is reflected sympathetically by the weather, which is unseasonably cold and rainy; when the clouds clear and the sun shines again, it is the prelude to Knightley's appearance and, eventually, his proposal. Such descriptions, with such an obvious dramatic function, are again exceptional in Jane Austen's work. Equally unusual is the expression in this passage of powerful feelings by means of what may be referred to as 'strong language': such phrases as 'the beginning of wretchedness', 'ruined happiness', 'Every other part of her mind was disgusting', are rare in this author, and gain emphasis from their rarity, suggesting the depths of emotion of which Emma is becoming aware for the first time and, as she thinks, too late. The use of such language is quite different here from the ironic account, in Sense and Sensibility, of the self-indulgent sufferings of the romantic Marianne. Finally, when Emma's depression is replaced by elation, the change of tone is marked by two instances of word-play, and the ambiguity is now not a means of making a moral point but a simple delight in punning, comparable to the high-spirited verbal

[15] This seems to be an exception to the rule, noted by M. Lascelles (*Jane Austen and her Art* (1939) 111), that Jane Austen is '*shy* of figurative language, using it as little as possible, and least of all in her gravest passages'.

humour of the letters, and having the effect of making the narrative style reflect the heroine's exhilaration. We are told, of her unsuspecting father's concern over Mr Knightley's having taken cold, that 'Could he have seen the heart, he would have cared very little for the lungs'; and there is a reference to the lovers going 'over the same ground again . . . literally and figuratively'. By such minor but perceptible variations in style are these stages of the novel's climax marked.

One other feature of the language of *Emma* calls for comment: as in *Mansfield Park*, we note the recurrence—too frequent to be fortuitous—of certain terms indicating qualities of character. *Clever*, for instance, which is the fourth word of the book, is applied first to the heroine, of whom we are later told that she is 'the cleverest of her family'. Cleverness, and by ironic implication the folly of which clever people are capable, is thus announced as one of the themes of the novel. Related to cleverness is *imagination*, not the supreme power that it was for the Romantic poets, but the result of a lively mind unaccustomed to self-control and to critical self-scrutiny. (Emma herself is at one point referred to by the nonce-word *imaginist*.) Both contribute to Emma's failures of *judgment*, another favourite word; 'mis-judgment' and 'error of judgment' both appear at the beginning of Chapter 16, after the Harriet-Mr Elton fiasco. Emma is not alone in being characterized by the use of recurrent terms: 'ease' is earmarked for Mrs Elton, and 'elegance' for Jane Fairfax, whilst even Mr Woodhouse has his revealing verbal mannerism in his addiction to the negative form (the phrase 'not unwholesome' for instance, occurs twice in his speech, the double negative aptly suggesting his timorous, hesitant attitude to life). In this and other ways we find that the relationship of the language of this novel to its themes is a more intimate one than obtains in the earlier books. Language is no longer both the object and the medium of parody, as it is in *Northanger Abbey*, or the external sign of inner weakness and folly, as it is in *Sense and Sensibility*. The firmness and precision of the words used and used again are now a token of the clear and unambiguous standards by which human behaviour is assessed. For ambiguity may serve as a valuable source of comedy, but the moral basis of the author's judgments, conveyed in her language, finds modes of expression which leave us in no doubt as to her standpoint.

Persuasion opens in a familiar vein of social satire, and Sir Walter Elliot may strike the reader as little more than a male re-incarnation of Lady Catherine de Bourgh; but the novel soon takes on a distinctive quality which is quite unlike that of any of its predecessors. This is largely due to the peculiar nature and situation of the heroine, and the way in which her consciousness —her inner life as it is lived from moment to moment—is brought before the reader. Anne Elliot is somewhat older than the other heroines and, most importantly, she has undergone a major emotional experience long before the action of the novel begins. Her sense of having been excessively 'persuadable' in rejecting her lover fills her with regret for the past, so that, where Emma is blooming with health, Anne is 'faded and thin'. This difference between them helps to account for an important difference in technique between *Emma* and *Persuasion*. Whereas Emma is confident, optimistic and gregarious, her impulses finding ready expression in speech and action, Anne is withdrawn, taciturn and often solitary, so that her most powerful feelings generally go un-expressed. She is sensitive to natural beauty and to poetry: per-haps the novel provides evidence of its author's new-found interest in the work of her contemporaries. Anne's condition is described with succinct accuracy in an observation she makes to Captain Harville on the constancy of a woman's love: ' "We live at home, quiet, confined, and our feelings prey upon us." ' (*P*, 232) Such a heroine demands in her presentation a technique which will make her thoughts and emotions, as well as her words and actions, accessible to the reader. It needs also to be a technique capable of recording with considerable sensitivity the delicate fluctuations of mood and emotional response: like Virginia Woolf more than a century later, Jane Austen in this final novel is aware of the overwhelming importance of the 'moment' of intense experience or insight. (A phrase in the cancelled Chapter 10, '. . . the evening seemed to have been made up of exquisite moments' (*P*, 261) has a distinctly Woolfian flavour.)

For this novel and this heroine, then, Jane Austen devised a style appropriate to the new purpose and different in many respects, therefore, from that of any of her previous novels. There is less wit and epigrammatism, less delight in individual and eccentric modes of speech, less dialogue in which characters find relish in conversation as a stimulating and delightful social activity. Instead, we encounter a style in which narrative, comment, dialogue (presented in various ways) and interior monologue very frequently and unobtrusively merge into one another. Without the abrupt changes of stylistic mode or form of presentation which are demanded by the more usual fictional methods of mingling speech and narrative, different voices and viewpoints are fused into a harmonious whole; and the speech and actions of other characters can be introduced without any displacement of the heroine's consciousness as the centre of focus. The slanting of the narrative through the mental life of the principal character, which is an important element in *Emma*, is here developed even further, and in the blending of narrative and dramatic styles *Persuasion* represents a full flowering of what can be seen, in a relatively undeveloped state, in the earlier novels.

Alongside this, Jane Austen has developed a syntax exceptionally sensitive to shifts in emotional tone. To an unprecedented extent, the narrative style has left behind the formal eighteenth-century sentence, with its elaboration of subordinate clauses and its emphatic patterning, and has moved towards a more relaxed and conversational manner, with a quiet intimacy which is in tune with the heroine's nature. In the account (in Chapter 7) of her reactions to the reappearance in her life of Captain Wentworth, we seem to experience as we read her breathless excitement as well as the painful suppression of strong feelings:

. . . And it was soon over. In two minutes after Charles's preparation, the others appeared; they were in the drawing-room. Her eye half met Captain Wentworth's; a bow, a curtsey passed; she heard

his voice—he talked to Mary, said all that was right; said something to the Miss Musgroves, enough to mark an easy footing: the
room seemed full—full of persons and voices—but a few minutes
ended it. Charles shewed himself at the window, all was ready,
their visitor had bowed and was gone; the Miss Musgroves were
gone too, suddenly resolving to walk to the end of the village with
the sportsmen: the room was cleared, and Anne might finish her
breakfast as she could.

'It is over! it is over!' she repeated to herself again, and again,
in nervous gratitude. 'The worst is over!' (P, 59–60)

This passage has been well described by Laurence Lerner as
'truly mimetic of emotion':[16] it not so much makes statements
about the fact of an emotional experience (there is a remarkable
restraint, a 'refusal to describe', about such phrases as the last
six words quoted), as suggests, by the movement of the prose, the
quality of the experience. Even the punctuation (reminiscent of
Sterne) indicates the dramatic element inherent in the sentence-
structure. Elsewhere, punctuation, and notably the marks of
exclamation and interrogation, is used to indicate a shift from
objective narrative to a prose which reflects the speech of one or
more characters. Thus the complaints of the disgruntled Mary,
for instance, find dramatic expression without a formal change-
over from narrative to dialogue:

When the plan was made known to Mary, however, there was an
end of all peace in it. She was so wretched, and so vehement, complained so much of injustice in being expected to go away, instead of
Anne;—Anne, who was nothing to Louisa, while she was her sister,
and had the best right to stay in Henrietta's stead! Why was not
she to be as useful as Anne? And to go home without Charles, too
—without her husband! No, it was too unkind! And, in short, she
said more than her husband could long withstand . . . (P, 115)

This begins and ends as narrative, but what intervenes is clearly
influenced by the tone and language of Mary's supposed remarks,
with their querulous repetitions and exclamations and their in-
dignant demand. Here is narrative prose which gains variety and

16 L. Lerner, *The Truth-Tellers* (1967) 169.

vitality from an infusion of the idioms and rhythms of speech; or, to put it another way, dialogue entering into an intimate relationship with narrative prose instead of standing resolutely and sometimes awkwardly outside it. This unobtrusively skilful and highly versatile blending of different elements was something new in the English novel, and surely constitutes one of Jane Austen's claims to be regarded as an innovator whose work looks beyond the Victorians to Henry James and the twentieth century.

There is also considerable interest in the 'cancelled chapter' of *Persuasion* for the light it throws on Jane Austen's technique, and specifically on her conscious rejection of one kind of narrative mode in favour of another. The tenth chapter of the second volume, originally the penultimate chapter of the novel, was replaced by the two chapters numbered 10 and 11 in Chapman's edition (22 and 23 where the numbering is continuous throughout). By rare good fortune, the discarded draft survived, was eventually published in the second edition of J. E. Austen-Leigh's *Memoir* (1871), and is reprinted as an appendix to R. W. Chapman's edition of *Persuasion*. The main trend of the revision is towards a fuller and more dramatic treatment of the scene, towards which the whole novel has been moving, in which Wentworth declares his love for Anne; but two specific changes are worth noting. The account of Wentworth's predicament in finding himself regarded as the lover of Louisa is converted, in the process of revision, from narrative to dialogue; and to set the two versions side by side is to see the gain in liveliness of style:

He found that he was considered by his friend Harville an engaged man. The Harvilles entertained not a doubt of a mutual attachment between him and Louisa; and though this to a degree was contradicted instantly, it yet made him feel that perhaps by *her* family, by everybody, by *herself* even, the same idea might be held, and that he was not *free* in honour, though if such were to be the conclusion, too free alas! in heart. He had never thought justly on this subject before, and he had not sufficiently considered that his excessive intimacy at Uppercross must have its danger of ill consequence in many ways; and that while trying whether he could attach

himself to either of the girls, he might be exciting unpleasant reports if not raising unrequited regard.

He found too late that he had entangled himself . . . (cancelled
version: *P*, 260)

'I found,' said he, 'that I was considered by Harville an engaged
man! That neither Harville nor his wife entertained a doubt of
our mutual attachment. I was startled and shocked. To a degree,
I could contradict this instantly; but, when I began to reflect that
others might have felt the same—her own family, nay, perhaps
herself, I was no longer at my own disposal. I was hers in honour
if she wished it. I had been unguarded. I had not thought seriously
on this subject before. I had not considered that my excessive intimacy must have its danger of ill consequence in many ways; and
that I had no right to be trying whether I could attach myself to
either of the girls, at the risk of raising even an unpleasant report,
were there no other ill effects. I had been grossly wrong, and must
abide the consequences.'

He found too late, in short, that he had entangled himself; . . .
(final version: *P*, 242–3)

The most obvious change here, apart from the shift from an impersonal narrative to a personal and dramatic form, is in sentence-structure. The three sentences of the earlier version (two
of which are above average in length) are broken up into nine
shorter sentences, with a gain in emphasis. The ponderous
Johnsonian antithesis of 'unpleasant reports . . . unrequited regard' is jettisoned; otherwise, lexically speaking, the two passages are not dissimilar, though the phrase 'startled and shocked'
is an addition. The effect of the first-person form, combined
with the shorter sentences, is to provide an increase in tempo
which the author rightly judged to be necessary at this point in
the scene.

For the climactic moment in which Anne learns of Wentworth's
love, however, a direct confrontation between the two is rejected
in favour of the writing and reading of a letter. At first sight,
this return to a Richardsonian convention may seem to involve
the opposite of an increase in dramatic power; but it does in fact

make possible the most fervent declaration of love in the Austen canon, since the letter, which is given in full, permits a more sustained and uninhibited expression of Wentworth's feelings than Jane Austen would have regarded as tolerable in dialogue. The original version, indeed, keeps the account firmly in the hands of the narrator, and the discovery of the truth is made through significant and revealing looks—'a silent but a very powerful dialogue'—rather than through speech, the actual dialogue in the central portion of the scene being confined to a single utterance of just five words. In the letter of the final version, however, neither Wentworth nor his creator suffers from any such restraint. Its style finds a correlate for the intensity of his emotion in its succession of short sentences ('You pierce my soul. I am half angry, half hope.'), with their imperatives ('Tell me not . . .', 'Dare not say . . .'), their rhetorical questions ('Have you not seen this? Can you fail to have understood my wishes?'), and their inversions: 'Unjust I may have been, weak and resentful I have been, but never inconstant'. The average sentence-length of 10.6 words is below that of most of the dialogue, as well as that of the narrative writing. The letter-form, in which Jane Austen had cast most of her early attempts at fiction, and which remains (as Chapter 5 will show) of importance throughout her work, is thus the medium through which her last novel reaches its climax.

These brief discussions of the juvenilia and the six novels have done little more than to raise some of the more important questions which need to be asked about the role of language in Jane Austen's fiction. If the exploration of particular questions has seemed to stop short precisely at the point at which it should have proceeded further, the chapters which follow have as their aim to examine and document them less inadequately.

CHAPTER TWO

'THE BEST CHOSEN LANGUAGE'

At the end of the fifth chapter of *Northanger Abbey*, Jane Austen exercises her authorial privilege and addresses the reader, at some length, in her own voice. The result is an essay (one of several, on various themes, in this early book) in defence of novel-reading; and, in the absence of prefaces in the Jamesian manner and of other developed statements on the art she was practising, it is probably the nearest we get to a direct expression of her views on fiction:

'And what are you reading, Miss ——?' 'Oh! it is only a novel!' replies the young lady; while she lays down her book with affected indifference, or momentary shame.—'It is only Cecilia, or Camilla, or Belinda;' or, in short, only some work in which the greatest powers of the mind are displayed, in which the most thorough knowledge of human nature, the happiest delineation of its varieties, the liveliest effusions of wit and humour are conveyed to the world in the best chosen language. (*NA*, 38)

'The best chosen language': the phrase seems to imply a rigorous selection from the language available to the writer, and invites comparison with the diction of the eighteenth-century poets with whom Jane Austen was familiar.[1] The reader of her novels who ponders this phrase soon becomes aware of, negatively, the con-

---

[1] One of Jane Austen's few surviving attempts at verse, *To the Memory of Mrs Lefroy* (quoted by J. E. Austen-Leigh, *A Memoir of Jane Austen* [1870] 76–8) uses not only the stock personifications of Augustan verse (*Fancy, Hope, Reason*) but also some of the recurrent nouns of the novels (*temper, genius, taste,* etc.).

spicuous absence of words referring to physical perceptions, the world of shape and colour and sensuous response; and, on the positive side, of the recurrence of a relatively small number of frequently-used words, mainly epithets and abstract nouns indicating personal qualities—qualities, that is, of character and temperament rather than outward appearance. Most of these words seem to express the standards she deems desirable in human conduct and social relationships, though of course they may in a given context be used either of those who exemplify, or of those who fail to measure up to, the implied standards. It is hard to think of another major novelist whose diction provides, to a comparable extent, a key to the qualities held to be desirable and, ultimately, to the moral attitudes behind the novels. (Perhaps Fielding provides one of the few comparable instances.) The most striking feature of Jane Austen's vocabulary is this group of terms, pointing in the same general direction: criteria of worth by means of which her characters, and the types and tendencies they represent, may be assessed. It is no exaggeration to describe these terms as *key-words*, of which Stephen Ullmann has written:

Most inquiries concerned with key-words are statistically orientated, but the concept can also be defined in qualitative terms. [G. Matoré] has described them as 'lexicological units expressing a society . . . denoting a person, a feeling, an idea which are alive in so far as society recognizes in them its ideal.' This approach can also be applied to individual authors. In this way, Corneille has been re-examined in the light of a small number of key-words epitomizing his ideals and aspirations: *mérite, estime, devoir, vertu, générosité*—and of course the famous *gloire* which, for a Cornelian hero, is the very breath of his nostrils.[2]

Jane Austen's key-words are different from those of Corneille, but they express her 'ideals and aspirations' no less: to possess *taste* and *judgment*, to be deemed *amiable* and *respectable*, may be said to be the very breath of an Austen heroine's nostrils, and the

[2] S. Ullmann, 'Style and Personality', *A Review of English Literature*, 6 (1965) 27.

importance of these words in her style is comparable to that of the Cornelian *gloire* or the Virgilian *pietas*. The usefulness of the present discussion is in proportion to the light shed on the under-lying attitudes and values of Jane Austen's work; what will be stressed, therefore, is the need to arrive at a precise sense of the meaning carried by these words for the writer and her contemporaries. And the fact that these are very common words for the most part should not lead us to undervalue their significance: as G. U. Yule has observed, 'Surely the colour and flavour of a text . . . are determined not by the exceptional words, unless these words taken together form a large class, but in the main by the common words used by the author, the words used by him over and over again?'[3]

In a useful discussion of the eighteenth-century taste for personification, B. H. Bronson has pointed out that we have, since that period, 'moved from a taste for the abstract—which (in other than aesthetic fields) is often supposed a mark of maturity— to a preference for the concrete'.[4] As one deeply committed in many respects to the linguistic inheritance of the century in which she was born, Jane Austen shares its 'taste for the abstract', a taste shared also by her favourite writers in prose and verse. As a novelist, on the other hand, she was necessarily involved with the concrete, since, at any rate on the surface, a novel must be concerned with specific individuals moving about in the material world. Inevitably, therefore, she writes of particular people in particular places—taking walks or making calls or visiting shops, giving and eating dinners, playing the pianoforte or picking strawberries. Yet the material solidity and circum-stantiality of this world is something that she has relatively little interest in rendering: there is in her novels almost none of the minute description of externals—people and their dress, houses and furniture and landscapes—that is such an important element

[3] G. U. Yule, *The Statistical Study of Literary Vocabulary* (Cambridge, 1944) 2.

[4] B. H. Bronson, 'Personification Reconsidered', *English Literary History*, 14 (1947) 165.

in creating the fictional worlds of Dickens and George Eliot and Hardy. We know Emma, for instance, intimately as a *mind*: in some respects we know her better than she knows herself; yet of her physical existence we know almost nothing, and the description of the heroine in Chapter 5 of *Emma* is, apart from a reference to her 'hazel eye', remarkably lacking in precise detail. In general, the reader intent upon creating mental pictures of fictional characters will find little evidence in this novelist to assist his imaginative efforts. This can be seen by comparing Miss Bates in the same novel with a character possessing some points of resemblance, Dickens's Miss Tox in *Dombey and Son*: when, in the third chapter of *Emma*, Miss Bates is introduced to the reader, he is told that she

enjoyed a most uncommon degree of popularity for a woman neither young, handsome, rich, nor married. Miss Bates stood in the very worst predicament in the world for having much of the public favour; and she had no intellectual superiority to make atonement to herself, or frighten those who might hate her, into outward respect. She had never boasted either beauty or cleverness. Her youth had passed without distinction, and her middle of life was devoted to the care of a failing mother, and the endeavour to make a small income go as far as possible. And yet she was a happy woman, and a woman whom no one named without good-will. It was her own universal good-will and contented temper which worked such wonders . . . The simplicity and cheerfulness of her nature, her contented and grateful spirit, were a recommendation to everybody and a mine of felicity to herself. She was a great talker upon little matters, which exactly suited Mr Woodhouse, full of trivial communications and harmless gossip. (*E*, 21)

This is highly informative, and Miss Bates's subsequent speech and behaviour illustrate but scarcely add to this assessment of her character. The method, however, is to relate her qualities to universal standards rather than to insist on those aspects of her appearance or behaviour which help to create her unique individuality. The balance-sheet of her deficiencies and virtues is scrupulously drawn up: the negative definitions of the first half of

E

the passage quoted (*neither, no, never, without*) are triumphantly cancelled by the declarations which follow, introduced by 'And yet she was a happy woman...'—declarations which resort to such abstractions as *good-will, temper, simplicity, cheerfulness*. When Mr Weston observes of Miss Bates, later in the novel, that ' "She is a standing lesson of how to be happy",' one sees the force of Jane Austen's mode of presentation: Miss Bates is not just a delightful example of humorous observation, but a model of one kind of moral excellence, and the language used necessarily reflects this purpose. Miss Tox is presented in very different terms:

The lady thus specially presented was a long lean figure, wearing such a faded air that she seemed not to have been made in what linen-drapers call 'fast colours' originally, and to have, by little and little, washed out. But for this, she might have been described as the very pink of general propitiation and politeness. From a long habit of listening admirably to everything that was said in her presence, and looking at the speakers as if she were mentally engaged in taking off impressions of their images upon her soul, never to part with the same but with life, her head had quite settled on one side. Her hands had contracted a spasmodic habit of raising themselves of their own accord as in involuntary admiration. Her eyes were liable to a similar affection. She had the softest voice that ever was heard; and her nose, stupendously aquiline, had a little knob in the very centre or key-stone of the bridge, whence it tended downwards towards her face, as in an invincible determination never to turn up at anything. (*Dombey and Son*, Chapter 1)

Figure, head, hands, eyes, voice, nose: Dickens offers us a catalogue of Miss Tox's physical oddities, sometimes deducing from these her mental habits; but our sense of the primacy of a physical presence is strong. (A further paragraph, too long to quote, describes in detail her dress and gait: her 'bonnets and caps', 'collars, frills, tuckers, wristbands', 'tippets, boas, and muffs', 'lockets', and so forth.) The visualization of Dickens's characters is, of course, exceptionally strong; but what is really remarkable in Jane Austen is the virtually complete absence of this element. This deliberate playing-down of the surface of life is her way of

relating the localized and limited world of the novel to those
wider issues of conduct which are, for her, all-important, and
which alone justify the claim of the novel to be taken seriously.
Attention is focused, therefore, upon speech and action, and the
analysis of their implications, rather than upon costume and
scenery; and stylistically this tendency is manifested in her preference for the abstract noun, or its related epithet, to the word
denoting substance or appearance. When actual physical objects
are mentioned, the reference is most often ironical or satirical, as
with the laundry-bills which caused Catherine Morland such
feverish excitement, or Miss Bates's concern over her mother's
spectacles, which is cleverly if unkindly parodied by Emma:
' "And then fly off, through half a sentence, to her mother's old
petticoat . . ." ' The concrete is thus equated with the trivial,
which cannot long occupy the attention of the well-regulated
mind and has no serious place in a novel which expects to be
regarded as more than ephemeral. For this preference for the
abstract is, it is perhaps necessary to add, partly a convention
of the kind of public discourse viewed as appropriate to the
novelist's art. In her private writings, as the Letters repeatedly
demonstrate, Jane Austen was quite capable of finding a source
of lively interest in the pattern of a new gown. In the novels, on
the other hand, there is a carefully-guarded frontier between the
serious use of abstract language by the narrator and those
characters who command respect, and the foolish or absurd or
suspiciously frivolous use of the concrete. This is obvious as soon
as one compares (say) the language of Mr Woodhouse, whose
conversational topics rarely rise above gruel and apple-tarts or
the state of the weather, with that of Mr Knightley, who constantly refers individual instances to the standards provided by
experience and reflection and embodied in abstractions. Mr
Woodhouse's universe is governed by his personal tastes and
timidities; Mr Knightley (whose very name suggests an abstract
and ideal virtue) tests the particular by reference to the general.
The same difference exists between Harriet and Emma: the
latter, though she behaves foolishly, is no fool, and the two friends

are shown speaking virtually different languages in, for example, their discussion of Mr Elton in Chapter 9.

Jane Austen's partiality for the abstract word has not passed altogether unnoticed; it has prompted a handful of brief references by critics mainly intent upon other matters, but has not received the detailed treatment its importance demands. C. S. Lewis, relating her work to the eighteenth century, remarks on 'the hardness—at least the firmness—of Jane Austen's thought . . . The great abstract nouns of the classical English moralists are unblushingly and uncompromisingly used . . . These are the concepts by which Jane Austen grasps the world. In her we still breathe the air of the *Rambler* and *Idler*. All is hard, clear, definable . . .' and Arnold Kettle points out that 'the precision of her standards emerges in her style. Each word has a precise and unambiguous meaning based on a social usage at once subtle and stable'.[5] However, the use of abstract words is not, of course, a stylistic virtue *per se*; and Lewis has reminded us elsewhere of the marked contrast between two kinds of style to be found in the novels of Jane Austen's contemporary, Sir Walter Scott: that of the dialogue passages (especially those put into the mouths of the characters from humble life)—vivid in vocabulary and vigorous in its rhythms—and the often turgid and long-winded style of many of the narrative and descriptive passages. Lewis adds that 'the early nineteenth century found English in a bloated condition. The abstract is preferred to the concrete. The word farthest from the soil is liked best . . .'[6] Although Jane Austen certainly shares her generation's fondness for the abstract word, 'bloated' is almost the last epithet one can justly apply to her style. Plainly, a preference for the abstract over the concrete cannot in itself be regarded as either a vice or a virtue of style: the question is a more complex one than this simple antithesis suggests, and involves a consideration of the strength and precision of the concepts that lie behind this class of diction.

[5] C. S. Lewis, 'A Note on Jane Austen', *Essays in Criticism*, 4 (1954) 363; A. Kettle, *Introduction to the English Novel*, Volume I (1951) 93.
[6] C. S. Lewis, *They Asked for a Paper* (1962) 102.

Taking these useful observations as starting-points, the need seems to exist for a more thorough description and analysis of this area of vocabulary, with an attempt to enumerate the most important words in question and to define them according to the senses they bear for Jane Austen. But before we consider what words are in question—what are the epithets and the 'great abstract nouns' which so largely convey the standards of her moral universe—it is important to take into account some of the obstacles to understanding which time and semantic change have erected. Speaking of the study of Greek, Edmund Wilson has asked 'what moral-aesthetic values were implied by the Greek abstract words that denoted human qualities?'[7] The English of Jane Austen is much nearer to us than the Greek of Plato, but there is nevertheless a gap to be bridged, which we ignore only at the cost of an incomplete apprehension of her meaning. For although Jane Austen may fairly be described (in so far as the phrase still remains meaningful) as a popular classic, familiar to the common reader as well as to the student and the critic, it can be argued that a full and accurate understanding of even the literal meaning of what she wrote may not be so easily and confidently arrived at as some may suppose. Many words, it is true, are employed in a sense which is hardly to be distinguished from that of the present day, though the word in question may now have acquired a formality which inhibits its frequent use by a modern writer or speaker. *Agreeable, benevolence, esteem, exertion, folly, rectitude, resolution* are some common examples. Time, that is, has not so much changed the world's basic meaning as rendered it less familiar, or at least less likely to occur (except with facetious intent) in informal contexts. Such words present no problems of comprehension, though they may contribute to an impression of precision, and perhaps of primness. Nor is the problem of the occasional obsolete word a serious one: if we are puzzled by references to negus or a barouche-landau, the matter can be quickly settled. There is more possibility of confusion when the word includes among its range of meanings both a

[7] E. Wilson, *The Bit between my Teeth* (New York, 1965) 599.

familiar modern and an archaic sense. When Mary Musgrove in *Persuasion* complains that the children's grandmother gives them 'so much trash and sweet things', the phrase has a distinctly contemporary ring and many readers no doubt unhesitatingly interpret *trash* in the present-day sense of 'rubbish', though it is likely that the meaning here is the more specific one of 'the refuse of sugar-canes after the juice has been expressed'. Some words, indeed, are used by Jane Austen in more than one sense: *address*, for instance, appears at different times with different meanings, archaic and modern. When Elinor says of Edward Ferrars that 'his address is certainly not striking', she is not referring to his place of residence, or to his skill or expertise in a particular field, though the word is elsewhere found in both these senses in Jane Austen's writings, but to his social manner and bearing. *Comfortable*, *elegant* and *expensive* are among many others which may from time to time bring the reader to a momentary halt, in order to resolve the unforeseen ambiguity.

The most serious possibilities of misunderstanding, however, spring from another category of words: those which, although still in everyday use, have undergone a more or less substantial shift of meaning in the century and a half since Jane Austen wrote. (As F. P. Wilson says of the same problem with regard to Shakespeare: 'The real danger comes with words to which it is possible to attach the modern meaning and make sense. But the sense is not Shakespeare's.'[8]) And since this category includes many words expressive of feelings and attitudes, standards and values, misunderstanding or incomplete understanding may be a serious matter. Often, though not always, the change has taken the form of 'deterioration', a decline from precision to looseness of meaning which seems to correspond to the decay of the traditional certainties and unquestioned assumptions on which the earlier meanings rested. It is a very common experience in reading eighteenth-century prose or verse to encounter a word used in a sense which obviously carries more weight and significance

[8] F. P. Wilson, *Shakespeare and the Diction of Common Life* (British Academy Shakespeare Lecture, 1941) 6–7.

than our own usage of the same word. What has been suffered is a loss of intensity, an enfeebling of the language. Consider the following, selected almost at random (the italics are mine in each case):

. . . that fine Taste of writing, which is so much talked of among the *Polite* World. (Addison)

. . . the whole magnificence of Nature, whether pleasing or *dreadful.* (Johnson)

Macpherson said he had strong and *nice* feelings . . . (Boswell)

The *decent* church that tops the neighbouring hill. (Goldsmith)

For who, to dumb Forgetfulness a prey,
This pleasing *anxious* being e'er resigned . . . (Gray)

These five epithets are still in common use, but have suffered a sea-change: such words as *nice* and *dreadful,* like Milton's *horrid,* now belong to the language of the nursery (or the cocktail party) rather than that of serious adult discourse, and demand a real effort of the linguistic imagination if we are to react to them in the way their authors expected and their original readers found entirely natural. Other words—*candid, complacent, genius, romantic* are familiar examples all used by Jane Austen—have changed even more radically, and in some contexts will strike the modern reader as hardly making sense according to present-day usage. (One wonders what the uninformed reader would now make of the phrase 'her candor was not to be surpassed' in the obituary notice published four days after Jane Austen's death.)[9] An alert consciousness of all these categories of words, with some awareness of their ancestry and their subsequent vicissitudes, is surely essential if we are not to be frequently misled as to the sheer meaning of the text. What this chapter seeks to do, therefore, is to elucidate some of the key items of Jane Austen's

[9] Cf. B. C. Southam, 'Jane Austen', *Times Literary Supplement,* No. 3170, 30 November 1962, 944.

vocabulary, and in the process to provide valuable insights into her moral and ethical preoccupations.

Her deeply-ingrained habit of sitting in judgment on character, and of recording this judgment in carefully-weighed words, may be traced throughout her writing career, in the juvenilia and the letters as well as the novels. Repeatedly, she effects a moral 'placing' by means of the classifications and distinctions provided by the language of her time, whether the character in question is that of a chance acquaintance in her daily life or a major fictional creation. To quote a handful of examples, from various sources and of different degrees of seriousness:

. . . his Sorrow was not without a mixture of Happiness, and his Affliction was considerably lessened by his Joy. (*MW*, 41)

I do not perceive wit or genius, but she has sense and some degree of taste, and her manners are very engaging. (*Letters*, 142)

She was sensible and clever, but eager in every thing; her sorrows, her joys, could have no moderation. She was generous, amiable, interesting; she was every thing but prudent. (*SS*, 6)

The indignities of stupidity, and the disappointments of selfish passion, can excite little pity. (*MP*, 464)

There is a range here from the public to the private use of language, and from the particular judgment to the general reflection, but there is also a common stylistic quality—an unusual dependence on a relatively small number of words of similar type—which is shared by innumerable other instances.

Some of the appearances of a single word in one of the novels may serve to illustrate in miniature the use of these terms to indicate, with sureness and precision, the social and moral standards deemed desirable. The notion of 'elegance' occurs often in *Emma*. The quality is one that the heroine both admires in others and seeks to exemplify herself; it is shown, too, by another character who serves as a foil to Emma: living with the Campbells, Jane Fairfax has enjoyed 'all the rational pleasures of an elegant society' and has profited by her experience. (We may note in passing the collocation of *elegant* with *rational*, entirely natural in Jane Austen but much less likely today.) Emma is surprised by the 'appearance and manners' of this social nonentity: 'Jane Fairfax was very elegant, remarkably elegant; and she had herself the highest value for elegance'. In contrast to Jane stands Mrs Elton: though at first spoken of in Highbury as 'handsome, elegant, highly accomplished, and perfectly amiable', she is judged very differently by Emma in the light of first-hand knowledge: 'She would not be in a hurry to find fault, but she suspected that there was no elegance; ease, but no elegance'. The last phrase quoted is typical of the frequent care taken to distinguish between qualities superficially similar and (by implication) often confused. In Emma's judgment of Frank Churchill in Chapter 38, benevolence is distinguished from friendship—a more precious and personal gift, to be bestowed less lightly—with similar scrupulousness.

Where elegance is concerned, Mr Elton comes off little better than his wife: Emma considers that 'with all the gentleness of his address, true elegance was sometimes wanting'; and Frank Churchill fares no better—his 'indifference to a confusion of rank bordered too much on inelegance of mind' in the eyes of the status-conscious heroine. 'Of *mind*': these examples make it clear that the quality of elegance, nowadays evoked mainly in sartorial and decorative contexts, entails for Jane Austen far more than smartness, sophistication, and social assurance: if we may come to know the word through the company it keeps, its yoke-fellows suggest that it is to be taken altogether more seriously, as an attribute of deeper value and more difficult attainment. In the essay already cited, Arnold Kettle defines elegance of mind as involving 'a genuine sensibility to human values as well as the more superficial refinements of polished manner',[10] and this definition sets a higher standard than the Eltons and their like are capable of achieving. Mere *ease* is commoner and ranks lower on a scale of moral values. Not unnaturally, words of this kind

[10] A. Kettle, *op. cit.*, 96.

are used in their shallower sense by characters whose own moral values are questionable. Mr Collins, for example, assuming that Elizabeth Bennet rejects his proposal only in order to inflame his passion further, attributes her behaviour to 'the usual practice of elegant females'; Elizabeth's notion of elegance is naturally very different, however, and she ironically disclaims any pretension to 'that kind of elegance which consists in tormenting a respectable man' (a phrase which neatly satirizes Mr Collins's corrupt usage of the term). The word recurs throughout this scene in *Pride and Prejudice* (Chapter 19) like a Wagnerian *leitmotiv*, and a few lines later Elizabeth determines to secure her father's co-operation in staving off her unwelcome suitor, since Mr Bennet's negative at least 'could not be mistaken for the affectation and coquetry of an elegant female'. As often, a firm distinction is drawn between the sense given to the word by Jane Austen—the best sense, that is—and the limited and falsifying meaning attached to it by those of whom she disapproves. There are class-distinctions in the use of language as well as in society.

As these few examples show, *elegance* is a much richer and more meaningful term used by Jane Austen than it can ever be in the hands of a present-day writer. Like many words which she uses for the most part with entire seriousness, it often carries nowadays an overtone of humour or irony. Moreover, its field of reference has become drastically restricted, whereas the contexts of the above quotations make it clear that for Jane Austen it can cover a range of senses, from the conventional coquettishness which is its meaning for Mr Collins (and from which the writer plainly dissociates herself), through the attractive dignity in appearance and social manner which Emma finds in Jane Fairfax, to that fine sensitivity and discrimination and instinctive good taste (without, again, any of the unfortunate overtones which the latter phrase has acquired) which constitute elegance of mind. Jane Austen is, then, exploiting a diction which is often qualitatively if not quantitatively richer than our own, and she does so with a fineness of perception of shades of meaning to which it is only too easy for us to be insensitive.

The full range of her vocabulary of characterization embraces aspects of personal appearance and manners, social qualities, intellectual endowment and cultivation, the practical application of common sense to behaviour, and the moral virtues. These are not, of course, sharply defined or mutually exclusive categories; and their significance can perhaps best be clarified in the process of specifying and examining instances from the novels.

References to personal appearance are limited, and almost invariably concern overall impressions rather than specific features. Among them, the usage of *handsome* and *pretty* perhaps calls for comment. Both have contracted their field of reference since Jane Austen wrote: the former, nowadays used generally of masculine, or of maturer feminine, charms, was defined by Johnson as 'beautiful with dignity' and is commonly used of female characters. It is, for instance, the first epithet applied to the young heroine in the opening sentence of *Emma*. *Pretty*, on the other hand, now almost exclusively feminine in usage, was once applied freely to both sexes, and 'pretty fellow' was a favourite eighteenth-century expression. It is thus used of both Emma and Mr Elton, though as it is Mr Woodhouse who describes the latter as 'a very pretty young man', the usage may already have had an old-fashioned ring. *Pretty* often suggests a degree of beauty inferior to *handsome*, and one detects a note of condescension in Lady Catherine de Bourgh's reference to Elizabeth Bennet as 'a very genteel, pretty kind of girl'. The two adjectives are used interchangeably by (significantly) the foolish Mrs Palmer in *Sense and Sensibility*: ' "I don't think her hardly at all handsomer than you . . . for I think you both excessively pretty . . ." ' Of appearance in more general terms, the nouns *manner* and *address* occur frequently, and suggest that quality of bearing and behaviour without which good looks are insufficient to achieve distinction. At the beginning of the novel just referred to, Edward Ferrars seems to Mrs Dashwood and her daughters to be without ' "any peculiar graces of person or address" '. The positive virtue of pleasing appearance and manner is *elegance*; but, as has already been suggested, mere fashionableness is no guarantee of elegance, and such characters as Lucy Steele (who 'was certainly not elegant') and Isabella Thorpe (who has 'stilishness' but not 'real elegance') strive for but fail to attain it.

Other epithets applied to manner are *agreeable*, *amiable*, *civil*, *courteous*, *easy*, *gallant*, *polite*. As in present-day usage, the difference between civility and politeness is one of degree, though a difference in social status may also be implied. The *OED* defines *civil* as decently polite . . . not (actually) rude'; and this is the sense in which we read of Emma's behaviour to Mr Elton: 'she could not be rude . . . she was even positively civil . . .' This implication of a minimal politeness is, however, surely not what is intended when we read, earlier in the same novel, that Mr Woodhouse is 'universally civil': the sense here seems to be rather of a formal, somewhat old-fashioned courtesy, and since Mr Woodhouse is the head of the most important family in Highbury, the word may be dictated by the considerations of relative status referred to above (one is civil to inferiors, polite to equals and superiors). A similar formality is implied by the statement that the 'intimacy' prevailing between Emma and Mr Elton would reasonably be terminated by his marriage: 'It would be almost beginning their life of civility again'. One has in such phrases a glimpse of a finely-graduated scale of controlled behaviour, with friends and acquaintances placed according to the relative warmth or coolness of manner judged as apropriate to the relationship, and with modifications in this placing made only after due consideration. On the same scale, *courteous* and *gallant* imply varying degrees of warmth. *Amiable* is a good example of a class of words used by Jane Austen with a precision which can only be recovered after scraping away the accumulated deposit of the past century and a half. The modern use of the word damns with faint praise: a bland, easy-going attitude to life can easily become fatuous, uncritical, and downright boring. In contrast, some idea of the force and dignity the word was capable of carrying in this period is suggested by Wordsworth's comment, in a letter dated 11 February 1805 which refers to his dead brother, that 'he was one of the most amiable of men'. In the novels, it is constantly used as a term of approbation: Charles Hayter in *Persuasion* is 'a very amiable, pleasing young man', and later in the same novel Captain Wentworth sums up Louisa Musgrove as 'a very amiable, sweet-tempered girl'. The word makes many appearances in similar company, and clearly carries the implication of qualities more positive than mere inoffensiveness. It is in fact explicitly defined by Mr Knightley—a character who is linguistically *sans reproche*:Emma's reference to Frank Churchill as 'an amiable young man' provokes the following remonstrance:

'No, Emma, your amiable young man can be amiable only in French, not in English. He may be very "aimable", have very good manners, and be very agreeable; but he can have no English delicacy towards the feelings of other people: nothing really amiable about him.' (*E*, 149)

The superficial Gallic associations of the word (which we may infer to have been influencing fashionable English usage) are contrasted with the more weighty English sense: in his speech, as in every other way, George Knightley seems intended to represent everything that Jane Austen regards as particularly admirable in the English gentleman.

It is Mr Knightley, again, who observes ' "I love an open temper" ' (his comment is provoked by Jane Fairfax's apparent lack of this quality); and it is Frank Churchill's 'very open temper' that Mrs Weston finds pleasing in early acquaintance with that young man, who fails to live up to the promise of his Christian name. Both the noun and the adjective in these expressions deserve attention. Three further quotations will show that the quality of *openness* is shared by characters of very different kinds. In *Northanger Abbey*, Henry Tilney ironically describes the character of Miss Thorpe as 'open, candid, artless, guileless . . .'; in *Mansfield Park*, Edmund Bertram finds an agreeable 'openness of heart' in Mary Crawford; and in *Sense and Sensibility*, we are told of the 'openness and heartiness' of Mrs Palmer's manner. The openness that Mary Crawford appears to possess, and Jane Fairfax to lack, is a straightforwardness, an 'absence of dissimulation' (in the words of the *OED*), in her dealings with others. With Mrs Palmer, on the other hand, something more like sociability and on uninhibited ease of manner is suggested. The opposite of openness is *reserve*, an antithesis made explicit in Chapter 27 of *Sense and Sensibility*: 'Elinor, distressed by this charge of reserve in herself, which she was not at liberty to do away, knew not how, under such circumstances, to press for greater openness in Marianne'. In the same novel *reserve* is used frequently of Edward Ferrars, in the company of such words as *shyness* and *coldness*; on one occasion, Elinor does her best to reassure him that Marianne, who has just used the word to his face, is not the soundest judge of a less demonstrative nature than her own: ' "Do you not know she calls every one reserved, who does not talk as fast, and admire what she admires as rapturously as herself?" ' *Rapture* is indeed a key-word for Marianne's character, and a warning-signal of her lack of necessary self-control. Jane Fairfax, who has already been cited as wanting 'openness', is also frequently described as 'reserved', which again is coupled with such epithets as *cold* and *cautious*. On first making her acquaintance, Emma concludes that 'She was disgustingly, was suspiciously reserved'; and in a discussion of Jane between Emma and Frank Churchill in Chapter 25, *reserve* and *reserved* are used six times in less than a dozen lines. Jane Fairfax's own consciousness of this quality is expressed near the end of the novel, when she tells Emma, ' " ... I know what my manners were to you. So cold and artificial! I had a part to act. It was a life of deceit! I know that I must have disgusted you." ' In this sense, reserve is morally reprehensible in so far as it is potentially destructive of the knowledge and trust upon which right relationships must be built.

If Jane Fairfax is repeatedly found to be *reserved*, Harriet Smith in the same novel is by contrast *artless*. She possesses an unspoiled innocence which reflects the limitations of both her experience and her intelligence. When she speaks it is with 'a very interesting naïveté'; her grief at being disappointed over Mr Elton is 'truly artless' (genuine and without mercenary motive); and

Mr Knightley, who is always to be relied on as a judge of character, describes her as 'an unpretending, single-minded, artless girl' and again as 'an artless, amiable girl'. The word seems to suggest in Harriet a quality of unaffected simplicity and sincerity of feeling and conduct, in contrast to (for example) the 'artful' Lucy Steele, who is found guilty of 'want of real . . . artlessness'. As so often, one feels the weight and firmness of a word whose significance has by our time deteriorated almost to vanishing-point: we are unlikely to use *artless* or *artful* except whimsically, but for Jane Austen both still carry the force of a moral standard.

The same loss of verbal precision can be detected in the subsequent history of *temper*, which also for Jane Austen represents an important quality of character and social behaviour. It is true that she occasionally uses the word in the modern sense of ill humour, as when Mr Weston speaks of the exasperating invalid Mrs Churchill as having 'the devil of a temper'; and a slightly different but related sense is implied when Henry Tilney, referring to his father's attitude towards his deceased wife, comments: ' "though his temper injured her, his judgment never did" ', where the variable and unreliable element of *temper* is contrasted with the more stable quality of *judgment*. Normally, however, the sense is of *good* temper—and this not merely as a passing mood, but as a settled, consistent feature of the individual temperament, a happy blending of self-control and good humour in one's relationships with others, and hence one of the most important qualities of the truly agreeable personality. Thus, Mrs Elton remarks of 'that excellent Mr Weston': ' "I do not know his equal for temper" '—an observation which bears a sense the reverse of present-day usage. When Frank Churchill shows signs of tender feelings for herself instead of for Harriet, Emma 'had difficulty in behaving with temper'. *Temper* in this sense is a guarantee of the needful quality of benevolence, which in *Emma* is carefully distinguished, as a prime social virtue, from the more personal and private quality of friendship: 'General benevolence, not general friendship, made a man what he ought to be'.

Benevolence, in turn, has much in common with *candour*,

which (with *candid*) is very commonly used in a sense which might disconcert the modern reader who was not attuned to the substantial shift in meaning that these words have undergone. Johnson defines candour as 'sweetness of temper, kindness' and candid as 'free from malice, not desirous to find faults'. This is the sense intended in Pope's line (in the *Essay on Man*) 'Laugh where we must, be candid where we can'; and according to Susie Tucker it is 'the usual eighteenth-century sense'.[11] The *OED* lists the sense 'freedom from malice, kindliness' as obsolete, and offers a quotation from Johnson himself, 'sincere, but without candour' (1751) which neatly demonstrates the drastic effect of the shift in meaning, since the phrase is rendered nonsense by the present-day meaning. The following examples will illustrate Jane Austen's usage, which is firmly in line with that of the eighteenth century: 'candidly and generously', 'candour and generosity', 'candour and indulgence', 'neither reasonable nor candid'. The collocations are revealing, and to interpret these usages in the modern sense would seriously distort the meaning: one wonders how many readers have misunderstood the spirit of Elinor's observation of Willoughby, ' "It is my wish to be candid in my judgment of every body" '. The word is defined for us by Elizabeth Bennet when she tells her sister Jane that

Affectation of candour is common enough;—one meets it every where. But to be candid without ostentation or design—to take the good of every body's character and make it still better, and say nothing of the bad—belongs to you alone. (*PP*, 14–15)

R. W. Chapman claims that, in Jane Austen's writings, '*candid* and *candour* seem never to mean telling the truth without regard to consequences';[12] but there is at least one instance of *candidly* in the modern sense. Significantly, it is the upstart Mrs

[11] S. Tucker, *Protean Shape: a Study in Eighteenth-Century Vocabulary and Usage* (1967) 213.

[12] R. W. Chapman, *The Novels of Jane Austen*, Volume 1, 393. (The Appendix on 'Miss Austen's English' is almost entirely devoted to lexical questions. See pages 388–421 of that volume.)

Elton who gives the word its modern usage, evidently in the process of ousting the one generally favoured, when she observes, ' "I candidly told you I should form my own opinion" '.

The man or woman whose social qualities reach the required standard is deemed *respectable*, another word which has suffered a drastic devaluation and diminution of force since Jane Austen used it. It is one of a class of words (*worthy* is another) of which Susie Tucker observes that 'whereas they used to be generous, they are now grudging'.[13] The opening paragraph of *Sense and Sensibility* tells the reader that the Dashwoods have lived at Norland Park in a 'respectable' manner 'for many generations'. The sense is obviously not just that of a decent cleanliness, honesty and sobriety: the Dashwoods enjoy considerable social status and the esteem of their neighbours ('the general good opinion of their surrounding acquaintance'). Again, Colonel Brandon is described as 'a very respectable man' and the Middletons as 'a very respectable family'. The word strikes somewhat oddly today, used of members of such a social class; and, encountering these passages, one is again conscious of an adjustment to the familiar meaning, a revaluation upwards, that must be made before the writer's intention can be successfully grasped. In the sense in which Jane Austen uses it, *respectable* seems to have established itself as late as the mid eighteenth century, and to have embraced social and moral qualities alike: 'worthy of respect by reason of moral excellence' (from 1755), and 'of good or fair social standing, and having the moral qualities appropriate to this' (from 1758), according to the *OED*.[14] The word was not long, however, in shedding its association of moral qualities with social status; certainly by the time Dickens came to describe Mr Vholes in *Bleak House* (1853) as 'respectable', it had acquired strong overtones of carefully-guarded and somewhat insecure lower-middle-class standing. Something similar has happened to *genteel*,

---

[13] Tucker, *op. cit.*, 229.

[14] The following quotation, however, dated 1749, from Lord Chesterfield (Letter 1653 in B. Dobrée's edition), seems to antedate the examples given in *OED*: 'a merry fellow was never yet a respectable man'.

F

which has largely lost its associations (still operating in Jane Austen's use of the word) with the moral attributes of gentility, and retains only those of a somewhat disparagingly regarded class-consciousness.

Among intellectual qualities, *knowledge*, *understanding* and (in one of its senses) *genius* occur frequently. Knowledge is, of course, acquired by diligent study, whereas understanding (now largely displaced by 'intelligence') is natural mental capacity: ' "Nature gave you understanding" ', as Mr Knightley tells Emma. *Genius* is also used in the sense of 'natural ability or capacity' rather than in the Johnsonian sense of 'characteristic disposition'. We read in *Persuasion* of Captain Wentworth's 'genius and ardour' which have enabled him to rise quickly in his profession; and Marianne Dashwood's enquiry, with reference to Willoughby, has already been quoted: ' "What [are] his pursuits, his talents and genius?" ' She also observes of Colonel Brandon that he 'has neither genius, taste nor spirit'. This is the usual sense for Jane Austen, though *Mansfield Park* contains an example of the modern usage: '. . . aware that he must not expect a genius in Mr Rushworth'. Among related epithets are *clever* and *well-informed*. *Clever* has not always been as widely-used as it is today: originally a colloquialism and a dialect word (Sir Thomas Browne cites it (1682) as a Norfolk term) with the sense 'nimble-handed', its meaning seems to have been extended to mental dexterity early in the eighteenth century. In *Emma* (which provides the *OED* with one of its examples) it is a key-word, not only applied to the heroine (e.g., in the opening sentence of the novel, and in Mr Knightley's remark that ' "Emma is spoiled by being the cleverest of [her] family" '), but used positively or negatively of several other characters. Mr John Knightley was 'a very clever man', but it is made clear that Miss Bates lacks cleverness and that Harriet Smith too 'certainly was not clever'. The opposites of well-informed are *ignorant* and *illiterate*, the latter bearing the general sense of 'uneducated' rather than the narrower, technical sense now usual.

With the word 'clever' echoing in his ears, the reader of *Emma* is likely to reflect that cleverness is not enough; and the importance of common sense in Jane Austen's scheme of values is suggested by the frequent appearances of such adjectives as *sensible, rational, prudent,* and the favourite noun *judgment.* In spite of Johnson's comment on *sensible,* that in 'low conversation it has sometimes the sense of reasonable; judicious; wise'[15] this is the meaning that seems to have become acceptable by Jane Austen's time, as when we are told that Mr Knightley is 'a sensible man', and (by Mr Knightley) that Harriet is 'not a sensible girl'. Similarly, Edmund Bertram speaks of 'sensible women', and the epithet is several times applied to Mr Elliot in *Persuasion* ('a sensible, discerning mind', etc.). It is used memorably by Elizabeth Bennet, when she asks her father, after they have perused Mr Collins's self-introductory letter, ' "Can he be a sensible man, sir?" ' and it is echoed a few pages later, when Mr Collins appears: 'Mr Collins was not a sensible man . . .' *Rational* is sometimes used in the sense of 'civilized' or 'cultivated', as when we learn that Jane Fairfax has enjoyed 'all the rational pleasures of an elegant society'. But it is also used to refer to a quality which is favourably contrasted with the free indulgence of the feelings: 'Elton may talk sentimentally, but he will act rationally'; '. . . the woman whom he had rationally, as well as passionately loved'. Rationality is a central concept in Jane Austen's thought, and is evidently not inconsistent with the deepest and strongest feelings. There is a poignant example of the word in one of her last letters (*L*, 496), where she observes that she is now out of bed and able to 'eat my meals with aunt Cass[andra] in a rational way'.

The reverse of 'sensible' behaviour is *imprudence,* or, more strongly, *folly,* though even the latter is less grievous than *vice,* as a comparative reference to Julia and Maria Bertram in Chapter 47 of *Mansfield Park* shows. As prudence is the keynote of Elinor Dashwood's character, so the lack of it characterizes her sister: 'She was generous, amiable, interesting: she was every thing but prudent'. At many points in the same novel, Marianne's

---

[15] Tucker, *op. cit.*, 250.

lack of prudence is stressed, with a notable use of the word *romantic* (as when Elinor says of her, ' "her opinions are all romantic" '). *Romantic*, in the eighteenth-century rather than the Wordsworthian sense, is common in the earlier writings: characteristic phrases are 'girlishly romantic' and 'romantic non-sense' (*MW*, 132, 294). It again collocates with *prudence* in the criticism of Mrs Dashwood's character: 'Common sense, common care, common prudence, were all sunk in Mrs Dashwood's romantic delicacy'. Marianne's failings are evidently inherited. The key-word *sensibility* belongs to the same group: it appears *passim* in *Love and Freindship*, and at one point in *Sense and Sensibility* is explicitly equated with 'indulgence of feeling'.

There remains an important group of words which denote the qualities of the truly admirable mind and character: *benevolence*, *candour* and *temper* have already been discussed, and to these should be added *delicacy*, *firmness*, *integrity*, *principle*, *rectitude*, *resolution*, *self-command*, *steadiness*. Repeatedly, these words provide standards by which important distinctions of moral worth may be made. In Chapter 33 of *Mansfield Park*, for in-stance, Fanny's 'delicacy' is contrasted with Crawford's 'want of delicacy'; and in later chapters the same word recurs in such phrases as Fanny's 'natural delicacy' (Ch. 41) and Mary Craw-ford's 'blunted delicacy' (Ch. 47). The successive appearances of such a word have the effect both of furnishing the reader with a moral yardstick, and of refining the word itself as a precision instrument.

The words, some forty-five in number, that have so far been cited do not constitute a comprehensive list of the recurring nouns and epithets used by Jane Austen in the analysis of character. Others might have been added, and the illustrative instances multiplied many times over. They do perhaps, however, go some way towards suggesting, by positive and negative defini-tion, an embodiment of the civilized virtues as Jane Austen saw them. It has been shown that a given word is likely to recur, both within a stretch of text (a novel or part of one) and within the corpus of her work as a whole. It has also been suggested that this limited but highly important vocabulary is employed with a precision that was rendered possible by the state of the language as well as by the writer's own fastidious and critical concern for the integrity of the words she used, but which would not have been possible a few years later, and would certainly not be so today. For most of the terms to which she attaches moral weight have since lost a good deal of their force: it is only a small minority (*disgusting* and *stupid* are common examples) regarding which Jane Austen's usage seems less emphatic than our own. An obvious corollary of this is that a patient act of adjustment to the significance of many recurring words is demanded of the reader who wishes to grasp the meaning of the novels. Study of this vocabulary also lends support to the view of Jane Austen as the heiress of the eighteenth century: in the novels (the letters are quite another question) usages tend to be backward-looking, except for a few colloquialisms used in dialogue with an evident eye to their modernity. The experience of reading these novels with the *OED* at one's side provides many examples of a word used in an eighteenth-century sense which was, even as she wrote, in the process of being lost. In some cases (*candour* has been cited in this connexion) she offers us the old and the new senses side by side. In one celebrated passage, the rearguard action that is being fought against verbal imprecision is made quite explicit. In Chapter 14 of *Northanger Abbey* there occurs a discussion by the hero and heroine of the novel on a linguistic question: the use of the epithet *nice*, which the enthusiastic but unreflecting Catherine has applied to *The Mysteries of Udolpho*:

'Very true,' said Henry, 'and this is a very nice day, and we are taking a very nice walk, and you are two very nice young ladies. Oh! it is a very nice word indeed!—it does for every thing. Originally perhaps it was applied only to express neatness, propriety, delicacy, or refinement;—people were nice in their dress, in their sentiments, or their choice. But now every commendation on every subject is comprised in that one word.' (*NA*, 108)[16]

[16] C. J. Rawson has pointed out a similarity between this passage and a passage in Richardson's *Correspondence* (published, in Mrs Barbauld's

It is clear that Tilney's creator shares his feeling that a word which 'does for everything' is good for very little. Time and colloquial usage have favoured Catherine rather than Henry; but the principle of such a protest remains a valuable one.

Tilney's sister warns Catherine that they are in danger of being 'overpowered with Johnson and Blair all the rest of the way', and the mention of these names suggests another implication of the phrase which was taken as the starting-point of the present chapter. 'The best chosen English' implies not only the choice between more and less desirable alternatives, but also some principle of selection, and desirably some authority to settle doubtful cases. The development of awareness of the standard language, and of deviations from it, is discussed in a later chapter;[17] but it will be relevant at this point to refer to the lively interest, in the late eighteenth century and early nineteenth centuries, in what the period was fond of callng 'synonymy'—the drawing of fine distinctions between words of approximately similar meaning. One of the earliest publications on this subject may be taken as representative. John Trusler's *The Difference between Words Esteemed Synonymous in the English Language; and the Proper Choice of them Determined* . . . (1766) bears on its title-page the promise that it will be 'Useful, to all, who would, either, write or speak, with PROPRIETY, and, ELEGANCE'; and the pages that follow proceed to distinguish between such terms as *air, mien, carriage, address, manners, behaviour* and *deportment*, to a total of 370 groups of words in all. Many of these are among the staple items of Jane Austen's vocabulary. Later examples of what was obviously a popular and lucrative type of publication include Mrs Piozzi's *British Synonymy; or an Attempt at Regulating the Choice of Words in Familiar Conversation* (1794) and works by James Leslie (1806), G. H. Poppleton

---

edition, in 1804), in which Lady Bradshaigh comments on the use and abuse of the word *sentimental* ('*Nice* and *sentimental*: a parallel between *Northanger Abbey* and Richardson's *Correspondence*', *Notes and Queries*, 209 [1964] 180).

[17] See pp. 147–50 below.

(1812), William Taylor (1813) and George Crabb (1816). The interest in this aspect of language outlived Jane Austen: its climax was reached in the publication of Roget's *Thesaurus* in 1852, but it was still active enough in 1920 to justify a centennial edition of Crabb's oft-reprinted book. Fine discrimination was, evidently, not a private monopoly of Jane Austen's but part of the linguistic climate in which she grew up.

A very important element in her vocabulary, then, is the result of a wish to make everyday words convey an exact and substantial meaning: she uses *amiable* or *elegant, taste* or *prudence*, with the same attention to their proper significance that makes her reject the vagueness and imprecision of colloquial and 'low' language. A familiar word can thus carry unusual weight; and normally she has no need of emphatic language to make her points cogently. Her habitual tone is quiet, avoiding declamation and rhetoric; and when 'strong' language is used, it is generally a signal of either ironic intent or some exceptionally crucial moment in the story. Perhaps the best example of the latter occurs near the end of *Emma*, when the heroine suffers her first real and instructive unhappiness. Believing that her ingenious manoeuvrings have only succeeded in losing for her the man she wishes to marry, she finds her serenity and complacency turn to misery and shame, and we read of her 'wretchedness' and her 'ruined happiness' in a passage which also contains such words as *agony, cruel* and *melancholy*—words commonplace in the Romantic poets who were Jane Austen's contemporaries, but exceptional enough in her work, at least in their serious senses, to strike the reader's attention. And here they are clearly to be taken seriously: strong language is justified by the exceptional nature of the heroine's predicament, and the words quoted gain additional effect from their rarity. More frequently, however, language of this kind is used ironically, to suggest a lack of proper balance, a disproportion between cause and effect resulting from lack of self-awareness and self-control. An extended example of this, the 'excessive affliction' of Marianne in *Sense and Sensibility*, has already been discussed in Chapter 1. Marianne, at any

rate in her own estimation, suffers 'wretchedness' and 'agony'
—the vocabulary closely resembles that applied to Emma's
emotional crisis; but the context makes it clear that she is merely,
and deservedly, reaping the harvest of a foolish taste for romantic
sentiment.

Typical of such words is *rapture*, which (with *rapturous*) is
nearly always a warning sign to the reader that a character's
actions or reactions are being called into question. A phrase in the
juvenilia, 'his transports, his Raptures, his Extacies' (*MW*, 169),
suggests the characteristic tone of its appearances. It is used of
the Miss Bertrams in *Mansfield Park*, who feel a 'rapturous'
admiration for Mr Crawford; of Mr Elton in *Emma*, who is 'in
continual raptures' over Emma's portrait of Harriet, and of
whom Emma scathingly observes to herself, ' "You know nothing
of drawing. Don't pretend to be in raptures about mine" '; of
Miss Bingley in *Pride and Prejudice*, whose 'raptures' are dismissed by Darcy with the same scepticism; and of Mrs Bennet
in the same novel, her husband being described as 'fatigued with
the raptures of his wife'. Rapture was a legitimate emotion, and
rapture a word capable of serious use, for the poets from Milton
to the Romantics; but Jane Austen's suspicion of the unbridled
expression of feelings leads her to associate rapture with insincerity (cf. Emma's ' "Don't pretend . . ." ') or a tiresome and
embarrassing excess of enthusiasm. A more puzzling use of the
word occurs in connexion with Fanny Price: we are told, when
she learns that she is to revisit her family in Portsmouth, that
'Had Fanny been at all addicted to raptures, she must have had a
strong attack of them . . .'—the sense here being ironical, and the
implication being that she was healthily free from such undesir-
able displays of emotion; yet what are we to make of Fanny's
own use of the word in her eloquent response to the beauty of a
starry night: ' "Here's what may tranquillize every care, and
lift the heart to rapture!" ' It is not self-evident that Jane Austen
is here ridiculing her heroine's artless emotion: Fanny's sincerity
is beyond question; but the passage occurs early in the novel (in
Chapter 11) when she is still young and inexperienced, so that a

hint of ironic comment is probably intended—an interpretation confirmed by Edmund's reply (' " I like to hear your enthusiasm, Fanny" '), which makes use of another word which habitually carries ironic overtones.

Our gradually deeping sense of Jane Austen's vocabulary as we read her novels, and our experience of her characteristic usages, serious and ironic, make an important contribution to the impressions we form of her characters and of their speech and behaviour. The apparently colourless noun or epithet is capable of carrying a weight of significance derived partly from its context and partly from its appearance elsewhere; a limited vocabulary thus becomes not a stylistic weakness but a device for expressing clearly-articulated moral attitudes.

The quotation from C. S. Lewis earlier in this chapter reminds us that Jane Austen inherited the eighteenth-century fondness for the abstract word of precise and reasonably constant meaning. This taste for the abstract word is of course shared not only by her favourite Dr Johnson and other prose writers, but by the poets of the age, and it is to be found in the informal writings that have survived from that period, such as the familiar letter and the journal, as well as in the public forms of the periodical essay and the novel. Many of these usages, that is to say, belong to Jane Austen's *milieu* and to a common stock of vocabulary available to all: the diction we have been concerned with in this chapter was not the monopoly of any individual writer, but a significant element in the language ready to be drawn on whether the composition in question were an ode, a sermon or a letter to a friend. One finds it, for instance, in the letters of Cowper, who, like Jane Austen in her novels, analyses character by invoking nouns and epithets which imply a commonly accepted standard. Thus Lady Austen is 'placed', in a letter dated 26 September 1781, by reference to her 'fine taste and discernment', her 'gratitude' and 'sense of obligation', and her 'vivacity'; and in a letter of 3 July 1786, Lady Hesketh is 'always cheerful and sweet-tempered . . . This disposition in her is the more comfortable, because it is not the humour of the day, a sudden flash of benevolence and good spirits, occasioned merely by a change of scene; but is her natural turn . . .' And when Cowper describes, with obvious distaste, the climax of a fox-hunt, gentlemen and hounds contemplating the victim's corpse with 'the most rational delight' (letter of 3 March 1788), a familiar epithet is given an ironic overtone in what was soon to become very much the Austen manner.

In the novelists, too, a similar vocabulary is to be found. Two brief quotations from Fanny Burney will show that these hard-worked words fall at times thick and fast from the writer's pen:

His conversation was sensible and spirited; his air and address were open and noble; his manners gentle, attentive, and infinitely engaging; his person is all elegance, and his countenance the most animated and expressive I have ever seen. (*Evelina* (1778))

Lady Margaret received her with a coldness that bordered upon incivility; irascible by nature and jealous by situation, the appearance of beauty alarmed, and of cheerfulness disgusted her. (*Cecilia* (1782))

In Maria Edgeworth these terms cluster less thickly, but still form an important ingredient of her language. The opening paragraph of *Belinda* (1801), a novel which earns honourable mention in the quotation from *Northanger Abbey* with which this chapter opened, may be examined as a sample of the ease and flexibility of her style which invites comparison with Jane Austen. Miss Edgeworth's tone is as sprightly as her heroine, but her diction has its roots in the century that had just ended: behind such phrases as 'a well-bred woman' and 'the highest company', which may strike the modern ear with a certain hollowness, lies a consensus as to what constitutes these ideals. Similarly, the introduction of the heroine with an escort of four epithets ('handsome, graceful, sprightly, and highly accomplished'), in a sentence which Jane Austen may have been echoing in the opening words of *Emma*, is evidence of a continuing tradition.

Some understanding of the linguistic climate of her immediate *milieu* may be deduced from two further sources. The more

familiar of these is the letters she wrote, particularly those ad-
dressed to her sister Cassandra, many of which reveal a consciously critical and often satirical attitude to language comparable
to that which has already been illustrated from her fiction. It
seems certain that such observations found a ready response in
the recipient, and it is probably reasonable to deduce that this
was a shared habit which characterized their unrecorded conversation as well as their correspondence. The habit must also have
extended to some at least of the Austen brothers. For a less widely-
known but very revealing source is the weekly periodical *The
Loiterer*, which the novelist's eldest brother James Austen
edited, and largely wrote, at Oxford in 1789–90, and which was
published in the latter year as a collection of sixty essays in two
slim volumes.[18] We may be sure that Jane Austen perused these
productions very closely; perhaps she was present when some of
them were in the process of composition. Several of the essays
show a critical and ironic attitude to language and to conventions
of discourse and style, and an interest in clarifying the meanings
of words which have suffered corruption in common usage.
Number 19, for example, light-heartedly scrutinizes some of the
clichés of well-bred conversation, such as the description of a
young girl wed to 'a battered rake of family and fortune' as
well-married. The concern, that is to say, is not only with the
word but with the social and ethical assumptions behind it. Another number (29) turns again to the theme of marriage for love
versus marriage for 'prudential motives'—a theme that James'
sister was soon to make one of the main preoccupations of her
fiction. Suggesting that the old appear to believe that, in marriage, material gain is all that need be considered, the essayist
adds wryly that 'the *young* have taken it into their heads to
imagine that Youth and Beauty, Good Temper and Good Sense,
are the best recommendations in a Wife'—a sentence that brings

---

[18] *The Loiterer: a Periodical Work in Two Volumes, First Published at
Oxford in the Years 1789 and 1790* (Oxford, 1790). See also A. W.
Litz, '*The Loiterer*: a Reflection of Jane Austen's Early Environment'
Review of English Studies, 12 (1961) 251–61.

us close to the language as well as the sentiments of the novels.

What distinguishes Jane Austen's style, then, is not the fact that she makes use of this area of vocabulary, but the exceptional fineness and sureness with which she employs the common diction of her time, and the consistency and subtlety with which she enlists it for the analysis and exposure of human character. Saintsbury refers to 'the tolerably stationary state of manners, language, etc., such as her kind of novel requires',[19] and one may regard this feature of her style as representing a major effort of conservation directed against the menace of 'the general mess of imprecision of feeling'. As a later chapter will illustrate more fully, a generation later, in the work of the early Victorian novelists, the firmness and certainty of these words had disappeared for ever, and in Dickens, Thackeray and the Brontës the language of characterization has suffered a sea-change. Under the impact of the social and intellectual upheavals of the early nineteenth century, with their inevitable impact on moral ideas, the old standards, once widely agreed, have largely collapsed, and with them a whole area of vocabulary has been thrown into doubt. To speak of taste or judgment, of amiability or openness, is no longer as meaningful as it was, and with succeeding generations it became ever more meaningless. To make, at this stage, the most forceful contrast possible: how far the change had gone a hundred years after Jane Austen can be seen by setting two passages of fiction side by side. The first, from *Persuasion*, shows a large number of words of the type discussed in this chapter used in a brief extract which is characteristic of many others:

Though they had now been acquainted a month, she could not be satisfied that she really knew his character. That he was a sensible man, an agreeable man—that he talked well, professed good opinions, seemed to judge properly and as a man of principle—this was all clear enough. He certainly knew what was right, nor could she fix on any one article of moral duty evidently trans-

[19] G. Saintsbury, *The English Novel* (1913) 211–12.

gressed; but yet she would have been afraid to answer for his conduct . . .

Mr Elliot was rational, discreet, polished—but he was not open. There was never any burst of feeling, any warmth of indignation or delight, at the evil or good of others. This, to Anne, was a decided imperfection. Her early impressions were incurable. She prized the frank, the open-hearted, the eager character beyond all others. Warmth and enthusiasm did captivate her still . . .

Mr Elliot was too generally agreeable. Various as were the tempers in her father's house, he pleased them all . . . (*P*, 160–1)

The key-words used here each denote a distinct area of meaning and express a single aspect of character or behaviour, whilst showing through their inter-relationships the complex of human personality. Behind the language, indeed, is the basic assumption that personality is susceptible to such dissection and to the corresponding 'naming of parts'; that 'character' is a meaningful and tolerably constant term; and that the language provides labels which correspond to realities that can be detected by observation and reflection. The extent to which Jane Austen relies on such concepts of social and moral excellence, and how little she has recourse to other kinds of description or commentary, can be illustrated by comparing the above with an extract from D. H. Lawrence's *Sons and Lovers* (1913):

Walter Morel seemed melted away before her. She was to the miner that thing of mystery and fascination, a lady. When she spoke to him, it was with a southern pronunciation and a purity of English which thrilled him to hear. She watched him. He danced well, as if it were natural and joyous in him to dance. His grandfather was a French refugee who had married an English barmaid —if it had been a marriage. Gertrude Coppard watched the young miner as he danced, a certain subtle exultation like glamour in his movement, and his face the flower of his body, ruddy, with tumbled black hair, and laughing alike whatever partner he bowed above. She thought him rather wonderful, never having met anyone like him . . . She was a puritan, like her father, high-minded, and really stern. Therefore the dusky, golden softness of this man's sensuous flame of life, that flowed off his flesh like the flame from a candle, not baffled and gripped into incandescence by thought and spirit as her life was, seemed to her something wonderful, beyond her.

This is powerful prose, but its effectiveness depends on its imagery and its power of evoking a sense of physical presence; the words expressing moral qualities (*high-minded*, *stern*) are relatively weak. Words have lost the exactness, the satisfyingly hard-edged moral and intellectual quality, that we find in Jane Austen: instead of *rational, discreet, polished*, we have *joyous, wonderful, mystery, fascination, glamour*. The repetition of a word (*rather wonderful, something wonderful*) is a rhetorical emphasis rather than a step in the direction of defining it more precisely. Explicit analysis of character is largely ousted by suggestive physical detail. Any difference in value between the two styles, or the two writers, is not of course the question at issue; what is being stressed is the difference in kind—a difference determined not only by individual choice and temperament, but by the radically altered nature of society as a whole and of the language which reflected that society—and the importance of bringing to each the kind of verbal awareness that is appropriate.[20]

Jane Austen's background, it has been suggested, was one in which a critical attitude to language was habitual: the Austen family, on the available evidence, were not accustomed to take words at their face value, but to examine the relationship between word and referent, and to castigate muddled or evasive expressions. Words were expected to possess, and to be used with strict attention to, precisely-defined meanings; even abstract words were not mere empty formulae, but stood for something recognizable, on the nature of which common agreement existed. Indeed, an abstraction was likely to be *more* valid, because more

[20] For an interesting discussion of D. H. Lawrence's language see D. Bickerton, 'The Language of *Women in Love*', *A Review of English Literature*, 8, 2 (1967) 56–67. According to a recent critic, 'Lawrence—despite his rude words about her—did not fail to learn a great deal from Jane Austen' (R. P. Draper, *D. H. Lawrence* [New York, 1964] 123). Cf. also W. T. Andrews, 'D. H. Lawrence's Favourite Jargon', *Notes and Queries*, 211 (1966) 97–8.

universally applicable, than a reference to the concrete and the specific. In this respect, the attitude of the eighteenth century was radically different from our own. Whereas we are apt to distrust abstractions, feeling that, by obscuring individual dfferences, they misleadingly oversimplify the truth, and perhaps erect a verbal façade behind which nothing real and substantial exists, the Augustans and their successors held fast to them as stressing the common element in men which it was the true province of literature to delineate.[21] Related to this is the absence (already noted) of references to the material world, of those descriptions of the externals of people and places, which are common in most novelists. For Jane Austen it is the *moral* life which is of supreme importance; and whereas the Romantics stressed the significance of individual experience, she constantly related the particular case to an agreed standard, conformity to which is judged desirable. She believes, that is, in absolute standards.[22] Not that these standards are necessarily those accepted by the society of her time: most obviously in the treatment of the marriage question, she makes it clear that conventional standards are insufficiently demanding. Charlotte Lucas's acceptance of Mr Collins in *Pride and Prejudice*, normal and defensible enough in terms of the ground-rules of her class and her period, is condemned as an offence against good sense and good judgment. What has been a primarily comic episode suddenly deepens in tone as Elizabeth learns that her friend intends to accept him: ' "Engaged to Mr Collins! my dear Charlotte,—impossible!" ': she is astonished and dismayed at Charlotte's willingness to sacrifice 'every better feeling to worldly advantage', and the discovery destroys their friendship ('Elizabeth felt persuaded that no real confidence could ever subsist between them again'). The individual has a duty to society at large, as the prominence of such words as *respectable* and *civil* makes clear, and to the smaller units of that

[21] Cf. Donald Davie, *Purity of Diction in English Verse* (1952) 44–5; C. F. Chapin, *Personification in Eighteenth-century English Poetry* (New York, 1955) 111.
[22] Cf. Ian Watt (ed.), *Sense and Sensibility* (New York, 1961) 231.

society, especially the family and the local community; but the first responsibility of the mature adult is to be true to himself. The moral acts which arouse our admiration, such as Fanny Price's refusal of Crawford in the face of Sir Thomas Bertram's overpowering displeasure, are assertions of the inner convictions of the individual in opposition to the demands of convention. A woman owes a duty to society to marry, if she can, and a duty to her family and her unborn children to marry as well as she can; but marriage without love is more serious than any of these considerations, since it is an offence against the moral dignity and self-respect of the individual. Yet the individual response is not something valued (as it was valued by Wordsworth or Byron) for its own sake, but according to its relationship to a code which demanded assent on account of its essential rightness.

If we inquire what was the source of Jane Austen's moral and ethical standards, the answer is likely to be found in terms of social rather than spiritual convictions. Of her religious beliefs we can speak only tentatively, from imperfect knowledge. Her letters, interesting though they are in many ways, tell us virtually nothing of her intellectual or spiritual existence: the problems they deal with are problems of fashion and domestic life rather than of ethics or theology, though of course the absence of documentary evidence of this kind permits us to draw no conclusions as to the writer's ideas and beliefs, or the lack of them. The evidence of those who knew her well stresses her religious orthodoxy; yet, as Laurence Lerner has pointed out, God is curiously absent from her work.[23] Apart from the 'ordination' theme in *Mansfield Park*, there are few references to the Church, or at least to its representatives, that are not comic or satirical. Superficially at least, religion in the novels means Mr Collins, who is a fool (and, over Lydia's elopement, a notably uncharitable one), and Dr Grant, who is out of temper when his dinner is not perfectly satisfactory and who comes closer to the Deadly Sins than the Christian Virtues. Nor is there any obvious use of Biblical allusions or parallels, such as we find in (for instance) Fielding's

[23] L. Lerner, *The Truth-tellers* (1967) 23.

version of the Good Samaritan story in *Joseph Andrews* or Dickens's introduction of the Lord's Prayer into the account of the death of Jo the crossing-sweeper in *Bleak House*. The Christian morality of Jane Austen's novels, if it exists, is conveyed more indirectly; and she is committed to no narrow doctrine in her assessment of moral worth. It has been said that, for her, the gravest offence is adultery; yet the character who is most uncompromisingly shown as flawed by moral inadequacy, and who seems to be presented with an unusual and barely-suppressed moral indignation, is the self-righteous Mrs Norris (the widow of a clergyman), whose offence is lack of charity.

More positively, Christian morality is mediated through the virtues of the class whose qualities, at their best, Jane Austen most admired and to which she herself belonged—the country gentry of her time. In the words of a recent historian, 'Honour, dignity, integrity, considerateness, courtesy and chivalry were all virtues essential to the character of a gentleman, and they all derived in part from the nature of country life'.[24] This is, in fact, a very closely accurate description of Mr Knightley. But, even as she wrote, changes in society were working in the same direction as changes in sensibility wrought by (as well as responsible for) the literary revolution of her lifetime. As the old ideals and the accepted values disintegrated, the language inevitably reflected the change—perhaps most obviously through semantic shifts to which words such as those discussed in this chapter were subjected. For this reason Jane Austen's vocabulary is more than a personal instrument of both delicacy and power: it is one of the last and finest products of a way of life and a way of thinking.

[24] F. M. L. Thompson, *English Landed Society in the Nineteenth Century* (1963) 16.

G

CHAPTER THREE

'VISION IN ACTION': A NOTE ON SYNTAX

Viewing Jane Austen's work as a whole, one has the sense of powers moving unfalteringly towards maturity, of the conscious artist setting herself new problems and finding appropriate solutions to them. Though the detailed chronology of the composition of these novels is still far from clear, and is likely to remain so, we have a clear enough picture of her working life to grasp the nature and extent of her achievement. From *Northanger Abbey* to *Emma*, or from *Sense and Sensibility* to *Persuasion*, is indeed not very far in years, but a considerable distance in the kind of sophistication of technique that has in recent years become widely recognized, and that is perhaps what G. H. Lewes had in mind when he referred to her (in the *Westminster Review* for July 1852) as 'the greatest artist that has ever written, using the term to signify the most perfect mastery over the means to her end'. This development can, of course, be seen at many levels, in the understanding and depicting of human behaviour as well as in questions of technique and style. To go no further for examples than her heroines: having created Elizabeth Bennet, she turned to a heroine as unlike her as possible, Fanny Price; and after showing Emma Woodhouse standing confidently on the threshold of life, she presented Anne Elliot, whose 'bloom' has already faded and whose major emotional crisis is already in the past when the novel opens. Subject-matter and style exist, naturally, in an inextricable interrelationship, and new devices of style come

into play not simply for the sake of linguistic experimentation—
the last thing to interest Jane Austen as an end in itself—but in
order to express new aspects of behaviour and to provide new
kinds of fictional experience. But whereas the psychological and
moral aspects have been repeatedly and exhaustively discussed,
the gradual maturing of her style awaits demonstration. Nowhere
is it more evident than in the syntax of her prose, which displays a
range and flexibility for which it has not always received credit.
When her style has not been ignored entirely, or dismissed as
unworthy of serious and sustained interest, it has been customarily
assumed that it comprises two principal modes or registers: a
colloquial one (in the dialogue) and a formal one (in the narrative
passages), the former earning wide praise for its 'naturalness' and
the latter being regarded as somewhat stiff and undistinguished.
There may well be room for questioning such a simplified account
of a complex phenomenon; but for the moment it will be sufficient to insist on the versatility of calculated syntactical effects of
which this prose is capable. If she often sounds like Dr Johnson,
she can also seem to look forward to Virginia Woolf: while many
passages, especially in the early writings, recall *Rasselas* and *The
Rambler*, there are others—notably in *Persuasion*, but also as
early as *Sense and Sensibility*—which may remind us of *Mrs
Dalloway*. Jane Austen commands a variety of sentence-patterns,
the loose as well as the highly-structured, the 'modern' kind of
sentence which traces in its construction the outline of a mental or
emotional experience as well as the symmetrical and harmonious
classical sentence. She can manipulate a sentence of more than a
hundred words in length without loss of lucidity, and can also
use the very brief sentence to telling effect; she can be dramatic as
well as analytic and epigrammatic. The subject invites fuller
treatment than a single chapter can afford. What follows, therefore, is offered as a 'note' indicating some of the more important
facets of the topic and providing some illustrative material,
rather than the kind of extended examination that, for instance,
has been given by W. K. Wimsatt to the prose of Johnson.[1]

[1] W. K. Wimsatt, Jr, *The Prose Style of Samuel Johnson* (New Haven,

It is with Johnson that one may begin in attempting to show the distance travelled by Jane Austen in her use of varieties of sentence-pattern. For her starting-point was the strongly-shaped eighteenth-century sentence which she absorbed from her youthful reading, and which is to be found in her earliest surviving compositions. It is still prominent in *Northanger Abbey*, and continues to appear, though with decreasing frequency, throughout her career. Her recorded relationship with the Johnsonian sentence begins, like so much else, in burlesque and mockery. In *Love and Freindship* (written at about the age of fifteen), we read of 'the determined Perseverance of disagreeable Lovers and the cruel Persecutions of obstinate Fathers'. The epithets are, somewhat ostentatiously, inserted for the sake of a precise balancing of phrase against phrase, and both the subject-matter and the obtrusive alliteration suggest parody. A more outrageous example from the same work is the warning to ' "Beware of the unmeaning Luxuries of Bath and of the stinking fish of Southampton" ', with its bathetic descent from the abstract to the particular, which seems to subvert the careful equilibrium with which nouns and epithets are matched. Such examples are not to be taken as a vote of no-confidence in Johnson as a stylistic model, however, but rather as an attack on the language of post-Richardsonian popular fiction, with its combination of formal syntax and false emotions which often descended into unconscious absurdity. This use of the balanced sentence for comic and satiric purposes survives in *Northanger Abbey*. The closing words of that novel resemble the kind of structure that is commonplace in Johnson's prose ('. . . to recommend parental tyranny, or reward filial disobedience'), but its ironic humour is, as has already been suggested, in keeping with the tone of the whole novel. A more extended example of balance as an ironic device occurs in the comments on Catherine Morland's reading of Gothic fiction and especially of 'Mrs Radcliffe's works':

1941); *Philosophic Words: a Study of Style and Meaning in the 'Rambler' and 'Dictionary' of Samuel Johnson* (New Haven, 1948).

Of the *Alps and Pyrenees*, with *their pine forests and their vices,* they might give a faithful delineation . . . But in the general part of England there was surely some security for the existence even of a wife not beloved, in *the laws of the land, and the manners of the age. Murder was not tolerated, servants were not slaves,* and *neither poison nor sleeping potions* to be procured, like rhubarb, from every druggist. Among the *Alps and Pyrenees*, perhaps, there were no mixed characters. There, such as were not *as spotless as an angel,* might have *the dispositions of a fiend.* But in England it was not so . . . (*NA*, 200; my italics)

The syntax here is highly-patterned, with its frequent antitheses (italicized above), its inversion (in the first sentence quoted), and its use in the third sentence of Jane Austen's favourite *oratio trimembris* or three-part structure. These features go some way towards endowing the passage with a Johnsonian weight and portentousness, but again the method is that of the saboteur, since the humour of the homely simile 'like rhubarb' (a characteristic example of quiet but effective deflation) and the zeugma of 'pine forests and . . . vices' work in the opposite direction. The final effect is quite different from that of the early burlesques, which employ formal syntax to expose absurdity by setting up a glaring contrast between style and thought, the structures with solemn associations being compelled to accommodate preposterous ideas. Here, the measured prose suggests that reason has replaced delusion in Catherine's mind: it is the voice of common sense that speaks in the accents of Johnson's prose; but at the same time the tone never becomes solemn.

Elsewhere in *Northanger Abbey*, the balanced sentence is used with greater seriousness for making a point briefly and economically ('Mr and Mrs Morland were all compliance, and Catherine all happiness'), or for giving wit and polish to the description of a scene whose dominating characteristic is its fatuous triviality, as in the brilliant single-sentence account of Mrs Allen. A little typographical rearrangement of the sentence in question will show how its syntax is dominated by the pairing of phrases. Catherine passes a somewhat tedious morning in the company of Mrs Allen,

whose vacancy of mind/and incapacity for thinking
    were such that
as she never talked a great deal,/so she could never be entirely silent;
    and, therefore, while she sat at her work,
if she lost her needle,/or broke her thread,
if she heard a carriage in the street,/or saw a speck upon her gown,
    she must observe it aloud,
whether there were any one at leisure to answer her/ or not. (*NA*,
    60–1)

The see-saw structure of this long sentence suggests the monotony
of Catherine's morning and conveys an implicit comment on
the decided limitations of Mrs Allen as a companion. At such
points, a syntactical device is used not only to provide stylistic
interest and variety but to serve the cause of characterization.

Johnsonian syntax is also important in *Sense and Sensibility*,
though less prominently so than in *Northanger Abbey*. The antithetical title of the former prepares the reader for a system of
contrasts which underlies its structure, and there is a notable
reliance on syntactical balance in the dialogue as well as the
narrative prose, coupled with an evident disparity in the extent
to which different characters employ the formal sentence in their
speech. Elinor, unlike her impulsive sister, is particularly fond of
such sentences, which have an obvious appropriateness to her belief in discipline and control as principles of conduct. Her syntax
is thus an index of her temperament. It is Elinor who says of Mrs
Ferrars that

$$\text{A} \qquad\qquad\qquad \text{B} \qquad \text{C}$$
'She would not be so weak as to throw away the comfort of a child,
$$\text{A} \qquad\quad \text{B} \qquad\quad \text{C}$$
and yet retain the anxiety of a parent!' (*SS*, 296)

in which the three elements (verb+noun+noun) of the first
half of that sentence are exactly paralleled in the corresponding
but contrasting elements of the second half. Again, she observes
to Willoughby,

$$\text{A} \qquad\quad \text{B} \qquad\qquad \text{B} \qquad\qquad \text{A} \qquad\quad \text{A}$$
'If their praise is censure, your censure may be praise, for they are

B   A   B

not more undiscerning, than you are are prejudiced and unjust.'
(*SS*, 50)

The two halves of this sentence are constructed in different but
equally mannered patterns, the chiasmus of the first two clauses
(ABBA) being followed by the more normal ABAB patterning of
the last two. The style thus formed, with its weightiness and its
lack of the spontaneous and the unexpected, is forceful but distinctly non-colloquial: in this novel perhaps only the priggish and
self-righteous Elinor could have uttered such a sentence, the rigid
syntax of which seems to mirror her moral inflexibility.

There is more ease in the balanced sentences of Edward
Ferrars, who has Elinor's rightness without her rigidity, and
whose concrete nouns also contrast with her abstractions, as in
the following expression of his lack of enthusiasm for romantic
fiction:

"I have more pleasure in a snug farm-house than a watch-tower
—and a troop of tidy, happy villagers please me better than the
finest banditti in the world." (*SS*, 98)

The second half of his sentence repeats the pattern of the first,
but mere repetition is avoided by strengthening the contrast between the elements displayed: *villagers/banditti* produces an
effect that is both comic and dramatic after the relatively mild
farm-house/watch-tower. The various elements are chosen, too,
with attention to the precision of the contrasts involved: the
compound *farm-house* makes its partner *watch-tower* structurally
as well as semantically appropriate, and *troop*, applied to the
villagers, looks forward (in another of its meanings) to the 'banditti', just as the ironical phrase 'the finest banditti in the world'
echoes the associations of the epithets applied to 'villagers'.
Edward's unaffected good sense is expressed, that is, by the use
of a structure at once formal and witty: he has precision without
pedantry, correctness without pomposity.

If Elinor is sometimes excessively formal, her sister's utterances
reveal, on the syntactic as well as other levels, a lack of discipline

and control that is, again, an index of her nature. Marianne's sentences often take the form of exclamations or questions, as in her rhapsody on the autumn leaves:

"Oh!" cried Marianne, "with what transporting sensations have I formerly seen them fall! How have I delighted, as I walked, to see them driven in showers about me by the wind! What feelings have they, the season, the air altogether inspired! . . .' (*SS*, 87–8)

This exclamatory style at times seems closer to poetic utterance than to rational discourse, and there is even a metrical element in such phrases as 'to see them driven in showers about me by the wind': we have left the world of Dr Johnson for that of Cowper's verse. Elinor's reaction to this outburst is characteristic—' "It is not every one," said Elinor, "who has your passion for dead leaves" '—and we may assume that it is the effusive style as well as the emotional content of Marianne's speech that provokes her damping comment. It is surely revealing, however, that after the illness that assists in her change of heart, Marianne, having learned wisdom through suffering, speaks in the language of sense rather than that of sensibility: her remark in Chapter 46, ' "Do not, my dearest Elinor, let your kindness defend what I know your judgment must censure" ', is not unworthy of Elinor herself, or, indeed, of Johnson. As so often, shifts in the moral and emotional tones of the novel are accompanied by appropriate modifications of style.

As late as *Mansfield Park*, the use of antithesis, though rarer, is still not uncommon in the narrative style. On Fanny Price's arrival at the great house, we learn that 'The grandeur of the house astonished, but could not console her', and at the other end of the novel there occurs a sentence which might have strayed from *The Rambler*:

The indignities of stupidity, and the disappointments of selfish passion, can excite little pity. (*MP*, 464)

The Idler is mentioned as among Fanny's reading; and another balanced sentence is introduced by a direct reference to the author of that work: after visiting Portsmouth, Fanny is tempted to apply to her two homes 'Dr Johnson's celebrated judgment as to matrimony and celibacy, and say, that though Mansfield Park might have some pains, Portsmouth could have no pleasures' (*MP*, 392). The sober and restrained tone of this novel perhaps makes the use of such syntax natural, particularly in the portions that relate to the country-house that provides its title: Mansfield Park and its owner, Sir Thomas Bertram, stand for the eighteenth-century virtues to which the Crawfords, like his own children, represent a threat. (Mary Crawford, for instance, exhibits in her speech an attitude that is informal to the point of offending against decorum: a characteristic remark, in a speech to Fanny, is ' "By the bye, Flora Ross was dying for Henry the first winter she came out" '.) It is fitting that eighteenth-century syntax should be invoked in such a context.

But the trend in Jane Austen's later work, seen as a whole, is away from formal syntax (except for special, often satiric, effects) and towards a freer and more dramatic kind. Some outstanding examples of the latter may be found in *Emma* and *Persuasion*, but the change was not of course an abrupt one, and instances occur even as early as *Sense and Sensibility*. Whilst Marianne is learning the importance of control and restraint, Elinor's education proceeds in the opposite direction: she, who has undervalued emotion (as in the autumn leaves passage already quoted), now finds herself assailed by feelings that her self-discipline is barely adequate to subdue. Some of these emotions are the result of Marianne's serious illness, as over the arrival of Colonel Brandon:

The comfort of such a friend at that moment as Colonel Brandon—of such a companion for her mother,—how gratefully was it felt!—a companion whose judgment would guide, whose attendance must relieve, and whose friendship might soothe her!—as far as the shock of such a summons *could* be lessened to her, his presence, his manners, his assistance, would lessen it. (*SS*, 311–12)

Since Elinor's feelings must remain unspoken (possibly in the original, epistolary version of the novel they were expressed in a letter to a confidante?), it is the narrative style that at such moments must be coloured by a stylistic quality which will differentiate passages of this kind from the general run of narrative. In this case Elinor's emotions are suggested by a marked departure from normal conventions of syntax; the paragraph quoted is in fact both preceded and followed by pasages of 'normal' prose. The power of feelings almost beyond her control is represented by a dislocation of the syntactical pattern, which is frequently interrupted, as the dramatic punctuation indicates. Yet even here formal patterning has by no means disappeared, as a selection of phrases and clauses from the sentence quoted will show:

... of such a friend ... of such a companion ...

... whose judgment would guide, whose attendance must relieve, and whose friendship might soothe ...

... his presence, his manners, his assistance ...

What we find is a tension between an incipient colloquial style (seen, for example, in the exclamations and the stressed *could*) and a structuring that for all its apparently fragmentary quality is still firm. Another example from the same chapter confirms this conclusion:

About noon, however, she began—but with a caution—a dread of disappointment, which for some time kept her silent, even to her friend—to fancy, to hope she could perceive a slight amendment in her sister's pulse;—she waited, watched, and examined it again and again;—and at last, with an agitation more difficult to bury under exterior calmness, than all her foregoing distress, ventured to communicate her hopes. (*SS*, 314)

Again, the dramatic punctuation is an obvious token of the dramatic syntax, which in turn records an intense emotional experience. The sentence, instead of proceeding smoothly toward an end that is foreseen from the opening, moves forward in a series of jerks, its hesitations and uncertainties reflecting the progress of Elinor's mood from doubt to hope, with her natural caution checking an excess of optimism. Such sentences justify the phrase used in the title of this chapter—a phrase applied by Tony Tanner to the syntax of Hemingway;[2] for syntax is here, as in the very different prose of the American writer, a medium for communicating, by imitation rather than summary or analysis, the outline of a passage of experience, and the structure of the sentence forces upon the reader, as he moves through it, a miming of the heroine's experience. Yet it is far from formless, and if the second thoughts and self-interruptions are stripped away, it can be seen that a strong sentence of a traditional type lies beneath; like many of Jane Austen's most effective sentences, it is tripartite, the divisions being marked by the two semi-colons.

Not all examples of 'dramatic syntax' are as long as these. Jane Austen can also handle the short, fast-moving sentence which makes its points with admirable economy of language:

The ball was over—and the breakfast was soon over too; the last kiss was given, and William was gone. (*MP*, 282)

They arrived, the carriage turned, the step was let down, and Mr Elton, spruce, black, and smiling, was with them instantly. (*E*, 114)

In the first of these, the rapidity of William's leave-taking is suggested by a series of brief statements in which detail is conspicuously absent, and in which the avoidance of personal verb-forms ('the last kiss was given' being preferred to 'William kissed Fanny for the last time') has a dehumanizing effect in harmony with the underlying notion of the relentless passing of time. The example from *Emma* also makes use of four statements, in the first three of which the stress falls on the verbs denoting physical action; the movement of the sentence is prevented from becoming purely mechanical, however, by the introduction into the final clause of three epithets which add precision without impeding the brisk progress to an emphatic conclusion ('instantly').

But it is, as has already been suggested in Chapter 1, *Persuasion* which offers Jane Austen's maturest experiments with dramatic syntax. The novel does indeed exhibit a remarkable variety of sylistic modes. When Anne Elliot observes that ' "There

[2] T. Tanner, *The Reign of Wonder* (Cambridge, 1965) 246.

is always something offensive in the details of cunning. The
manoeuvres of selfishness and duplicity must ever be revolting
..." ' (*P*, 207), she speaks the tongue that Johnson spake; but the
more emotional passages—and these are more numerous than
Jane Austen's reputation as pre-eminently a writer of social
comedy might suggest—are cast in a different mould. There is
an exquisite control of cadence in the passage, certainly not
dramatic in the usual sense but deeply infused with emotion,
which shows the lovers reunited after long separation:

> There they returned again into the past, more exquisitely happy,
> perhaps, in their re-union, than when it had been first projected;
> more tender, more tried, more fixed in a knowledge of each other's
> character, truth, and attachment; more equal to act, more justified
> in acting. And there, as they slowly paced the gradual ascent,
> heedless of every group around them, seeing neither sauntering
> politicians, bustling house-keepers, flirting girls, nor nursery-maids
> and children, they could indulge in those retrospections and acknow-
> ledgments, and especially in those explanations of what had directly
> preceded the present moment, which were so poignant and so
> ceaseless in interest. (*P*, 240–1)

This is surely a style which belongs both to the eighteenth century
and to the nineteenth: Dr. Johnson is still in sight (particularly in
the second sentence quoted), but for a comparable handling of
emotional tone we must seek parallels among the Victorians—in
the closing sentence of *Little Dorrit*, for instance, or that of
Wuthering Heights. Jane Austen has not renounced her birth-
right, and the second sentence is to a remarkable degree constructed upon the Johnsonian principle of balance:

And there,

as they slowly paced the gradual ascent,	heedless of every group around them,
seeing neither sauntering poli-ticians,	bustling house-keepers,
flirting girls,	nor nursery-maids and children,

they could indulge in those retrospections and acknowledgments,	and especially in those explanations of what had directly preceded the present moment,
which were so poignant	and so ceaseless in interest.

However, the pattern is dictated not by a mere mechanical fondness for the pairing of phrases and clauses, but by the artistic necessity of a quiet, restrained tone in which intense emotions can be exhibited for contemplation. The climax in the final clause is not a logical one—not the Johnsonian triumph of rationality—but an emotional climax, with the weight falling upon the two epithets ('so poignant and so ceaseless in interest') which are, for Jane Austen, unusually coloured by feeling.

I have dealt with the second sentence first because it reflects an earlier tradition to which Jane Austen was indebted, as well as looking forward to a new kind of romantic prose in fiction. The sentence which precedes it represents a more drastic departure from eighteenth-century syntax: its more urgent movement seems to suggest the first intensity of Anne's and Wentworth's feelings, just as the following sentence expresses the calmer state which succeeded. The strength and flexibility of the first sentence are derived partly from a relationship to the spoken language that the eighteenth-century sentence does not normally possess. Though it is far from being a 'colloquial' style in the sense in which that term is commonly applied to (say) Sterne or Hemingway, it owes its distinctive structure less to the demands of grammatical patterning than to the natural rhythms of the speaking voice, and the instinctive emphases of feeling and conviction. One might express the difference by saying that the dominance of the architectural qualities of the written sentence have largely given way to speech-derived patterns. The gentle insistence of the repeated 'more', like the discreetly stressed '*so* poignant . . . *so* ceaseless in interest', requires to be heard, if only by that 'inner ear' which, in the process of silent reading, 'listens' to the rhythms and inflexions of dialogue and of speech-based prose.

Other examples of Jane Austen's mature prose, even more nervously dramatic, will be cited in a fuller discussion of *Persuasion* in the next chapter; but it is clear by now that those who find in her style lack of variety or lack of distinction have not granted it the close attention that it demands. Herbert Read's complaint that it lacks action and speed and 'any mood of compulsion', for which its 'decoration' and 'mildly ironic comment' are insufficient compensations, seems to derive from a very partial recollection of what Jane Austen actually wrote; and the passage from *Emma* quoted and discussed by Read as a sample of her prose, though admirable in itself and entirely characteristic of *one* of her stylistic modes, will hardly stand as 'representative' of her style as a whole.[3] For, like most great writers, she has not one style but several, and to set a passage from Emma alongside one from *Wuthering Heights* (as Read does) in order to demonstrate the general superiority of Emily Brontë's prose is hardly a valid critical procedure.

More detailed analysis of the syntactical texture and variety of Jane Austen's prose must concern itself with such matters as sentence-length and typical structural patterns. The examples quoted have already made it clear that, whilst she often employs the complex sentence with its hierarchy of clauses that is the staple of her period's prose, she can also use to good effect sentences which are much shorter or much longer than the average. This immediately suggests that discussion should not stop at the sentence as the largest unit of language susceptible to investigation, since there is a meaningful element in the grammatical relationship of a sentence to its neighbours—a relationship that extends, of course, to internal structure as well as to length. In other words, the analysis of prose should be prepared to concern itself both with structure within the sentence-unit and with the 'gross anatomy' of the succession of sentences which make up the paragraph or other (generally nameless) larger unit. The deploying of statistical detail at length is beyond the scope of this book, but some idea of both the norm and the degree of variation

[3] H. Read, *English Prose Style* (1928) 118–20.

in sentence-length may be gained from an examination of characteristic passages. The third chapter of *Pride and Prejudice* (more suitable for the present purpose than the first two chapters, which contain much dialogue) can represent Jane Austen's mature narrative prose. If we ignore one sentence of dialogue, the first four paragraphs of that chapter contain eighteen sentences, which range from five to ninety-one words in length, with an average of thirty words. A norm of moderate length, that is to say, is combined with a wide degree of variation. Since half the sentences contain between twenty and forty words, the norm is firmly enough established to give a stability to the prose which heightens by contrast the effect of the occasional wide departures from that norm. There are examples of both the simple sentence ('Mrs Bennet was quite disconcerted.') and the double sentence ('In a few days Mr Bingley returned Mr Bennet's visit, and sat about ten minutes with him in his library.'). Most of the sentences are complex, however, and in the longer sentences a preference is shown for subordination over co-ordination. Even the longest sentence in the passage involves no loss of clarity, however, since the larger unit of ninety-one words is broken down into smaller units whose relation to each other is immediately apparent. This can be shown most clearly by taking some mild typographical liberties with the sentence in question:

A.1. The gentlemen pronounced him to be a fine figure of a man,
A.2. the ladies declared he was much handsomer than Mr Bingley, and
A.3. he was looked at with great admiration for about half the evening,

B.   till his manners gave a disgust which turned the tide of his popularity;

C.1. for he was discovered to be proud,
C.2.   to be above his company,
C.3.   and above being pleased;

D.1. and not all his large estate in Derbyshire could then save him
from having a most forbidding, disagreeable countenance,
D.2. and being unworthy to be compared with his friend. (*PP*, 10)

One sees very clearly here Jane Austen's fondness for three-part
structures. A.1.–3. record the initial reactions of the company
assembled at Netherfield to Darcy, A.3. acting as a summary of
the previous two clauses; all three are of approximately the same
length. B. is only slightly longer but gains greater force from the
two 'strong' nouns *disgust* and *popularity*, and acts as the pivot
on which the sentence turns. C.1.–C.3. are parallel to A.1.–A.3.,
indicating the unanimous change of heart in response to Darcy's
'manners', and suggesting by their greater brevity an offended
and dismissive attitude. The greater length of D.1.–D.2. gives an
air of finality to this social judgment; it also has internal patterning in the ironic antithesis of 'large estate' and 'disagreeable
countenance' (the implication being that the two are not, as a
general rule, closely correlated), and D.2. looks forward to the
next sentence, the subject of which is 'his friend'.

The opening of *Emma*, also examined from the point of view
of sentence-length, shows a similar norm and an almost equally
wide range. The first five paragraphs, for instance, contain fourteen sentences, ranging from three to sixty-six words, with an
average of 26.5 words. Here the disposition of sentences of varying lengths is rather striking. The fifth sentence is a short one, of
only nine words, but it is preceded by four sentences of average
and above-average length, and is immediately followed by the
longest sentence in the passage. Apart, therefore, from under-
lining by its brevity the importance of its contents (it stresses the
intimacy of Emma and Miss Taylor which the latter's marriage
has terminated, leaving a vacuum to be filled), it serves as a
resting-place at which the reader's attention can momentarily
pause—or the reader, if he is reading aloud, can recover his breath
—before passing on to the more demanding sentence that follows. Graphically represented, the passage shows an interesting
system of peaks (major and minor) and troughs:

Note particularly the position of the key-sentence, 'Miss Taylor married.'—the shortest but also one of the most important—marked * in the above diagram.

For special effect, Jane Austen can temporarily abandon both the normative length and the typical structures of her prose, as in the following from *Mansfield Park*:

It was a very proper wedding. The bride was elegantly dressed—the two bridemaids were duly inferior—her father gave her away—her mother stood with salts in her hand, expecting to be agitated—her aunt tried to cry—and the service was impressively read by Dr Grant. (*MP*, 203)

The unusually short first sentence allows unusual weight to fall on the epithet *proper*, and thus signals to the reader the irony that is to be sustained throughout the much longer sentence which follows. This second sentence rejects the customary subordination of clauses in favour of a series of self-contained and apparently neutral statements in which, again, the emphasis can fall successively on words which carry the main burden of the ironic intent: '*elegantly* dressed', '*duly* inferior', '*expecting* to be agitated', '*tried* to cry', '*impressively* read'. The technique is that of a series of snapshots (or, better, caricatures), and the language resembles a parody of upper-class nuptial jargon. The absence of subordination surely indicates the author's wish to appear detached: she is (it seems) not imposing upon the reader any interpretation or evaluation of this absurd scene, but simply

H

allowing it to speak for itself in all its insincerity, though of course the detachment suggested by the syntax is only illusory.

Somewhat differently, a succession of short sentences can often mark a period of excitement or suspense:

Not a syllable passed aloud. They all waited in silence for the appearance of their visitor. His footsteps were heard along the gravel path; in a moment he was in the passage; and in another, he was before them. (*SS*, 359)

In the process of reading such prose the reader is encouraged to relive, as it were, the emotions of those concerned—a response largely evoked by the syntactical structure. In the same chapter of *Sense and Sensibility*, we share the confused emotions of Elinor:

. . . the figure of a man on horseback drew her eyes to the window. He stopt at their gate. It was a gentleman, it was Colonel Brandon himself. Now she should hear more; and she trembled in expectation of it. But—it was *not* Colonel Brandon—neither his air—nor his height. Were it possible, she should say it must be Edward. She looked again. He had just dismounted;—she could not be mistaken; —it *was* Edward. She moved away and sat down. 'He comes from Mr Pratt's purposely to see us. I *will* be calm; I *will* be mistress of myself.' (*SS*, 358).

The average sentence-length here is 8.8 words, compared with an average of 28 in the opening paragraphs of the same chapter; and co-ordination has largely ousted subordination as a means of clause-linkage. This grammatical feature helps to suggest the nature of Elinor's perceptions: in 'It was a gentleman, it was Colonel Brandon himself' we are given in the two clauses (here in a paratactic rather than a co-ordinated relationship) the success-ive stages of her recognition—mistaken, as it turns out—of the visitor's identity. The syntax renders, that is to say, the experience of the instant rather than that experience viewed in the light of subsequent reflection, which might well have presented the first clause in a concessive relation to what follows, in some such form as 'Though she at first could see only that the stranger was a

gentleman, . . .' In other words, the sentence offers not an order-
ing of experience in retrospect but a dramatic re-enactment
through syntax of Elinor's experience. At such points the prose
technique is closer to Virginia Woolf or Hemingway than to
Addison or Johnson, and there is a more intimate relationship
than usual to speech which makes it not surprising that the style
moves within a few lines from narrative ('He had just dismounted'), through free indirect speech ('she could not be mistaken;—it *was* Edward') to direct speech.[4]

If the exceptionally short sentence, or succession of short sentences, can be used as the medium of particular dramatic or
ironic effects, Jane Austen also shows skill in manipulating the
longer than usual sentence. An example from *Emma* has already
been examined in Chapter 1 (pages 44–46 above), and without
being quoted in full here may be further discussed from the point
of view of its syntax. It presents, in 163 words, a complete account
of Elton's conquest of his bride, from first meeting to acceptance:
the compression of the material within a single sentence constitutes an ironic comment on the haste and determination with
which the business was, on both sides, pushed to a conclusion. To
read this sentence carefully is to become aware that it falls into
three sections, of respectively forty-three, twenty-seven and
ninety-three words in length. The first introduces the lady and
her 'fortune'; the second (introduced by 'the story told well')
celebrates Elton's success; and the third (from 'the first hour of
introduction . . .') enumerates the stages by which the prescribed
ritual from formal introduction to correct proposal had been
faithfully observed. The tempo of this long sentence is varied:
beginning in leisurely fashion with a unit of thirty-three words (as

---

[4] An important influence here is the epistolary style of Richardson:
Jane Austen admired *Sir Charles Grandison* and probably also knew
Clarissa. In such passages, one seems to detect a surviving fragment of the
novel-in-letters in which *Sense and Sensibility* originated. The setting
down of 'instant' impression, so that action and the letter-writing process
run alongside each other, is very characteristic of Richardson's style.
Here, however, this element is not presented as monologue (either spoken
or written), but is incorporated into the narrative.

far as the first semi-colon), it soon takes on a brisker movement by the appearance of several very short units, indicated by the dashes, and culminating in 'the lady had been so easily impressed—so sweetly disposed— . . .'; so that the syntax offers a 'miming' or verbal equivalent of the 'delightful rapidity' of this sardonically-observed courtship.

A more striking example of variety of movement within a single long sentence occurs a little earlier in the same novel, in the parallel account of Elton's unexpected proposal to Emma herself. The writer's task here is to suggest by stylistic means Emma's utter astonishment at this turn of events, and she does so by a marked shift of style in the course of a sentence of 125 words (it is followed, incidentally, by one of just four words):

To restrain him as much as might be, by her own manners, she was immediately preparing to speak with exquisite calmness and gravity of the weather and the night; but scarcely had she begun, scarcely had they passed the sweep-gate and joined the other carriage, than she found her subject cut up—her hand seized—her attention demanded, and Mr Elton actually making violent love to her: availing himself of the precious opportunity, declaring sentiments which must be already well known, hoping—fearing—adoring—ready to die if she refused him; but flattering himself that his ardent attachment and unequalled love and unexampled passion could not fail of having some effect, and in short, very much resolved on being seriously accepted as soon as possible. (*E*, 129)

Style, and especially syntax, reflect in their abrupt dislocation the unexpected change in Elton's behaviour. The sentence, and Emma, begin decorously enough: only the epithet *exquisite* suggests a certain strain; and until the first semi-colon, which takes the travellers as far as the sweep-gate, the prose is resolutely non-idiosyncratic. Then the more urgent rhythm of the repeated 'scarcely . . . scarcely . . .' introduces the reference to Emma's carefully objective conversation being 'cut up'; and from that point the sentence itself is indeed cut up: visibly by the dramatic punctuation, less obviously by the series of non-co-ordinated sentences and the emphatic present participles. Whereas the sentence opens with stress naturally falling on its nouns (*manner, calmness, gravity,* etc.), Elton's passionate language and behaviour call for emphasis on verbs (*cut up, seized, demanded,* etc.). Such phrases as 'ready to die' and 'flattering himself . . .', without explicitly presenting the substance of Elton's speech, are obviously intended to reflect his cliché-ridden language: the conventionality of his diction betrays his basic insincerity. The empty repetitions of 'ardent attachment and unequalled love and unexampled passion' have a similar effect. The dramatic syntax which in *Persuasion* is used for serious purposes is here put brilliantly to comic and satiric effect.

As earlier quotations have already illustrated, the use of sentences consisting of three clauses or other verbal units is widespread throughout Jane Austen's writings.[5] The following are further examples of different dates:

Your Husband I abhor—Reginald I despise—& I am secure of never seeing either again. (*Lady Susan*; *MW*, 307–8)

Design could never bring them in each other's way; negligence could never leave them exposed to a surprise; and chance had less in its favour in the crowd of London than even in the retirement of Barton . . . (*SS*, 213)

She was disheartened by Lady Bertram's silence, awed by Sir Thomas's grave looks, and quite overcome by Mrs Norris's admonitions. (*MP*, 14)

One may well ask why the triple sentence, rather than (say) the quadruple sentence, should occupy this favoured role. The answer may be, at least in part, that without extending the sentence to inordinate lengths, the three-part structure permits a pattern to be established and subtle but perceptible variations to be rung on that pattern: the first two parts of such a sentence establish an

---

[5] K. Sørensen, 'Johnsonese in *Northanger Abbey*: a Note on Jane Austen's Style', *English Studies*, 50 (1969) 390–97, has some useful comments on *oratio trimembris*. He suggests that the Johnsonian influence is particularly strong in *Northanger Abbey*, and that both writers have 'a very strong predilection for three-member structures' (392).

expectation which, by being in some respect disappointed in the third part, can produce an effect of surprise, whether the purpose is to be witty or dramatic. In each of the examples quoted above the impact of the triple sentence is in fact increased by other devices serving to strengthen its unity and underline its contrasts. In the first, from *Lady Susan*, the inversion of the first clause is repeated in the second, but the third departs from this pattern in a longer and more emphatic, because more final, statement that brings together the previous ones. In the next quotation, each of the three clauses is introduced by an abstract noun (*Design, negligence, chance*), but whilst the first two are similar in structure, the third breaks the pattern in favour of its own internal antithesis. The third example, from *Mansfield Park*, has both a formal patterning ('disheartened by . . . silence' is followed by the parallel phrases 'awed by . . . grave looks' and 'overcome by . . . admonitions') and a further significance in the disposition of the lexical items which occupy the key-positions at the end of each clause: reading the sentence, one seems to experience for oneself the increasingly heavy blows rained upon Fanny's sensibilities in the progression from 'silence', through 'looks', to 'admonitions'. Structure here is seen as an important component of meaning: the placing of the reference to 'Mrs Norris's admonitions' tells us something not only about Fanny but about that lady herself.

A less serious use of the triple sentence occurs in *Sense and Sensibility*, shortly after the introduction of Willoughby as the pseudo-hero:

His name was good, his residence was in their favourite village, and she soon found out that of all manly dresses a shooting-jacket was the most becoming. Her imagination was busy, her reflections were pleasant, and the pain of a sprained ancle was disregarded. (*SS*, 43)

As in some of the examples already quoted, the units within each sentence are arranged in order, the third being in both cases the longest (the sentences contain 4+7+16 words and 4+4+9 words respectively). Reading the first two clauses, one

has a sense of movement forwards and upwards, which seems to
slow down and level out on the long plateau of the final clause;
and it is in each case the final clause which makes the main
humorous and ironic point, the bathos of *name/residence/shoot-
ing-jacket* and *imagination/reflections/sprained ancle* conveying
its own comment on Marianne's behaviour.

Apart from the internal structuring of sentences on these lines,
a comparable element of patterning may also at times be dis-
cerned in the combination of sentences of different types within
a larger, multisentence unit. A passage of ironic narrative at the
end of Chapter 7 of *Sense and Sensibility* begins as follows:

Marianne's performance was highly applauded. Sir John was loud
in his admiration at the end of every song, and as loud in his
conversation with the others while every song lasted. Lady Middleton frequently called him to order, wondered how any one's
attention could be diverted from music for a moment, and asked
Marianne to sing a particular song which Marianne had just finished.
(*SS*, 35)

This well illustrates the two kinds of patterning under discussion:
that operating *within* the sentence, and that involving the *overall*
structure of a related group of sentences. The first sentence is a
single-unit statement uncoloured by irony or innuendo. The
second exposes the inconsistency of Sir John's behaviour by its
antithetical structure, his words being contrasted with his deeds,
and the repetition ('loud . . . as loud', 'every song . . . every
song'), as well as the sound-similarity of 'admiration . . . conversation', serving to reinforce this effect. The third sentence
performs a similar task by somewhat different means: Lady
Middleton's insincerity is not revealed until the bathos of the
final clause, and the three-part structure, with the units arranged
in order of increasing length (five, twelve and thirteen words
respectively), makes the anticlimax even more striking. The internal organization of these three sentences, then, is in each case
simple but effective. But if we go on to consider them not separately but as themselves constituting a larger three-part structure

—a sentence-group—we find them disposed in an order that is surely not fortuitous. A simple sentence is followed first by a double and then by a triple sentence, again in ascending order of length, so that the internal pattern of the third sentence is repeated in the group of three sentences as a whole. And whilst one would obviously not wish to suggest that Jane Austen herself paid the kind of conscious attention to prose structure that such analysis involves, it seems likely that she went beyond the minimal requirements of correctness and euphony, and carefully 'listened' to her prose as she composed it (even if this was a silent process), and that certain verbal conformations struck her as possessing distinctively pleasing and effective qualities.

Some other aspects of her syntax repay scrutiny but cannot receive extended discussion within the modest dimensions of the present chapter. In certain passages, syntax acts as a signal of parody, as when Catherine Morland returns home unceremoniously from Northanger Abbey:

A heroine in a hack post-chaise is such a blow upon sentiment, as no attempt at grandeur or pathos can withstand. Swiftly therefore shall her post-boy drive through the village, amid the gaze of Sunday groups, and speedy shall be her descent from it. (*NA*, 232)

The inversions of the second sentence quoted ('Swiftly . . . shall her post-boy drive . . . and speedy shall be her descent . . .') have a mock-heroic flavour, but the author seems to be laughing not at her heroine but at a familiar style of novel-writing, as the appearance of the word *sentiment* confirms. Another aspect of syntax that ought not to be overlooked is its use in dialogue in relation to character-presentation: the syntactical element is often an important one in the distinctive idiolects with which many of her characters are endowed, and which are more fully discussed in the next chapter.

A moment's consideration of such characters as Miss Bates and Mr Collins, Sir Thomas Bertram and Sir Walter Elliot, will justify this suggestion. A single quotation may be offered, from Mary Crawford in *Mansfield Park*:

'There is a beauty in every family.—It is a regular thing. Two play on the piano-forte, and one on the harp—and all sing—or would sing if they were taught—or sing all the better for not being taught —or something like it.' (*MP*, 288)

Even these few lines suggest the attractiveness and the radical moral unsatisfactoriness of the speaker: she is witty and *à propos*, but 'careless', and her carelessness—which, properly understood, involves a disregard for decorum—is manifested in the loose syntax of many of her speeches, for which we find no counter-part in the speech of the more morally responsible characters.

CHAPTER FOUR

'FREQUENT CONVERSATIONS'

Jane Austen is so often associated with the pleasures and virtues of rural life that there may be some difficulty in seeing her in the role of an enthusiastic theatregoer. Yet her letters contain many references to actors and plays: when she missed seeing Mrs Siddons owing to a misunderstanding, she remarked that she 'could swear at her with little effort for disappointing me', and of Don Juan she wrote: 'I must say that I have seen nothing on the stage who has been a more interesting character than that compound of cruelty and lust' (*L*, 275, 323). She was also fond of reading plays, and during her early years had had many opportunities of enjoying amateur theatricals, which seemed to excite less disapproval in the Austen household than at Mansfield Park.[1] Her interest in dramatic literature has left its mark on her novels in the brilliance and variety of their dialogue, as well as in certain features of their action and characterization. Possibly the influence of the stage is also mediated through the example of Richardson, whom she greatly admired, and whose novels contain strong dramatic elements. Ever since the *Monthly Review* observed, in its notice of *Emma* in July 1816, that 'the dialogue is easy and lively', the critic and the common reader have con-

---

[1] B. C. Southam lists plays performed at Steventon before 1790 (*Jane Austen's Literary Manuscripts* [Oxford, 1964] 8). Cf. also S. Rosenfeld, 'Jane Austen and Private Theatricals', *Essays and Studies*, 15 (1962) 40–51.

curred in finding the presentation of speech a source of delight in all the novels. Dialogue is always important, though not always equally so, and not always presented in the same forms.

Lengthy passages, even whole chapters, may be found which consist largely of direct speech. The opening chapter of *Pride and Prejudice* is one of the most celebrated of many examples of what are virtually ready-made dramatic scripts. At the outset one has a sense of the curtain rising on the Bennets' drawing-room and the assembled characters 'discovered'. By the time the final paragraph of authorial comment is reached, the reader has learned to know Mr and Mrs Bennet well enough to have no hesitation in assenting to the author's verdict on their respective natures. That verdict comes not as a surprise but as a confirmation of what has already been conveyed through their speech. He has also learned something of three of their daughters, as well as of Mr Bingley and the Lucases. The apparent ease and naturalness of the dialogue in this short scene conceals the substantial amount of necessary information it presents. So that this is not merely clever or amusing talk: it performs some essential functions in relation to plot and characterization. More than any earlier novelist, Richardson excepted, Jane Austen uses dialogue not as an occasional diversion but as a major resource for conducting the business of her fiction. Moreover, it is often of unprecedented realism (though the concept of realism, as applied to literary dialogue, needs to be handled with caution); and, yet again, we find her engaged, particularly in the later novels, in experiments of striking originality in the various modes of presenting speech and of combining it with other elements. It is likely to be rewarding, therefore, to look closely at Jane Austen's dialogue —at the linguistic techniques of its presentation, as well as at the literary uses to which it is put.

First, however, the notion of 'realism' in dialogue, already alluded to, needs to be examined, especially since it has often been evoked in relation to Jane Austen's art. Both early and later critics have praised the naturalness of the verbal exchanges between her characters. Shortly after her death, the *British Critic* published a long appreciation of her work which included the following comment on her use of speech:

Our authoress gives no definitions; but she makes her *dramatis personae* talk; and the sentiments which she places in their mouths, the little phrases which she makes them use, strike so familiarly upon our memory as soon as we hear them repeated, that we instantly recognize among some of our acquaintance, the sort of persons she intends to signify, as accurately as if we had heard their voices.[2]

This, published in 1818, is valuable contemporary evidence of Jane Austen's success in catching the tone of current speech, but the implication in the final phrase that she is offering little more than a transcript of such speech must be questioned. Later in the century, Fanny Kemble commented that 'She must have written down the very conversations she heard *verbatim*, to have made them so like',[3] and more recently a more impressive authority, H. C. Wyld, has ventured even further into hyperbole:

We have here the representation of actual life and dialogue as the author knew it. There can be no doubt that this is the real thing, and that people really spoke like this in the closing years of the eighteenth century ... It is not Miss Austen who is speaking, it is the men and women of her day.[4]

The shrewd observation of Jane Austen's dialogue is undeniable, and she rarely if ever provokes the kind of protest that the editor of *The Oxford Book of English Talk* makes against the dialogue of *Jane Eyre*, that it is 'literary' in the pejorative sense of being palpably unreal. At the same time, claims such as those quoted are in danger of confusing the means with the effect. Recent investigations into spontaneous speech suggest that it is altogether freer and looser, less patterned and organized and

[2] Quoted by C. B. Hogan, 'Jane Austen and her Early Public', *Review of English Studies*, 1 (1950) 47–8.

[3] *Ibid.*, 53.

[4] H. C. Wyld, *A History of Modern Colloquial English* (Oxford, 1936) 185.

more wasteful and repetitive, than has often been assumed; and, even making allowance for the greater formality that obtained in much of the polite speech of the upper levels of early nineteenth-century society, there seems good reason to doubt whether Jane Austen's contemporaries really spoke with the sureness and economy of effect which characterize the speech of even her foolish and vulgar figures. Less than twenty years after her death, Edward Bulwer made an interesting attempt to represent one form of spontaneous speech with more than usual accuracy, and the result, with its hesitations and confusions and all the phenomena which have been termed 'normal non-fluency', suggests something of the gulf that lies between 'real' speech and even the most 'realistic' fictional dialogue.[5] Inevitably, even when it is based on observation rather than literary convention, written dialogue is the result of a controlled and modified selection from the features of living speech: the uncertainties and misdirections of actual 'talk' are distilled into a concentration of effects that justifies their appearance in the very different medium of print and their perception through the eye rather than the ear. Thus, Miss Bates is no ordinary bore: her speech contrives to give simultaneously the impression of tedium and the liveliest pleasure. Observation is transmuted by art, so that what would be tolerable or merely commonplace in life becomes a source of interest. But this would clearly not be accomplished by merely transcribing the undoctored conversations of actuality: the dialogue we read has gone through a refining process, and one corollary of this fact is that caution needs to be exercised in basing conclusions about the nature of the spoken language in a given period upon the evidence of novels and plays.

The reference to the drama reminds us that the dialogue of the early novels often has a quality recalling eighteenth-century stage

[5] Cf. R. Quirk, 'Colloquial English and Communication', in *Studies in Communication* (1955) 181; A. H. Smith and R. Quirk, 'Some Problems of Verbal Communication', *Transactions of the Yorkshire Dialect Society*, 9 (1955) 10–20; D. Crystal and D. Davy, *Investigating English Style* (1969) Ch. 4

comedy. What follows is the opening of a long conversation between Catherine Morland and Isabella Thorpe in *Northanger Abbey*, and the scene, as in many an eighteenth-century comedy, is the Pump Room at Bath:

'My dearest creature, what can have made you so late? I have been waiting for you at least this age!'

'Have you indeed!—I am very sorry for it; but really I thought I was in very good time. It is but just one. I hope you have not been here long?'

'Oh! these ten ages at least. I am sure I have been here this half-hour. But now, let us go and sit down at the other end of the room, and enjoy ourselves. I have an hundred things to say to you ... Have you gone on with Udolpho?'

'Yes, I have been reading it ever since I woke; and I am got to the black veil.'

'Are you, indeed? How delightful! oh! I would not tell you what is behind the black veil for the world! Are not you wild to know?'

'Oh! yes, quite; what can it be?—But do not tell me—I would not be told upon any account ...' (*NA*, 39)

If this is triviality, it is triviality with a purpose, for we learn a good deal about Isabella and Catherine not only from what they say but from the stylistic qualities of their respective modes of speech. Although both make much use of questions and exclamations, there is a significant difference between the former's modish exaggerations (' "at least this age ... these ten ages at least" ') and the latter's sincerity and regard for truth. Sentence-length and sentence-structure are markedly different from those of non-dialogue passages: there is a preference for co-ordination rather than subordination, and for simple sentences and phrasal units. Similarly there are distinctive lexical features (*this age*, *wild to know*, etc.), especially in Isabella's speech. As in well-written dramatic dialogue, a brisk pace is obtained by contriving that one speech shall lead naturally to the next, the most common relationships being of question-and-answer and of statement-and-reaction. Many of Jane Austen's duologues consist of a rapid exchange of debating points, as in the famous confrontation between Elizabeth

Bennet and Lady Catherine in Chapter 58 of *Pride and Prejudice*. Only rarely is a character permitted to deliver a lengthy monologue, as Colonel Brandon does when he enlightens Elinor (and the reader) concerning Willoughby (*SS*, Chapter 31); a more usual device for a revelation of this kind is the interpolation of a letter given verbatim. Exits and entrances are often indicated as in dramatic texts, but the concomitants of speech such as movement, gesture and facial expression are rarely referred to: when Edward Ferrars shows his anxiety by snipping nervously with a pair of scissors (*SS*, 360) the exceptional use of significant detail takes us by surprise. It is language itself, often subtle departures from the norms of vocabulary and syntax, which usually carries the burden of meaning and suggestion. We must not assume that Jane Austen was insensitive to the external aspects of human behaviour or to their expressive potential; more probably, she preferred to leave such matters to the reader's imagination, rather than to risk distracting the attention from what is said to the manner of its saying. Whereas Richardson, for instance, makes very frequent use of references to stylized gestures presumably originating in the theatre, we are not often invited to visualize Jane Austen's characters in the act of delivering their speeches. In the same way, her dialogue suggests such features of the spoken language as vocal quality, stress, pause, tempo or intonation relatively rarely, and there are very few indications of idiosyncratic pronunciation. Whereas in Dickens, to take another example, paralinguistic qualities may not only reinforce but at times contradict the spoken word, revealing the hollowness of a verbal façade, the irony and criticism in Jane Austen's intention find expression within the actual language of the dialogue. At the same time, this is dialogue which subjective experience shows to be constantly making an appeal to the mind's ear: it belongs to that category of speech which is 'written to be read as if heard'.[6] Her art is primarily conceived in aural rather than visual terms: one suspects that few readers ever *see* her characters or settings with

[6] Cf. M. Gregory, 'Aspects of Varieties Differentiation', *Journal of Linguistics*, 3 (1967) 177–98.

much vividness. A revealing comment in a letter to her sister Cassandra dated 4 February 1813 (*L*, 299) suggests that her own conception of dialogue in fiction included an element of voice-quality. The experience of hearing her mother read aloud the newly-published *Pride and Prejudice* provokes the comment that 'though she perfectly understands the characters herself, she cannot speak as they ought'.

The use of direct speech is traditionally, though not invariably, signalled by graphological means; yet it would be wrong to assume that what is placed within quotation marks is always to be taken as a record of the actual words spoken. (It would be pedantic to insist on saying, here and elsewhere, 'words which are to be supposed to have been spoken', but it perhaps needs pointing out that one is often conscious of speaking elliptically, and sometimes misleadingly, in discussing fictional dialogue.) Eighteenth-century practice, as exemplified in, for example, the novels of Fielding, was often to make use of quotation marks (e.g., for various kinds of indirect speech) where these would not nowadays be employed. Beyond this, however, there is an interesting special case which deserves mention. Consider Catherine Morland's anxious reflections on the weather (*NA*, 83): on hearing the clock strike twelve, she remarks:

'I do not quite despair yet. I shall not give it up till a quarter after twelve. This is just the time of day for it to clear up, and I do think it looks a little lighter. There, it is twenty minutes after twelve, and now I *shall* give it up entirely . . .'

There can surely be no intention of suggesting that this speech was delivered in the form in which it is presented, as the references to the passing of time make quite clear: twenty minutes elapse within a couple of lines, but what is given does not prevent us from assuming that there must have been other, intervening remarks which are left unrecorded. In spite of the apparent similarity to direct speech, this is something different from what usually passes by that name: not a transcript of conversation but a selection from it, a number of speeches which we may suppose to have been uttered *seriatim* being conflated within a single set of quotation marks for the sake of vividness and economy. The author has performed, as it were, an editorial rather than a purely recording function. This was an early solution to a technical problem of dialogue writing which engaged Jane Austen's interest throughout her career: how to give the impression of a sequence of speeches without such loss of narrative pace as might be damaging to the rhythm of an episode. Another example occurs later in the same novel, when Catherine questions Miss Tilney about the latter's deceased mother:

'Was she a very charming woman? Was she handsome? Was there any picture of her in the Abbey? And why had she been so partial to that grove? Was it from dejection of spirits?'—were questions now eagerly poured forth;—the first three received a ready affirmative, the two others were passed by . . . (*NA*, 180)

Again the context makes it perfectly clear that Catherine's eager questions were asked and answered, or not answered, separately; but the novelist has chosen to present them as a single speech, and to avoid a protracted ding-dong dialogue, partly to emphasize her heroine's consuming curiosity, and partly to gain speed for the narrative.

Direct speech is only one method, though the commonest, of suggesting the exchange of conversation. Indirect, or reported, speech may be the result of the wish to keep a character in the background, to reduce loquacity and diffuseness to economy and order, or to preserve narrative speed by giving the gist of a dialogue in the narrator's words without allowing it to occupy a disproportionate amount of space. Or the indirect form may be deliberately used in contrast to the direct form, to suggest the difference between two speakers. Thus, when Mrs Bennet (on the first page of *Pride and Prejudice*) presses her unwelcome conversational attentions upon her husband, his coolness is suggested by the indirect form:

'My dear Mr Bennett,' said his lady to him one day, 'have you heard that Netherfield Park is let at last?'
Mr Bennet replied that he had not.

I

Another example occurs in *Emma*, when Mrs Elton's effusive and officious anxieties over Jane Fairfax (in direct speech) are highlighted by the quiet restraint of Jane's reply in the less dramatic, reported form:

'My dear Jane, what is this I hear?—Going to the post-office in the rain!—This must not be, I assure you. You sad girl, how could you do such a thing?—It is a sign I was not there to take care of you.'
Jane very patiently assured her that she had not caught any cold.

Not all the instances of indirect speech in Jane Austen's novels, however, observe the traditional conventions of that form (i.e., the use of a verb of saying or thinking, followed by a dependent clause, often introduced by the relative 'that', with its pronouns in the third person and its verbs in a past tense.) A useful example occurs in the famous second chapter of *Sense and Sensibility*, where by gradual degrees the John Dashwoods resolve to do nothing for the widowed Mrs Dashwood and her daughters. The triumph of avarice over conscience is depicted dramatically, in a long passage of dialogue; but there is an introductory paragraph which covers a good deal of ground in a few words:

Mrs John Dashwood did not at all approve of what her husband intended to do for his sisters. To take three thousand pounds from the fortune of their dear little boy, would be impoverishing him to the most dreadful degree. She begged him to think again on the subject. How could he answer it to himself to rob his child, and his only child too, of so large a sum? . . .

The first sentence quoted is straight narrative, in the 'voice' of the author; the third sentence is normal indirect speech; but the second and fourth are what is usually described as free indirect speech. Mrs John Dashwood's statement and her rhetorical question are presented in a form which lacks the introductory verb of saying, yet which retains some of the other grammatical qualities of indirect speech; at the same time, it suggests the lexical and syntactical qualities of the hypothetical 'original' (in, for instance, the phrase 'dear little boy', and the colloquial pattern of 'to rob his child, and his only child too') to an extent not generally found in indirect speech, where a neutral reporting style is favoured. The free mixture of different modes of speech-presentation, of which we have here an early example, is very characteristic of this novelist. In this case it provides an initial impetus which launches the dialogue more rapidly than could have been contrived had direct speech been used from the outset. After this brief summarizing paragraph, the curtain rises, so to speak, on a conversation already under way, and with the audience fully informed as to its topic and tone.

Free indirect speech (known also as *style indirect libre* and *erlebte Rede*) is widely used by Jane Austen, particularly in her later work.[7] It combines detachment and economy with dramatic vividness and stylistic variety—to some extent, that is, the best of both worlds of the direct and indirect forms—and many later novelists have exploited its advantages. It is now widely agreed that the two traditional categories already discussed are far from adequate to describe all the forms in which speech is presented in fiction. Michael Gregory has suggested not only that two further categories already familiar to students of style must be taken into account (free direct speech and free indirect speech) but also that 'These "free" categories have to cover what prescriptively might be termed "a multitude of sins", probably a wider variety of significantly different groupings of linguistic features than the older categories whose criteria have been more precisely stated'.[8] One need look no further than the novels of Jane Austen to discover that the four existing categories provide a very unsatisfactory framework for the discussion of speech-

[7] On free indirect speech, see W. Bühler, *Die 'erlebte Rede' im englischen Roman: ihre Vorstufen und ihre Ausbildung im Werke Jane Austens* (Zurich, 1937). L. Glauser, *Die erlebte Rede im englischen Roman des 19. Jahrhunderts* (Zurich, 1948), surveys its use in the work of eight other nineteenth-century novelists. Cf. also S. Ullmann, *Style in the French Novel* (Cambridge, 1957) Ch. 2, and *Language and Style* (Oxford, 1964) 134–6; R. Quirk, *The Use of English* (1962) 246–9. According to Ullmann, free indirect speech is 'comparatively rare' in French literature in the first half of the nineteenth century (*Language and Style*, 134).

[8] M. Gregory, 'Old Bailey Speech in *A Tale of Two Cities*', *A Review of English Literature*, 6 (1965) 55.

presentation. It will be argued that free indirect speech in particular is used with remarkable flexibility for a variety of fictional purposes whose distinctive linguistic features and mode of functioning may be identified and described.

Jane Austen's contribution to the use of this form of speech was not altogether that of an innovator, since brief examples may be found in such eighteenth-century novelists as Fielding and Fanny Burney. However, she undeniably developed and extended its role, and was the first major novelist to make considerable use of it. It occurs occasionally in the earlier novels: 'The man believed Miss Tilney to be at home, but was not quite certain. Would she be pleased to send up her name?' (*NA*, 91). Here the servant's question retains the form in which it would be cast in direct speech (though the pronouns are changed), but merges readily into the narrative, which pursues the tenor of its way without the interruption of an insignificant character asserting his individuality. Sometimes quotation marks are retained, in the eighteenth-century manner, as when General Tilney refers angrily to a servant who fails to open a door for Catherine: ' "What did William mean by it? He should make a point of inquiring into the matter".' (cf. *NA*, 185). A later passage, from *Emma*, shows the use of free indirect speech in quotation marks combined with the device of conflating a number of speeches which has already been referred to. When Frank Churchill makes small talk to Emma, the author's purpose is to give the substance of a trivial conversation without permitting it to occupy more than a few lines:

'Was she a horse-woman?—Pleasant rides?—Pleasant walks?— Had they a large neighbourhood?—Highbury, perhaps, afforded society enough?— . . . Balls—had they balls?—Was it a musical society?' (*E*, 191)

These are the notes of a dialogue rather than the dialogue itself: we are left to infer Emma's replies and to reconstruct the original form of Frank's questions, since we are surely not to assume that he, like Dickens' Jingle, actually used such telegraphic phrases as ' "Pleasant rides?—Pleasant walks?" ' Yet the passage, whilst gaining economy, does not forfeit dramatic quality entirely: it has a liveliness which the mere authorial statement that such a conversation took place would lack.

Free indirect speech is used in strikingly different proportions in different novels, in a way that cannot be accounted for solely in terms of Jane Austen's growing interest and skill in speech-presentation but seems to be more intimately related to the tone of a particular novel and the viewpoint of its narrative. *Pride and Prejudice*, with its fondness for the dramatic mode and its ebulliently extrovert heroine, employs it very little, whereas *Mansfield Park* offers a large number of examples, and *Persuasion* even more. A handful of examples from, firstly, *Mansfield Park* will illustrate more fully some of the uses and varieties of this form of speech:

(1) A few inquiries began; but one of the earliest—'How did her sister Bertram manage about her servants? Was she as much plagued as herself to get tolerable servants?'—soon led her mind away from Northamptonshire . . . (*MP*, 385)
(2) He was after her immediately. 'She must not go, she must allow him five minutes longer,' and he took her hand and led her back to her seat . . . (301)
(3) She proclaimed her thoughts. She must say that she had more than half a mind to go with the young people; it would be such an indulgence to her; she had not seen her poor dear sister Price for more than twenty years . . . (372)
(4) 'What if they were among them to undertake the care of her eldest daughter, a girl now nine years old, of an age to require more attention than her poor mother could possibly give?' (5)
(5) 'There could be no harm in her liking an agreeable man——every body knew her situation—Mr Crawford must take care of himself.' (44)

The first two quotations suggest the facility with which free indirect speech can be incorporated into narrative writing, with far less interruption of its flow than direct speech would cause. In (1), Mrs Price's questions retain the flavour of speech, yet are smoothly accommodated into the sentence. Words such as 'plagued' and 'tolerable', like the expressions 'more than half a mind' and 'her poor dear sister Price' in (3), reflect the language of their respective speakers: little attempt has been made to iron out the idiosyncrasies of a particular idiolect—indeed, they are carefully reproduced, thus securing a vividness and variety not normally achieved by ordinary indirect speech. This becomes obvious as soon as one tries the experiment of recasting sentences of free indirect speech into the more usual indirect form: not only does the latter tend to be more long-winded, but the characteristic patterns (e.g., question and exclamation) as well as the characteristic diction tend to disappear in the neutral reporting style. By using the freer form, Jane Austen succeeds in suggesting in (1) the harassed mother's querulous and self-pitying enquiries; that is to say, free indirect speech makes a real contribution to character-portrayal.

(2) suggests the dramatic urgency of Henry Crawford's speech and at the same time makes possible the more extended rhythm of the sentence in which it appears, the whole conveying admirably the suddenness with which Fanny finds herself listening to his proposal. A glance at the context in which (4) appears shows that it is preceded by indirect speech and followed by direct speech: it thus serves to ease the transition from one to the other, without the kind of dislocation of the narrative line which a change of form sometimes involves. In this case the style suggests speech-idiom without reproducing it very closely, for alongside elements which seem to echo Mrs Norris's speech ('her poor mother') are others which constitute an intervention by the authorial voice (e.g., the explanatory phrase 'a girl now nine years old'). (5) seems to differ from the rest in representing either the conflation of several short speeches, or perhaps an abridgement of a long one—again making possible an effect that combines the dramatic quality of direct speech with the succinctness of the indirect form. In four of these five examples, quotation marks surround passages of free indirect speech; although later novelists generally dispensed with them, Jane Austen's practice seems to lack consistency.

But it is *Persuasion* that offers the fullest and most important use of free indirect speech in Jane Austen's work, and represents a remarkable and fascinating step towards technical experiment-ation at the end of the novelist's life. The description of this novel by a recent critic as Jane Austen's 'least dramatic work'[9] may well be questioned. It is surely misleading to make the use of direct speech the criterion of dramatic quality: there is a kind of inner drama which, as we shall see, can often be best communi-cated by other means. Even so, considerable portions of the novel are cast in dramatic form, and there are many passages of direct speech in the earlier manner. In the following, Anne Elliot has just received, and read, a long-awaited letter from her sister Mary:

'How is Mary?' said Elizabeth; and without waiting for an answer, 'And pray what brings the Crofts to Bath?'

'They come on the Admiral's account. He is thought to be gouty.'

'Gout and decrepitude!' said Sir Walter. 'Poor old gentleman.'

'Have they any acquaintance here?' asked Elizabeth.

'I do not know; but I can hardly suppose that, at Admiral Croft's time of life, and in his profession, he should not have many acquaintances in such a place as this.'

'I suspect,' said Sir Walter coolly, 'that Admiral Croft will be best known in Bath as the renter of Kellynch-hall. Elizabeth, may we venture to present him and his wife in Laura-place?'

'Oh! no, I think not . . .' (*P*, 165–6)

As so often, we are not far from the accents of stage-comedy: although the authorial voice is silent, the complacency and condescension of Sir Walter's tone (e.g., in his ' "Poor old gentleman" ') are unmistakable, and both his character and that of his elder daughter are quietly but bitingly delineated through their speech, the author confining her comments mainly to the provision of 'stage-directions' ('as he laid down the newspaper', 'rising and pacing the room').

At many points, however, the rhythm of the novel demands a more versatile treatment of speech. In the next example, an

[9] W. Craik, *Jane Austen: the Six Novels* (1965) 171.

account of a lengthy discussion is presented within the compass
of a single paragraph, free indirect speech being readily inter-
spersed with other elements such as narrative and comment, as
well as with occasional excursions into direct speech. The result
is an unusual flexibility, combining the immediacy of speech with
the unslackened narrative pace made possible by the free mingling
of diverse elements:

It now became necessary for the party to consider what was best to
be done, as to their general situation. They were now able to speak
to each other, and consult. *That Louisa must remain where she was,
however distressing to her friends to be involving the Harvilles in
such trouble, did not admit a doubt. Her removal was impossible.*
The Harvilles silenced all scruples; and, as much as they could, all
gratitude. They had looked forward and arranged every thing,
before the others began to reflect. *Captain Benwick must give up his
room to them, and get a bed elsewhere—and the whole was settled.
They were only concerned that the house could accommodate no
more*; and yet perhaps by 'putting the children away in the maids'
room, or swinging a cot somewhere', *they could hardly bear to
think of not finding room for two or three besides, supposing they
might wish to stay; though, with regard to any attendance on Miss
Musgrove, there need not be the least uneasiness in leaving her to
Mrs Harville's care entirely. Mrs Harville was a very experienced
nurse; and her nursery-maid, who had lived with her long and gone
about with her every where, was just such another. Between those
two, she could want no possible attendance by day or night.* And all
this was said with a truth and sincerity of feeling irresistible.
(*P*, 112–13)

Four elements, definable but not always easily separable, may be
distinguished here: narrative (as in the first two sentences quoted);
authorial comment (as in the final sentence of the paragraph);
free indirect speech (as in the sentences italicized); and direct
speech, the quotation marks amounting to an apology for the
colloquial nature of the expressions used. (Fanny Burney employs
a comparable device when she italicizes certain words and phrases
in Evelina's letters, to indicate that these expressions, although
not strictly belonging to dialogue, are to be taken as having been

used by others; for example, at a ball her heroine is 'accosted by another, who *begged the favour of hopping a dance* with me' (*Evelina*, Letter 50).) The borderline between the second and third of these four elements is of a fluctuating nature that the defining of categories, for convenience of discussion, should not be allowed to obscure. For example, the first sentence italicized, although carrying the implication that speech has taken place, is closer to interpretative comment than the sentence that follows ('Her removal was impossible'). Throughout, the language of the sentences in free indirect speech is not necessarily to be taken as being close to that used in the supposed conversation on which they are based, since by tradition indirect speech is more formal than direct speech, and even the free form may be expected to partake of this quality; nevertheless, the sense of a dialogue having taken place is strong as one reads, and is confirmed by the final sentence: 'And all this was said . . .' To spell out a dialogue of this length, using the normal machinery of direct speech, would produce a passage of considerable length; added to which, authorial comments could only be made at the expense of a certain clumsiness. As it is, such a sentence as the one beginning 'They were only concerned . . .' not only creates, by its use of what may be termed summary-effect, the illusion of social relationships being worked out through discussion, but simultaneously presents the author's judgment on the generous behaviour of the Harvilles.

This passage is immediately followed by another which will serve to illustrate a different and more dramatic manner of suggesting, within a few lines, the exchange of speeches within a group:

Charles, Henrietta, and Captain Wentworth were the three in consultation, and for a little while it was only an interchange of perplexity and terror. 'Uppercross,—the necessity of some one's going to Uppercross,—the news to be conveyed—how it could be broken to Mr and Mrs Musgrove—the lateness of the morning,— an hour already gone since they ought to have been off—the impossibility of being in tolerable time.' At first, they were capable of nothing more to the purpose than such exclamations; but, after a while, Captain Wentworth, exerting himself, said:

'We must be decided, and without the loss of another minute...'
(*P*, 113)

As in the previous example, the problem is to achieve an effect of concentration without the loss of immediacy which a bald summary entails. An earlier quotation from *Emma*, superficially similar to the present one, presented in telegraphic form one side of a conversation (Frank Churchill's questions, but not Emma's replies); here, however, the purpose is not simply one of economy but of dramatic vividness, and the effect that comes over is the theatrical one of a confused hubbub of excited voices. The passage begins with narrative and ends with normal direct speech. What lies between is less easy to define, but it appears to consist of fragments of free indirect speech, the exclamatory nature of the conversation being conveyed by the use of nominal groups and subordinate clauses rather than complete sentences: the use of main verbs is suspended as action is temporarily paralysed by the shock of the accident, and only static, apparently unproductive expressions of dismay are possible ('At first, they were capable of nothing more...'). The transition to direct speech is also a transition to a different kind of grammatical structure, and Wentworth's firm 'We must be decided' (the result of the exertion to which authorial tribute has been paid) shows that command of syntax at such a time is related to qualities of character. The passage is at once highly dramatic and remarkably economical, in a way that could hardly have been accomplished by the more customary modes of speech-presentation.

Where the intention is not to produce the impression of an entire conversation having taken place, but simply to present the speech or thought of a single character, the use of free indirect speech produces what is tantamount to a temporary shift in point of view. Thus the final paragraph of Chapter 8 of the second volume gives us Anne's reactions to the abrupt departure of Wentworth; the variety of modes of speech-presentation within a few lines can be best illustrated by extending the quotation to include the sentences which immediately precede this paragraph:

... she found herself accosted by Captain Wentworth, in a reserved yet hurried sort of farewell. 'He must wish her good night. He was going—he should get home as fast as he could.'

'Is not this song worth staying for?' said Anne, suddenly struck by an idea which made her yet more anxious to be encouraging.

'No!' he replied impressively, 'there is nothing worth my staying for;' and he was gone directly.

Jealousy of Mr Elliot! It was the only intelligible motive. Captain Wentworth jealous of her affection! Could she have believed it a week ago—three hours ago! *For a moment the gratification was exquisite. But alas! there were very different thoughts to succeed.* How was such jealousy to be quieted? How was the truth to reach him? How, in all the peculiar disadvantages of their respective situations, would he ever learn her real sentiments?—It was misery to think of Mr Elliot's attentions.—Their evil was incalculable. (*P*, 190–1)

In the two short sentences italicized, the authorial voice makes its intrusion into this brief episode with unusual terseness, whilst speech and thought-speech are presented in three different ways: by ordinary direct speech in Anne's question and Wentworth's reply; by free indirect speech (enclosed by quotation marks) in Wentworth's 'reserved yet hurried sort of farewell'; and by free indirect speech, without quotation marks, for the final paragraph, in which we are given an insight into Anne's consciousness that is the fictional equivalent of the dramatic soliloquy, and which re-calls Professor Ullmann's comment that free indirect speech 'supersedes the borderline between narrative and inner speech, so that the two imperceptibly merge into one another'.[10]

Each of these three methods has its own specific effect. The direct speech has an immediacy which lends effectiveness to Wentworth's exit line and to the succinct stage-direction which follows ('he was gone directly'). (The theatrical terminology offers

[10] S. Ullmann, *Style in the French Novel*, 119.

itself naturally and revealingly.) The modified free indirect speech of his earlier farewell has, in its abruptness, an appropriate flavour of dramatic urgency, yet leaves in reserve a quantum of directness for the two speeches that follow. Finally, the analysis of Anne's state of mind is more economically and at the same time more dramatically performed through the medium of free indirect speech, with its retention of the questions and exclamations that belong more properly to direct speech, than would be possible in ordinary indirect speech (the more usual fictional medium for an effect of this kind), in which the sharp edge of her desperation would be blunted, and (for instance) the urgent demand 'How was the truth to reach him?' would become the placid statement 'She wondered how the truth was to reach him'. On the other hand, the flexibility of the chosen medium also makes possible, what direct speech would not so easily permit, authorial comment of the kind italicized above. In other words, the peculiar advantages of both direct and indirect speech are combined to fashion a medium which brings the reader close enough to the character's consciousness to have a sense of something at times resembling interior monologue, yet at the same time preserves the kind of objectivity, and the frequent reminders of an impartial authorial presence, which make explicit comment possible. Nor, it may be added, is this flexibility solely on the grammatical level: lexically, free indirect speech is generally closer to the direct than to the indirect form, and here such words as *misery* and *evil* surely reflect Anne's state of mind and embody *her* view of the situation in the intensity of the moment, rather than the author's objective judgment.

A less dramatic passage in which, within a brief space, the point of view similarly shifts from objective narrative to the unspoken thoughts of a character, and back again, will illustrate the unobtrusive ease with which this is accomplished. The weakness of Charles Musgrove's character and his capacity for self-persuasion are shown by the rapid collapse of his sense of paternal duty: a few lines earlier he has protested his inability to leave the injured child (the sentences are numbered for ease of reference):

(1) The child had a good night, and was going on well the next day. (2) It must be a work of time to ascertain that no injury had been done to the spine, but Mr Robinson found nothing to increase alarm, and Charles Musgrove began consequently to feel no necessity for longer confinement. (3) The child was to be kept in bed, and amused as quietly as possible; but what was there for a father to do? (4) This was quite a female case, and it would be highly absurd in him, who could be of no use at home, to shut himself up. (5) His father very much wished him to meet Captain Wentworth, and there being no sufficient reason against it, he ought to go; and it ended in his making a bold public declaration, when he came in from shooting, of his meaning to dress directly, and dine at the other house. (*P*, 55).

The straightforward narrative of (1) continues in (2), with the additional implication in the more formal language of the latter that the surgeon's words are being echoed, if not quoted verbatim: that is to say, we have a form of narrative coloured, slightly but perceptibly, by speech. In the middle of the third sentence comes a change to free indirect speech, which continues throughout (4); and here the more colloquial idiom appropriate to the reflections of the easy-going Charles (*quite a female case, highly absurd*) is underlined by the contrast with the formal terms of (2) (*ascertain, increase alarm*), Charles's casualness being set against the surgeon's gravity. The insight into Charles's thoughts continues as far as the semi-colon in (5), after which the narrative is briskly resumed and his 'public declaration' (the language has the flavour of parody, emphasized by the bathos of what follows) is conveyed through ordinary indirect speech. The question in (3), the specious reasoning in (4), and the self-deception masquerading as manly resolution in (5)—he has shifted his position from finding 'confinement' irksome to deciding that he 'ought to go'— show syntax communicating the workings of his mind with considerable sensitiveness. What is notable here is not only the unusual pace and economy but the variety of effects obtained by movement between styles of different degrees of formality. Another quotation will show how the particular qualities of different patterns of syntax are exploited for a similar purpose. This time it is Mary Musgrove's selfish and querulous nature that is revealed:

(1) Captain Wentworth now hurried off to get every thing ready on his part, and to be soon followed by the two ladies. (2) When the plan was made known to Mary, however, there was an end of all peace in it. (3) She was so wretched, and so vehement, complained so much of injustice in being expected to go away, instead of Anne; —Anne, who was nothing to Louisa, while she was her sister, and had the best right to stay in Henrietta's stead! (4) Why was not she to be as useful as Anne? (5) And to go home without Charles, too —without her husband! (6) No, it was too unkind! (7) And, in short, she said more than her husband could long withstand; and as none of the others could oppose when he gave way, there was no help for it: the change of Mary for Anne was inevitable. (*P*, 115)

As before, the movement is from straightforward narrative (in the first two sentences) to a markedly different style in (3), where the more vigorously colloquial structure of the opening phrases ('so wretched, and so vehement'), reinforced by a deliberate exaggeration of language, prepares the reader for the change to free indirect speech in mid-sentence. This continues in (4) (5) and (6), which, with their repetitions, questions, and exclamations, contrast syntactically with the narrative style with which the passage opened; until the narrative takes over again in (7), which begins by effectively summarizing ('in short') the remainder of what might clearly have been a long passage of dialogue—the summary itself constituting a comment on the tediousness of Mary's complaints. Within the paragraph, then, the point of view has shifted from the author to Mary, and back again; though, as the retention of third-person pronouns throughout indicates, it is never so wholly abandoned to Mary as to amount to an abdication of the function of judgment everywhere implicit. For Jane Austen, this is perhaps the supreme virtue of free indirect speech: that it offers the possibility of achieving something of the vividness of speech without the appearance for a moment of a total silencing of the authorial voice.

A final example from the second chapter of the novel will show how a variety of modes of speech-presentation can be employed, with easy transitions from one to another, in a short passage. The subject is Sir Walter Elliot's reluctance to accept the inevitable and reduce his style of living:

How Anne's more rigid requisitions might have been taken, is of little consequence. Lady Russell's had no success at all—could not be put up with—were not to be borne. 'What! Every comfort of life knocked off! Journeys, London, servants, horses, table,—contractions every where. To live no longer with the decencies even of a private gentleman! No, he would sooner quit Kellynch-hall at once, than remain in it on such disgraceful terms.'

'Quit Kellynch-hall.' The hint was immediately taken up by Mr Shepherd, whose interest was involved in the reality of Sir Walter's retrenchng ... 'Since the idea had been started in the very quarter which ought to dictate, he had no scruple,' he said, 'in confessing his judgment to be entirely on that side ...' (*P*, 13)

The authorial comment of the opening sentence gives place, in the course of the second sentence, to a manner which is unmistakably imitative of Sir Walter's speech, though the verbs are in the past tense. At the same time, the change of style is marked graphologically (by the dashes), lexically (by a more colloquial idiom), and syntactically (the telegraphic phrases condensing replies of perhaps much greater length). We then move into quotation marks, though there is no introductory verb of saying or attribution to a speaker; we are now closer to the words that Sir Walter may be taken to have uttered, and the forms here are of two kinds: at first what appear to be the actual words used, quoted verbatim (' "What! Every comfort of life knocked off!" '), but in the final sentence of the paragraph a clear example of free indirect speech, with verb and pronoun in the appropriate tense and person. In the second paragraph, a phrase from Sir Walter's implied remark is quoted to introduce a sentence combining narrative and comment. The rest of the paragraph (not quoted here in full) at first sight resembles direct speech, with the graphological indications and the use of 'he said'; but the verbs are in the past tense, and the third person is used; so that the ultimate effect is of a past conversation reported rather than one taking place as we read. In less than twenty lines, a considerable range of effects has been deployed with a total absence of fuss— so unobtrusively, indeed, that their existence has not often been commented on; and, when comment has been made, justice has not been done to their variety. Andrew Wright, for instance, uses the omnibus term 'indirect discourse' for what he describes as 'the more or less verbatim report, in the third person, of a conversation'. He goes on to suggest that this form, or multiplicity of forms, is used for two reasons: 'to abbreviate what would otherwise be rather tediously conventional dialogue', and 'to present verbal interchanges which she cannot quite trust her ear to reproduce exactly'.[11] One may feel that this appraisal, which dwells on the negative rather than the positive advantages of the free forms, does something less than justice to Jane Austen's technical skill and artistic purposes. What *Persuasion* surely and repeatedly exemplifies is the power of free indirect speech to embody dramatic elements within the flow of the narrative.

Persuasion has been discussed at some length because it offers an impressive range of methods of speech-presentation, deployed singly or in combination, for a variety of subtle effects. Though the novels which preceded it do not show an equally striking concern with experiment in this direction, they provide many instances of devices which were to become widely used only much later in the nineteenth century. Jane Austen's handling of free indirect speech has been emphasized because it possesses exceptional advantages as an instrument for the rendering of speech as one element in the depicting of a scene or a state of mind. Its capacity for being quietly integrated into a narrative which is focused from a particular point of view may be illustrated by a final quotation from *Emma*; when Mr Knightley arrives unexpectedly,

[11] A. H. Wright, *Jane Austen's Novels: a Study in Structure* (1953) 74–5.

There was time only for the quickest arrangement of mind. She must be collected and calm. In half a minute they were together. The 'How d'ye do's,' were quiet and constrained on each side. She asked after their mutual friends; they were all well.—When had he left them?—Only that morning. He must have had a wet ride. —Yes.—He meant to walk with her, she found. 'He had just looked into the dining-room, and as he was not wanted there, preferred being out of doors.'—She thought he neither looked nor spoke cheerfully ... (*E*, 424)

As we near the emotional climax of the novel, narrative and speech merge almost imperceptibly: the reader has the unmistakable sense of a conversation taking place, but Emma's consciousness remains the centre of interest, so that Knightley remains 'he' whether he is the subject of Emma's thoughts or is shown (by the rules of free indirect speech) as referring to himself in his own speech. At such moments we are concerned not with a mere technical device of linguistic interest, but with a mode of story-telling that is both distinctive and strikingly 'modern'. Such, at least, must be the justification for the space devoted to free indirect speech in this chapter.

The importance of speech in all its forms does not mean that, at certain moments, Jane Austen does not deliberately avoid its use. Her playing-down of episodes involving a declaration of love has often been pointed out. ' "I cannot make speeches" ', Mr Knightley tells Emma (though he does very creditably in the circumstances), and for Emma's reply to his proposal we are obliged to be satisfied with

What did she say?—Just what she ought, of course. A lady always does. (*E*, 431)

More generally, it may be suggested that Jane Austen tends to renounce dialogue when events seem about to precipitate a scene with considerable emotional potential. One should not, however, conclude too quickly that this necessarily implies a distrust of her own powers to render such a scene successfully. Emma's disclosure to Harriet that she has completely misunderstood Mr

K

Elton's intentions is narrated in a single sentence (*E*, 141), thus avoiding a long dialogue which would not only be painfully, even distastefully, lachrymose (as it is, 'Harriet's tears' earn only the briefest mention), but would bring Harriet and her feelings to the centre of the stage, to the jeopardy of whatever sympathy we may feel for the heroine. The stages of Emma's folly are minutely laid bare, but Jane Austen was surely wise not to dwell on its results. Another example, which seems to demand a different explanation, is found in the ninth chapter of *Sense and Sensibility*, when Marianne, having sprained her ankle, is rescued by the fortuitous but covenient arrival of the handsome unknown who turns out to be Willoughby. He appears from nowhere, offers his services, carries her home, introduces himself to her surprised mother and sister, exchanges social pleasantries, and is enthusiastically discussed after his leave-taking—all without the use of a singe word of direct speech. The whole adventure occupies little more than a page, and at first sight one is struck by Jane Austen's self-denial in rejecting the opportunity for what might easily have become a substantial and dramatic episode. Probably she was aware that it would have been difficult to develop such a scene without slipping into parody: the situation contains, after all, many of the ingredients of that romantic fiction which she had been mercilessly ridiculing since childhood (J. M. S. Tompkins cites a late-eighteenth-century novelist who cannily promised the reader 'no sprained ankles'),[12] and it is obviously important for the future development of the Marianne-Willoughby story that the reader should not be discouraged at the outset from taking it seriously. Its dramatic potential remains, therefore, deliberately unrealized.

Again, though Jane Austen's characters exist most vividly and memorably through their dialogue, she does not regard the gift of speech as an unqualified blessing. There are many examples of idle chatterboxes (like Mrs Allen in *Northanger Abbey*) and of pompous speechifiers (like Sir Walter Elliot in *Persuasion*). While

[12] J. M. S. Tompkins, *The Popular Novel in England 1770–1800* (1932) 58.

social relationships are maintained and developed through conversation, and the ability to speak with ease and precision is highly valued, mere fluency is in itself suspect. Of Lady Susan, who confesses that 'If I am vain of anything, it is of my eloquence', we are told that she 'talks very well, with a happy command of language, which is too often used I beleive to make Black appear White' (*MW*, 268, 251). In contrast, the ideal is represented by Mr Knightley, who, in a novel where so much of the dialogue exposes the triviality or pretentiousness or equivocation of the speakers, consistently uses a 'plain, unaffected, gentleman-like English'. Jane Austen would doubtless have endorsed the praise given by her brother James, in the opening number of *The Loiterer*, to 'a decent reserved demeanour, just half way between the extremes of pert garrulity and solemn dullness'.

There are, of course, very few who satisfy this prescription; and everyday conversation, with all its deficiencies, remains the staple of her dialogue. Yet her concern for the precise and meaningful use of language often brings the fatuities of such speech under gentle attack. On the visit to Sotherton in *Mansfield Park*, Mr Rushworth points out, 'with the sort of self-evident proposition which many a clearer head does not always avoid', that if ' "we are *too* long going over the house, we shall not have time for what is to be done out of doors" ' (*MP*, 89); and in the same chapter the looseness of colloquial usage is commented on by Edmund, when Mary Crawford asks him whether the church is 'never chosen', and he replies: ' "*Never* is a black word. But yes, in the *never* of conversation which means *not very often*, I do think it" (*MP*, 92).

Behind Jane Austen's dialogue, then, lies an alertness to the nuances of everyday speech, combined with an awareness that many people reveal their inadequacies through their own lips. Her skill in dialogue has been widely praised, but what has not so often been remarked on, and hardly at all investigated in detail, is the subtle yet sure differentiation she effects between the speech of various characters. Her purpose is not simply to exploit idiosyncrasies for their own sake, but to enlist speech in the cause of more refined character-portrayal. Nor are these differences exaggerated: Mary Lascelles has observed, in a felicitous phrase, that in these novels speech is 'modelled . . . in very low relief'; and Macaulay recognized the same important truth a hundred years earlier when he wrote that Jane Austen's characters are 'all such as we meet every day' yet are 'all as perfectly discriminated from each other as if they were the most eccentric of human beings'.[13] She works, that is, by hints rather than by emphatic strokes; and the scale of variation is so finely adjusted that even slight departures from the norm modify our attitude towards the speaker. The delicacy of her art, and the rejection of any tendency towards caricature, can be seen by a comparison between Admiral Croft of *Persuasion* and other naval characters in fiction such as Tom Bowling in Smollett's *Roderick Random*, or Captain Cuttle in Dickens' *Dombey and Son*. These novelists devise for their sailors a broad occupational dialect of the 'Shiver my timbers' variety, which often verges on parody. (They can, of course, be defended by the argument that it was the purpose of both novelists to create eccentrics.) Jane Austen, in contrast, creates a form of speech which is unlike that of any other character in the novel, and which succeeds in conveying the bluff heartiness of her Admiral, yet which strikes the reader as in no way resembling a stage dialect. The main features of his idiolect are the use of unusually short and direct statements, a preference for concrete over abstract vocabulary, and the absence of description and analysis: he has learned wisdom practically, on the quarter-deck, not theoretically, in the library:

'Did you say that you had something to tell me, sir?'

'Yes, I have. Presently. But here comes a friend, Captain Brigden; I shall only say, "How d'ye do," as we pass, however. I shall not stop. "How d'ye do." Brigden stares to see anybody with me but my wife. She, poor soul, is tied by the leg. She has a blister on one of her heels, as large as a three shilling piece. If you look across the

---

[13] M. Lascelles, *Jane Austen and her Art* (1939) 94; Macaulay, 'Madame D'Arblay', *Edinburgh Review*, 76 (1843) 561.

street, you will see Admiral Brand coming down and his brother. Shabby fellows, both of them! I am glad they are not on this side of the way. Sophy cannot bear them . . .' (*P*, 169–70)

In other places, Admiral Croft's speech is marked by one or two unusual words, which serve to remind the reader of his naval background. He employs the term *younker*, for instance, which has both the wider sense of 'young man' (and is used thus by Richardson) and the specialized sense of 'boy or junior seaman on board ship'; he also twice uses the epithet *snug*, which according to the *OED* was 'first recorded as a naval term' (it is used, in a different and newer sense, by the vulgar Mrs Jennings of *Sense and Sensibility*). The writer's personal interest in and knowledge of the navy was no doubt strong enough to make her unusually sensitive to the distinctive flavour of such words. But this flavouring is carried out with notable restraint and discretion: the Admiral's speech never verges on caricature, and the nautical seasoning is never permitted to dominate the dish.

Occupational varieties of speech, as reflected in the dialogue of (among others) sailors and lawyers, affect only a minority of characters, however; and regional differences, which her contemporary Scott used so extensively and effectively in the Waverley Novels, seem to have interested Jane Austen not at all. She differs from many English novelists, that is, in using a relatively narrow range of varieties for the speech of her characters: there is nothing in her work to approach the class and regional dialects, or the individual eccentricities, depicted by Fielding or George Eliot or Hardy, though the range of class dialects is perhaps wider than has sometimes been supposed. Nevertheless, within the area she has chosen to cultivate, human variety is unobtrusively but surely demonstrated; and a speech by any one of her characters cannot easily be mistaken for that of any other. An analysis of the language of several characters will illustrate some of the means by which this is accomplished.

Mr Woodhouse is allocated fourteen speeches in the opening chapter of *Emma*, and a selection from the phrases he employs will show that his characteristic tone is quickly established: 'poor Miss Taylor' (three times), 'poor James', 'What a pity', 'a sad business'. What superficially appears to be tenderness and sympathy for others is soon seen as a self-indulgent sensibility and a somewhat factitious melancholy. At the outset, the reader is alerted to distrust Mr Woodhouse's judgments, even to discount them as based entirely subjectively on a vision of the world that does not extend beyond his own armchair. He begins by expressing a series of idle wishes and imaginary difficulties: when Emma suggests a wedding-visit to Mrs Weston, ' "I could not walk half so far" ', and when the carriage is proposed, ' "James will not like to put the horses to for such a little way" '. As these quotations show, his habitual mode of expression is in the negative form (there are ten negatives in his speeches in this opening chapter), and this surely provides a linguistic clue to character: the implication is of a timidity in the face of experience, a shrinking from positive commitment to life. His philosophy begins and ends with the desire to avoid change: his first words deplore Miss Taylor's marriage—and the novel is, of course, very largely *about* marriage—and three volumes later Emma's forthcoming marriage provokes a similar complaint: ' "Why could not they go on as they had done?" ' Another group of phrases from his first appearance indicates a further aspect of Mr Woodhouse's nature: 'a shocking walk', 'a vast deal of rain', 'it rained dreadfully hard', 'break up one's family circle grievously'. He is repeatedly guilty of the offence for which Boswell was castigated by Dr Johnson on one occasion, and which Jane Austen herself rarely allows to pass unridiculed. No doubt she had read the following anecdote in Boswell's *Life*:

I happened to say it would be terrible if he should not find a speedy opportunity of returning to London, and be confined to so dull a place. JOHNSON. 'Don't, Sir, accustom yourself to use big words for little matters. It would *not* be *terrible*, though I *were* to be detained some time here.'[14]

[14] Boswell, *Life of Johnson* (Oxford, 1953) 333.

In Mr Woodhouse's limited universe, trivialities assume alarming proportions—a shower of rain is seen as a threat to safety—and the process is paralleled by his use of inflated language, which in Jane Austen is an invariable sign of foolishness or worse. Nor does his language show any modification in the course of the novel: his nature, self-centred but not self-aware, is incapable of change, and its linguistic manifestations simply reiterate the qualities announced at the opening.

Like Mr Woodhouse, Mrs Norris in *Mansfield Park* reveals her nature through her speech in the opening chapter of the novel. In her case it is a betrayal as well as a revelation, since there is a plain disparity between what she says of herself and what the actual language of her speeches tells us about her. Mr Woodhouse is, at least, guileless in his selfishness; but Mrs Norris seeks to play a role which is belied by the words she utters. ' "I am a woman of few words and professions" ' she says near the beginning of her very first speech; but that speech runs to a full page, the opening sentence to eighty-seven words, and the whole is assertive and presumptuous: she has Miss Bates's garrulity without her good nature, just as the latter's entertaining preoccupation with trifles has somehow gone sour with Mrs Norris and turned into a symptom of her incorrigible meanness of spirit. The context of this first speech is also significant: it occurs as an interruption of the stately Sir Thomas; it seems that Mrs Norris's conviction of her own rightness renders her insensitive to decorum, that key-concept of the novel. Thereafter her speeches are commonly accompanied by the direction 'cried Mrs Norris', and although Jane Austen is sparing of information about vocal manner, the suggestion seems to be of a shrill and noisy officiousness. (The use of *cried* rather than *said* is generally reserved for the vulgar or disagreeable characters.) Two kinds of sentence, the rhetorical question and the hasty assurance of agreement with her interlocutor, occur frequently. She says of Fanny, ' "Is she not a sister's child? and could I bear to see her want, while I had a bit of bread to give her?" ', and the emotion behind her words is obviously as hollow as the sentimental rhetoric in which it is expressed. Her speeches often begin with such expressions as 'I perfectly comprehend you', 'I thoroughly understand you', 'Very true', 'That is exactly what I think' (these examples are all from the first chapter), which represent clumsy attempts at diplomacy and persuasiveness. Like Mr Woodhouse, she is preoccupied by petty domestic and practical details, but her preoccupation springs not from concern for others or even personal anxiety, but from a wish to inflate her own importance and, often, from avarice. Few characters display so much energy in obtaining possession of trivial objects. This falsifies her judgments disastrously: her concern over economizing on green baize and curtain rings blinds her completely to the moral issues represented by the theatricals during Sir Thomas's absence, and when he returns home unexpectedly (Chapter 19) she is shown as 'trying to be in a bustle without having any thing to bustle about, and labouring to be important where nothing was wanted but tranquillity and silence'. Her bustle and labour often take verbal form, and her speeches are full of tiresome fussiness and a wish to organize the lives of others without expense to herself.

Thirdly, Mr Collins in *Pride and Prejudice* is given a form of speech in which comedy springs from incongruity. It lacks that ready adaptation to company and occasion which the well-regulated mind will always make: on the most informal and even intimate occasions, he is formal to the point of pedantry; and when he proposes to Elizabeth Bennet in Chapter 19, he uses the register of his Sunday sermons rather than that of courtship. In the drawing-room at Netherfield (Chapter 18) his notion of small-talk is an address, or spoken essay, of some length on 'the profession of a clergyman'; and his tendency to enumerate the points of his discourse recurs when he informs Elizabeth of his reasons for marrying. He is addicted to faded clichés of literary or clerical origin—his home is a 'humble abode', music an 'innocent diversion', death a 'melancholy event'—and when he tells Elizabeth that he hopes to lead her 'to the altar ere long', one feels that he has sealed his doom with the phrase. Mr Collins is

given a further and related 'voice' as a letter-writer; his epistolary
style is discussed in the next chapter. As with the previous examples, there is an evident correspondence between qualities of
mind and character and qualities of language: speech that is both
pompous and trite is the index of a personality which possesses
similar limitations.[15]

If Jane Austen has the power to make Mr Woodhouse's fret-
tings entertaining, she can also prompt the reader to feel affection and even respect for the vulgar Mrs Jennings, in *Sense and
Sensibility*. Most of the characteristics of her speech and external
behaviour are such as invite censure at other times; yet her noisy
vulgarity is redeemed by her genuine good humour and generosity
of spirit, for she has none of the self-seeking ambition of Mrs
Elton and Lucy Steele. She is an older woman with an assured
income, and those who see Jane Austen as depicting a society
motivated by economic considerations may reflect that it is Mrs
Jennings' 'ample jointure' which, by removing the need for her
to flatter or impress and by giving her the confidence stemming
from financial security, enables her to emerge as a thoroughly
likeable character. She is exceptional in Jane Austen's gallery in
being given dubious linguistic habits which nevertheless carry no
overtones of moral censure, and also in having bestowed upon her
a physical presence which has not been granted to most of the
other characters. She is, we learn, 'a good-humoured, merry, fat,
elderly woman, who talked a great deal, seemed very happy, and
rather vulgar' (*SS*, 34). She resembles those other stout and
cheerful figures, Juliet's Nurse and Mrs Gamp, not only in being

---

[15] There have been some interesting speculations about the origins of
Mr Collins' speech. B. C. Southam ('Jane Austen and *Clarissa*', *Notes
and Queries*, 208 (1963) 191–2) has pointed out a resemblance between
the style of Mr. Collins and that of the Rev. Elias Brand, Richardson's
'pedantic young Clergyman'; he has noted, in particular, the occurrence
twice in Richardson's novel of Mr Collins' hackneyed reference to the
'olive branch' (*PP*, 63). D. J. Greene ('Jane Austen and the Peerage',
Publications of the Modern Language Association, 68 (1953) 1022) suggests another possible source: Collins' *Peerage of England*, the fulsome
dedication of which shows some resemblance in tone to Mr Collins.

very loquacious (one of her speeches, in Chapter 37, runs to about a thousand words) but also in reflecting on life in homely terms:

'Aye, it is a fine thing to be young and handsome. Well! I was young once, but I never was very handsome—worse luck for me. However I got a very good husband, and I don't know what the greatest beauty can do more. Ah! poor man! he has been dead these eight years and better . . .' (*SS*, 163)

More often, however, her mind deals in tangibles and practicalities: when she thinks of Marianne marrying Colonel Brandon, it is not love and romance that occupy her thoughts but his income and the arrangements for disposing of 'the little love-child', as well as the convenience of the butcher 'hard by in the village' and the mulberry tree in the garden: ' "Lord! how Charlotte and I did stuff the only time we were there!" ' It follows that her vocabulary consists mainly of concrete terms, with few of the abstract nouns and related epithets that represent the habitual thought-patterns of the more serious characters. Other features of her idiolect are the frequent use of exclamations (particularly 'Lord!') and of the conjunctions 'so' and 'and so'. She can narrate an incident briskly and vividly, and has a keen eye for a dramatic situation:

'Nancy, she fell upon her knees, and cried bitterly; and your brother, he walked about the room, and said he did not know what to do. Mrs Dashwood declared they should not stay a minute longer in the house, and your brother was forced to go down upon *his* knees too, to persuade her to let them stay till they had packed up their clothes. *Then* she fell into hysterics again, and he was so frightened that he would send for Mr Donavan, and Mr Donavan found the house in all this uproar . . .' (*SS*, 259)

The indications of stress on certain words, and the characteristic syntactical patterns (e.g., the co-ordination in the last sentence quoted, and the colloquial quality of 'your brother, he walked about the room') give passages like this an unusual closeness to spontaneous speech. One senses, too, a pleasure in the act of telling the tale, even when the subject-matter is distressing. Her language is often colourful, if not always in strict propriety: inquiring as to the progress of her daughter's pregnancy, she observes with satisfaction ' "I warrant you she is a fine size by this time" ', and she offers Colonel Brandon what the author drily refers to as a 'vigorous sketch of their future ennui': ' ". . . how forlorn we shall be, when I come back!—Lord! we shall sit and gape at one another as dull as two cats" '. All this is evidence that Mrs Jennings enjoys a freedom of language that is denied to characters with a more serious function in the novel. She is more than a study in colloquial speech or in innocent vulgarity, however: when Marianne is in real distress, her sympathy may be somewhat comically expressed but it is none the less real: ' "I wish with all my soul his wife may plague his heart out," ' she says of Willoughby. ' "And so I shall always say, my dear, you may depend on it. I have no notion of men's going on in this way; and if ever I meet him again, I will give him such a dressing as he has not had this many a day" ' (*SS*, 192).

All these examples—and every reader of Jane Austen will be able to suggest many others—show the congruence that exists between character and features of speech; we learn to know these figures through their distinctive idiolects, which very skilfully combine individuality with plausibility.

Mrs Jennings also serves to raise the problem of Jane Austen's use of social varieties of speech. Although English society was changing rapidly during Jane Austen's lifetime, the hierarchical structure of 'the old society' had not disappeared, particularly in southern England. Its more obvious manifestations have been described thus:

Differential status was part of the given, unquestioned environment into which men were born, and they proclaimed it by every outward sign: manner, speech, deportment, dress, liveried equipage, size of house and household, the kind and quantity of the food they ate.[16]

Of all these tokens of status, it is speech which plays the most

[16] H. Perkin, *The Origins of Modern English Society, 1780–1800*, (1969) 24–5.

important role in the novels. Her awareness of the differences to be found at various levels of society, as well as in various settings and among the members of various professions, was gained from an experience that, thanks to her talented, proliferating and far-flung family, was wider than is often supposed. Social dialects thus provide an exceptionally rich area of stylistic interest. And, because she tends to identify the members of particular class with moral excellence (Mr Knightley, say, rather than Mr Elton, or Elinor Dashwood rather than Lucy Steele), a class dialect is liable to become more than a sociolinguistic phenomenon, and speech becomes an index of moral qualities: men and women demonstrate their virtues, or betray their weaknesses, out of their own mouths.

Let us first consider some of the characters whose speech exhibits a degree of nonconformity to accepted standards. In the context of English society, conformity and nonconformity in the spoken language have traditionally been interpreted as badges of social status or social aspirations; and it is true that Jane Austen makes a good deal of comic and satiric capital out of this attitude. She goes further than this, however, and in her fiction these finely-controlled variations in speech often indicate moral as well as social nuances—so that the point about, say, the vulgarisms of Lucy Steele in *Sense and Sensibility* is not merely that they reveal her as belonging to a level of society which most of the characters (and, one presumes, the author) regard as inferior, but, more damagingly still, that they betray a lack of the civilized virtues of intelligence, taste and self-awareness. A 'low' expression tends, therefore, to be symptomatic of unsatisfactory moral or ethical standards. Jane Austen is, of course, far from being blinded by class prejudice, and is well aware that similar characteristics may be encountered at different levels of society—that vulgarity and foolishness are not the monopoly of a single class. As Lord Chesterfield had pointed out, in his description of 'good company', people of the 'very first quality' can be 'as silly, as ill-bred, and as worthless, as people of the meanest degree'.[17] Although

[17] Letter 1596 in B. Dobrée's edition of Chesterfield's *Letters* (1932).

Chesterfield is perhaps the last writer in whom one might expect to find democratic sentiments, he sees right social behaviour—of which speech is a very important component—as by no means an automatic concomitant of rank; and Jane Austen, too, finds affection and folly at many levels, and exposes it to ridicule and censure wherever it is found.

This claim is supported by an analysis of her use of slang and colloquial language—a hazard which a surprisingly large number of characters fail to avoid. (For once, one must disagree with Mary Lascelles in her observation that Jane Austen 'tends to suggest social variants in speech by syntax and phrasing rather than by vocabulary'.[18] Like a good disciple of Dr Johnson, she does what she can to resist the encroachment of the new and fashionable word, regarding it as a threat to the purity and stability of the English vocabulary. She shares, indeed, in the spirit of the second half of the eighteenth century, during which there developed a keen awareness of the standard language and of various kinds of deviation from it, as affecting the spoken as well as the written medium. Her lifetime saw the publication of Francis Grose's *Classical Dictionary of the Vulgar Tongue* (1785), which drew attention to slang as a distinctive subdivision of the language's lexical resources, and of Samuel Pegge's *Anecdotes of the English Language* (1803), which contains what is probably the first full discussion of colloquialisms and vulgarisms. Significantly, too, it saw the appearance in the language of the word *slang* to denote 'the cant or jargon of a certain class or period' (1802). Perhaps Jane Austen had read Dr James Beattie's protest (1790) at the 'new fangled phrases and barbarous idioms that are now so much affected'.[19] Certainly there was no shortage of warnings against this kind of offence from eighteenth-century writers on language: Campbell had gravely suggested that such improprieties often arise from 'affectation of an easy, familiar, and

---

See also F. W. Bradbrook, 'Lord Chesterfield and Jane Austen', *Notes and Queries*, 203 (1958) 80–2.

[18] M. Lascelles, *op. cit.*, 95.

[19] Quoted by E. Partridge, *Slang Today and Yesterday* (1950) 78.

careless manner',[20] and the influential Blair, who earns honourable mention in *Northanger Abbey* as an authority on correctness,
thus defined purity and propriety in language:

Purity, is the use of such words, and such constructions, as belong to
the idiom of the language which we speak; in opposition to words
and phrases that are imported from other languages, or that are
obsolete, or new-coined, or used without proper authority. Propriety,
is the selection of such words in the language, as the best and most
established usage has appropriated to those ideas which we intend
to express by them. It implies the correct and happy application of
them, according to that usage, in opposition to vulgarisms, or low
expressions . . .[21]

To the same period belongs the celebrated *English Grammar* of
Lindley Murray (1795), for long a standard text-book. As K. C.
Phillipps says, 'By Jane Austen's time grammarians like Lowth,
Priestley and Lindley Murray, not to mention, in a wider sphere,
Dr Johnson and Lord Chesterfield, had done their work.'[22] And
although their prescriptive doctrines, like Blair's reference to
'proper authority', strike the ear somewhat quaintly in our own
epoch of linguistic permissiveness, their importance in relation
to Jane Austen's notions of acceptable verbal behaviour should
not be underrated.

It has already been suggested that what unites the various
characters who are guilty of this kind of linguistic sin is not
membership of a single social group (though a number of them
belong to a socially ambitious lower middle class), but a common
tendency, to a greater or lesser degree, towards intellectual or
moral inadequacy. The use of such language may reveal lack of
taste or discretion, a brash modishness, or a more serious indifference to right conduct and sound principles. A revealing
comment on one offender, Mary Crawford in *Mansfield Park*,

[20] Quoted by S. A. Leonard, *The Doctrine of Correctness in English
Usage, 1700–1800*, (Madison 1929) 176.
[21] Blair, *Lectures on Rhetoric and Belles Lettres* (1825) 118.
[22] K. C. Phillipps, 'Lucy Steele's English', *English Studies*, 1969 Supplement, lxi.

accuses her of being of a 'careless' nature, and her carelessness is seen to extend to her use of language. (The word, like many others of its class, has since lost most of its force, and is now more likely to be used to reprove a negligent schoolgirl than to censure a woman whose morality is radically defective.) The implication is that the man or woman who is careless about language, the dress of thought, is likely to be careless about everything else. Mary Crawford is intelligent, so her abuse of language must be regarded as wilful: she is capable, for instance, of using a vulgarism whilst recognizing it as such, as when she writes in a letter to Fanny Price that Mrs Rushworth will feel 'to use a vulgar phrase—that she has got her pennyworth for her penny' (*MP*, 394). The letter is described as being written with 'some degree of elegance', but the offending expression, like the joking on serious matters, suggests a certain hardness in the user. In the same novel, it comes as no surprise to the reader that Tom Bertram, who in the early chapters can perpetrate such insensitivities as predicting that Dr Grant ' "would soon pop off" ', reveals himself later in the novel as fundamentally lacking in *gravitas* and a due sense of responsibility. The colloquial expression is not just an offence against restrictive notions of decorum in language, but a symptom, small but significant, of a defect of character.

Not every case is of equal seriousness, of course. Sometimes, as with Mrs Elton in *Emma*, loose language reveals nothing worse than vulgarity of mind, bred by a combination of ambition and ignorance often associated in the novels with the prosperous tradesman class. Mrs Elton's origins—she is the daughter of a tradesman and has been brought up, ominously enough, 'in the very heart of Bristol'—prepare us for the diverse and diverting solecisms which abound in her speech, and which so exasperate Emma:

'A little upstart, vulgar being, with her Mr E., and her *caro sposo*, and her resources, and all her airs of pert pretension and underbred finery.' (*E*, 279)

Emma's indignation springs partly from snobbery and partly from affronted pride, as Jane Austen is well aware, but this does not prevent her from being right about Mrs Elton. The objectionable reference to her husband as 'Mr E.' is only surpassed, in the view of the well-bred Miss Woodhouse, by the presumptuous intimacy of her reference to Mr Knightley:

'Knightley!—I could not have believed it. Knightley!—never seen him in her life before, and call him Knightley!'

One is reminded forcibly that forms of address, which are still not without social potency in the twentieth century, were regarded in this period as very important and very revealing: the code determining which forms might and might not be used in the context of different relationships was, in well-bred society, a strict one.[23] (Another striking instance occurs in *Sense and Sensibility*, where Elinor immediately deduces, from Willoughby's casual use of her sister's Christian name, that a secret engagement exists between them.) Mrs Elton's use of foreign phrases such as *caro sposo* and *carte-blanche* seems also intended to place her among the linguistically impure; the use of French words and phrases is, in the novel, a common sign of affectation, though the author's own frequent use of them in her letters suggests that this was a fictional convention rather than an aversion to them *per se*. The pretentious element in her speech, with its fulsome epithets and hackneyed metaphors, is brought vividly before the reader in the account of her description of 'a most desirable situation' for Jane Fairfax. By a masterly stroke of economy, the novelist gives Mrs Elton's speech, not in full, but reduced ruthlessly to the offending elements: 'Delightful, charming, superior, first circles, spheres, lines, ranks, every thing . . .' (*E*, 359). This is a brief but telling anthology of her verbal offences, in which the juxtaposition of incongruous items exposes the falsity of her language and of the attitudes behind it.

[23] Cf. R. W. Chapman's appendix on 'Modes of Address' in Volume 2 of his edition of the novels (*Pride and Prejudice*, 409–412). I have discussed the subject briefly in 'Forms of Address in Dickens', *The Dickensian*, 67 (1971) 16–20.

Although Mrs Elton is a mature and successful example of the use of colloquial language as a form of social criticism and moral censure, the method is most widespread in the early novels, which show a lively curiosity concerning this as well as other aspects of language. One of the earliest and most interesting examples is John Thorpe in *Northanger Abbey*: he is characterized as 'a rattle', and like his sister is addicted to exaggerated and affected speech, which is quickly seen as a symptom of his irresponsibility and immaturity. John and Isabella Thorpe represent the masculine and feminine versions of fashionable empty chatter. Her conversation, which has already been briefly quoted in this chapter, is sprinkled with such epithets as *delightful* and *horrid*, *charming* and *vile*, *heavenly* and *frightful*. Her language knows no moderation: she is 'sick of Bath' and 'wild with impatience' to see Henry Tilney, whose own comment to Catherine in relation to Isabella stands as a condemnation of all these glib, conventional and unmeaning expressions: when Catherine naïvely expresses surprise that Isabella has not kept her word (' "Isabella promised so faithfully to write directly" '), Tilney's reply may perhaps be taken as a shaft directed against the absent Isabella: ' "Promised so faithfully!—A faithful promise!—That puzzles me.—I have heard of a faithful performance. But a faithful promise—the fidelity of promising!" ' (*NA*, 195–6).

John Thorpe's vocabulary is different from his sister's: in place of her automatic and monotonous hyperboles, which seem to anticipate the smart society talk of the 1920s as satirized by Evelyn Waugh, Thorpe shows a fondness for the cant terms of the man of fashion, the dandy or blood. He is equally capable of an oath (a much rarer phenomenon in Jane Austen than in Maria Edgeworth),[42] a disrespectful reference to an older man (' "Old Allen is as rich as a Jew, is not he?" '), and an indecorous simile:

[24] See, for example, the speech of Sir Philip Baddely in Chapter 7 of Maria Edgeworth's *Belinda*, which is liberally sprinkled with oaths in a way that Jane Austen prefers to leave to the reader's imagination.

'She is as obstinate as—'

Thorpe never finished the simile, for it could hardly have been a proper one. (*NA*, 101)

What stands is enough to condemn him, however: we may be sure that Henry Tilney or George Knightley would never have begun it. He also uses such recent arrivals in colloquial language as *famous* (in the sense 'excellent') and *tittupy* (unsteady), for both of which *OED* gives 1798 for the earliest appearance; and he uses *quiz* (on page 49) in a sense which seems to be peculiar to this writer. It is hardly surprising that his indifference alike to linguistic decorum and to simple truthfulness leave the inexperienced Catherine somewhat bemused, for 'she had not been brought up to understand the propensities of a rattle' (*NA*, 65). A large measure of both the characterization and the unsparing criticism of the two Thorpes is conducted through their speech and its deviations from established standards.

Sense and Sensibility is particularly rich in language of this kind, and such characters as Lucy Steele and Mrs Jennings are linguistic sisters to Mrs Elton and the Thorpes. Lucy's addiction to the modish word *beau* is sufficient to put the reader on his guard. After she has used it five times within a few lines, Elinor, who is very much the purist in questions of propriety of speech, remarks to her: ' "Upon my word . . . I do not perfectly comprehend the meaning of the word" ' (*SS*, 124), and her tone makes it clear that, like Lady Bracknell and the spade, she is glad not to be acquainted with it, though her ignorance is perhaps surprising, since the word had been current at least since 1720. *Beau* (which is used also by Mrs Elton) is typical of a class of words which represent a hangover from eighteenth-century fashionable talk. The process by which, during this period, certain words, after enjoying a vogue as hallmarks of status and elegance, gradually fell in the social scale is a familiar one. J. Platt has noted the 'abandonment by educated speakers of certain idioms to pretentious, semi-educated speakers who had previously imitated their use' as a phenomenon of the late eighteenth- and early nineteenth-century linguistic scene.[25] The aping by social climbers of the language of their betters seems to have had the result of spoiling this to some extent for the genuinely genteel, who were forced to seek new status-words to replace those contaminated in the mouths of their inferiors. Another instance is the intensive use of *vast* and *vastly*, to be found in the speech of Lucy Steele, Mrs Elton, Mary Crawford and Isabella Thorpe— a socially heterogeneous group, but plainly sisters under the skin. These usages date from the end of the seventeenth century, and are redolent of the fop and the fine lady in the Restoration and eighteenth-century comic drama. In 1754 Chesterfield described them (in their intensive use) as 'fashionable words of the most fashionable people',[26] but by the time Jane Austen wrote they had evidently degenerated into signs of the would-be fashionable. It may be noted that Lucy Steele's written style is a fitting complement to her speech: the letter quoted in Chapter 49 of *Sense and Sensibility* is a patchwork of trite phrases, of which 'we are just returned from the altar' is a fair example.

The vigour of Mrs Jennings' speech in the same novel has already been referred to. At one point she is described as 'hallooing' a long speech through an open window, and the language she uses is of a piece with such indecorous behaviour. She is fond of homely, proverbial expressions such as 'to have the whip hand' and to 'plague his heart out': again Jane Austen's attitude resembles that of Chesterfield, who refers to phrases of this kind as 'the flowers and rhetoric of a vulgar man', and, elsewhere, as 'so many proofs of having kept bad and low company'.[27] Proverbial phrases, while not restricted to those of dubious social standing (they are also to be found, for instance, in the speech of Sir John and Lady Middleton), are resolutely

[25] J. Platt, 'The Development of the English Colloquial Idiom during the Eighteenth Century', *Review of English Studies*, 2 (1926) 76–7.
[26] In *The World* for 5 December 1754 (quoted by J. H. Neumann, 'Chesterfield and the Standard of Usage in English', *Modern Language Quarterly*, 7 (1946) 470).
[27] Letter 1661; Letter 701 (Dobrée).

avoided by all those who enjoy the author's approbation. (The only notable exception is, predictably, Elizabeth Bennet—no respecter of persons or phrases.) When they occur in the narrative, it is generally in an ironical sense, as when we are told, of Harriet Smith in *Emma*, that a collection of riddles was 'the only mental provision she was making for the evening of life'.

Hackneyed language is often accompanied by triteness or triviality of subject-matter. The best conversation, in Jane Austen's judgment, relates individual instances to general principles and universal truths; but all too common is the variety described in *Emma*:

... the usual rate of conversation; a few clever things said, a few downright silly, but by much the larger proportion neither the one nor the other—nothing worse than every day remarks, dull repetitions, old news, and heavy jokes. (*E*, 219)

Northanger Abbey anatomizes the inanities of middle-aged domesticity:

... in what they called conversation, but in which there was scarcely ever any exchange of opinion, and not often any resemblance of subject, for Mrs Thorpe talked chiefly of her children, and Mrs Allen of her gowns. (*NA*, 36)

One detects a note of personal exasperation behind this account of intellectual mediocrity, but more good-humoured is the passage a little earlier in the same novel in which Henry Tilney parodies the rituals of polite conversation: he tells Catherine Morland

'I have hitherto been very remiss, madam, in the proper attentions of a partner here; I have not yet asked you how long you have been in Bath; whether you were ever here before; whether you have been at the Upper Rooms, the theatre, and the concert; and how you like the place altogether. I have been very negligent—but are you now at leisure to satisfy me in these particulars? If you are I will begin directly.'

'You need not give yourself that trouble, sir.'

'No trouble I assure you, madam.' Then forming his features

into a set smile, and affectedly softening his voice, he added, with a simpering air, 'Have you been long in Bath, madam?'

'About a week, sir,' replied Catherine, trying not to laugh.

'Really!' with affected astonishment.

'Why should you be surprised, sir?'

'Why, indeed!' said he, in his natural tone—'but some emotion must appear to be raised by your reply, and surprise is more easily assumed, and not less reasonable than any other.—Now let us go on . . .' (*NA*, 25–6)

What Tilney does in jest, others do in earnest, and there are some characters who hardly seem to rise above the everyday remark, the social formula and the dull repetition. Equally liable to censure are those radically limited minds which are incapable of transcending a preoccupation with minor practicalities and material details. Mrs Price in *Mansfield Park* is characteristic, and the tedium and triviality of her mother's conversation is not the least of Fanny's trials when she revisits her old home at Portsmouth:

'And now I am afraid Campbell will be here, before there is time to dress a steak, and we have no butcher at hand. It is very inconvenient to have no butcher in the street. We were better off in our last house . . .' (*MP*, 379)

Man cannot live by butcher's meat alone, and, with the example of Mansfield Park (as represented by Edmund and Sir Thomas) vividly in her memory, Fanny feels the mental and moral narrowness of her mother's universe. Of a similar kind is Mrs Elton's recommendation of a post as governess: ' "Wax-candles in the school-room! You may imagine how desirable!" '—as if wax-candles were, to Jane Fairfax, a sufficient recipe for happiness. As has already been suggested, the specifying of material circumstances, and the preoccupation with material objects, is nearly always evidence of seriously restricted horizons, whether it is Mr Woodhouse praising the virtues of soft-boiled eggs, Harriet Smith sentimentalizing over a piece of court-plaster, or finding gratification in 'a Robert Martin's riding about the

country to get walnuts for her', or Sir John Dashwood's indignation over Willoughby's behaviour:

'Such a scoundrel of a fellow! such a deceitful dog! It was only the
last time they met that he had offered him one of Folly's puppies!
and this was the end of it!' (*SS*, 215)

All these, slight in themselves, are used by Jane Austen to imply
a radical defect in a character's sense of values.

It may be suggested, then, that the speech of Mrs Elton, Lucy
Steele, and their like is the target of Jane Austen's satire because
it represents more than offence against linguistic decorum: in its
up-to-the-minute smartness and its disregard for established
convention it is the outward token of inner folly and falsity.
Simultaneously, that is, it betrays their improper social aspirations—they are anxious to rise more rapidly than the natural
processes of society permit, and without the justification of exceptional merit, out of the class to which by birth and education
they belong—and their moral shortcomings. The obverse is the
'gentleman-like English' (and *gentleman* is not a word used
lightly by Jane Austen) of Mr Knightley, who provides an un-
wavering standard against which the language of his moral inferiors may be measured. Such English avoids the homely, the
hackneyed and the merely fashionable; it shuns the meretricious
attractions of the new word, and does not succumb to the temptation to call little things by big names.

These discriminations are important, but Jane Austen goes
beyond them in depicting the social varieties of speech, the range
of which in her novels is not quite as narrow as has sometimes
been suggested. Apart from examples of the servant class such as
Thomas in *Sense and Sensibility* and the old coachman in
Mansfield Park—both appear briefly, but have a share in the
dialogue—there is an obvious social gulf, clearly manifested in
their speech, between Mrs Jennings and Mr Darcy, or Mrs Elton
and Sir Walter Elliot. It is worth while examining specimens from
both ends of her range, taking an example already briefly alluded
to—the Prices in *Mansfield Park*—as representative of the lower

end. Fanny's parents are not socially ambitious; her mother, indeed, has dropped in the social scale since her marriage. Their speech, which in at least one important chapter (38) is a major ingredient in the impression they create, contributes to the overwhelming sense of contrast between Portsmouth and Mansfield Park which Fanny quickly comes to feel: a contrast not merely of material surroundings—squalor and muddle versus grandeur and order—but of values. Portsmouth is 'home', and might be expected to satisfy a profound need that the ceremonious atmosphere of the country-house has left unsatisfied. That this is not how things actually work out is quickly made clear—and largely through the dialogue. Mrs Price is, of course, the sister of Lady Bertram and Mrs Norris, and, as a result of her 'imprudent marriage', has come off definitely worst of the three. Her plight, as Jane Austen makes clear, is brought about by a combination of temperament and circumstance: 'She might have made just as good a woman of consequence as Lady Bertram, but Mrs Norris would have been a more respectable mother of nine children, on a small income.' (*MP*, 390) The Portsmouth home is noisy, untidy, and inefficiently run—the antithesis in every respect of Mansfield Park: *propriety* is the keynote of the latter, but the Prices' is 'the abode of . . . impropriety'. Fanny's initial enthusiasm and affection as she returns to the scene of her early childhood quickly give way to an unspoken admission of its shortcomings:

Yet she thought it would not have been so at Mansfield. No, in her uncle's house there would have been a consideration of times and seasons, a regulation of subjects, a propriety, an attention towards every body which there was not here. (*MP*, 382–3)

The 'impropriety' of Portsmouth is not just stated but is dramatized through the dialogue, especially in the first of the nine chapters (38–46) which cover the Portsmouth visit. It is Chapter 38 which records Fanny's first impressions and which also contains most of the dialogue of this episode: appropriately so, for it is the sheer hubbub of voices (apart from the fact that

so many of the speeches are insensitive in content and indecorous
in language) that has, right at the outset, such a shattering effect
on Fanny's nerves. (There is evidence, in the Letters and elsewhere, that Jane Austen was exceptionally sensitive to the unpleasant effects of noise.) One sees why D. H. Lawrence had no
time for Jane Austen: Fanny's family, so far from representing
the deep, intimate warmth of a closely-knit lower-class family life,
contrasts very unfavourably with the orderly if somewhat austere
and passionless atmosphere of Mansfield Park.

Particularly in Mrs Price's speech, this lack of propriety is
suggested with great skill. Her language is not blatantly vulgar in
the manner of, say Mrs Jennings, for she has, after all, seen
better days. Rather, she is betrayed by frequent minor lapses into
a homely colloquial idiom—a linguistic correlate of the process
whereby her whole style of living has been insidiously corrupted
over a long period by poverty and fecklessness. Such expressions
as 'quite in a worry' do not properly belong to slang: Mrs
Price is no Lucy Steele, yet her phrases would never, we feel,
be found on the lips of a woman of taste and discernment—a
woman such as Fanny herself has become. Later she talks of
'a sad fire' (Mrs Elton uses *sad* in this colloquial sense when she
addresses Jane Fairfax as 'You sad girl'); of their being 'starved
with cold'; and of 'a bone of contention' (as usual, the
proverbial expression, with its stale metaphor, is suspect). She
asks questions and continues without awaiting a reply, and she
constantly slips into irrelevant digressions and repetitive complaints. Most distressingly of all, she is capable of a maudlin
parade of sentimentality in speaking of her dead child and of the
stock philosophizing that the memory prompts (' "Well, she was
taken away from evil to come" '). When Fanny's honesty com-
pels her to face the truth about her mother, it is significant that
'no conversation' is one of the charges she silently lays against her.
Mrs Price's sense of relative values is fairly indicated by a speech
which expresses her reaction to the news of Maria Rushworth's
adultery:

'Indeed, I hope it is not true,' said Mrs Price plaintively, 'it
would be so very shocking!—If I have spoke once to Rebecca about

that carpet, I am sure I have spoke at least a dozen times; have not I, Betsey?—-And it would not be ten minutes work.' (*MP*, 440)

At such moments, more is at issue than a failure to employ 'the best chosen language'. The conventional response ('so very shocking') is followed by the prompt transfer of her thoughts to a familiar domestic grievance, showing the impossible narrowness of her moral vision.

Mr Price's speech is delineated in bolder strokes. His voice, again, is 'loud', his manner brusque (his welcome to his son— ' "Glad to see you" '—is at the opposite pole from the formal addresses of Sir Thomas), and he swears freely, probably more freely indeed than any other character in Jane Austen's novels. Fanny finds her delicacy continually offended, and his speech is a fair index of his personal limitations: 'he swore and he drank, he was dirty and gross'. The portrait of Mr Price, to which his dialogue makes a substantial contribution, is a salutary corrective to the view, still occasionally encountered, of Jane Austen as never venturing outside the drawing-rooms of polite society. The effect of the Portsmouth visit is to cure Fanny of an illusion, the idealized memory of the home she has left; and, in the process, to set in a clearer light the distinctive virtues for which Mansfield Park stands. The contrast involves much more than speech: it is two ways of life, two opposing sets of habits and values, that are in question; but in the dramatic presentation of the heroine's awakening from her sentimental dream, the role of her parents' speech is a very important one.

Apart from a few brief speeches by servants, the Prices represent Jane Austen's lowest point of descent in depicting the social varieties of speech; and though they are far from belonging to the lowest stratum of early nineteenth-century society (they are even employers of labour), Chapter 38 of *Mansfield Park* may fairly be described as unique in her novels. More frequently, even when a character of relatively humble status has a role of some significance, dialogue is avoided. Robert Martin, the prosperous farmer in *Emma*, for instance, is seen but not heard.

At the other end of the social scale, we are given some memor-

able examples of upper-class speech, of which three—Sir Thomas
Bertram, Sir Walter Elliot, and Lady Catherine de Bourgh—
may be examined more closely. Sir Thomas's first speech, in the
opening chapter of *Mansfield Park*, sets the tone for nearly all
his subsequent utterances:

'There is a great deal of truth in what you say,' replied Sir
Thomas, 'and far be it from me to throw any fanciful impediment
in the way of a plan which would be so consistent with the relative
situations of each. I only meant to observe, that it ought not to be
lightly engaged in, and that to make it really serviceable to Mrs
Price, and creditable to ourselves, we must secure to the child, or
consider ourselves engaged to secure to her hereafter, as circumstances may arise, the provision of a gentlewoman, if no such
establishment should offer as you are so sanguine in expecting.'
(*MP*, 7)

This is good sense, but the manner of its expression tells us a
good deal about the speaker's mind and temperament. The long
sentences, with their carefully-ordered structures of parallel
phrases and subordinate clauses have a quasi-legal flavour, as
have such words and phrases as 'hereafter' and 'as circumstances
may arise'. The second sentence quoted, indeed, seems in its con-
voluted syntax to be alien to the spoken medium. Such a mode of
delivery implies habits of reflection and deliberation, together
with a sense of the importance of his own utterances, which his
later behaviour serves to confirm. Lexically, his style shows a fondness for abstractions and for the ready-made and time-honoured
phrase—not, of course, the homely proverbial idiom of some of the
less aristocratic characters, but the clichés of the man of affairs ('not
to be lightly engaged in'). He avoids the concrete and the specific,
being always much readier to fall back upon an established
phrase than to venture upon a personal observation. All these
qualities may be seen not just as a natural expression of his
formality and pomposity, but as a linguistic manifestation of his
innate Toryism. He judges by immutable standards, and conveys
his judgments in language which is as much concerned to preserve
the existing order as his politics. One feels that an original epithet

or a vivid metaphor would cause him the same displeasure as a Radical idea. Yet he is more complex than this: how complex, and how Jane Austen resists the temptation to turn him into a caricature, may be seen by comparing him with another fictional baronet, Dickens' Sir Leicester Dedlock in *Bleak House*. Sir Thomas is as much a prisoner of his inflexible syntax and conservative diction as of his frigid manner; these are manifested even when his basic impulse is generous and humane, and to this mode of speech, as well as to his habitually distant manner, must be attributed some of his failure as a father. When he returns unexpectedly from Antigua (Chapter 19), he makes an effort to be 'happy and indulgent', but his speech even so is still formal. But perhaps the best example of this uniformity of his manner is the scene (Chapter 32) in which he informs Fanny that Mr Crawford is seeking her hand, and then reproaches her with ingratitude for her refusal. In the early part of the scene his tone is kindly, but even his kindness is expressed in stilted terms: when he finds her sitting without a fire, he observes ' "Here is some great misapprehension which must be rectified" '. Later, when Fanny is most in need of sympathetic understanding, he turns his verbal big-guns upon her:

'. . . . I had thought you peculiarly free from wilfulness of temper, self-conceit, and every tendency to that independence of spirit, which prevails so much in modern days, even in young women, and which in young women is offensive and disgusting beyond all common offence . . .' (*MP*, 318)

Fanny is, understandably, crushed beneath the weight of his abstract nouns.

Jane Austen's achievement in creating the speech of Sir Thomas was to devise an idiolect that could express with accuracy the mental universe of a Tory landowner without slipping into comedy or parody. He is an impressively serious creation, retaining respect even where he does not win affection. The purpose behind Sir Walter Elliot of *Persuasion* is surely quite different. For him we can feel little but contempt, as the embodiment of snobbery, of placing importance on externals and mistaking appearances for realities. The words *snob*, *snobbish*, and *snobbery*, in the sense under discussion, emerged only in the generation after Jane Austen, but the phenomenon was obviously real enough at least by the end of her lifetime. Like Sir Thomas Bertram and Sir Leicester Dedlock, Sir Walter is concerned to preserve a status quo that is in the process of changing in spite of him: his mentality is distinctly backward-looking, and it is revealing that the first reference to him is in connection with his favourite book, 'the Baronetage', in studying which he can gratify a pleasant scorn for 'the almost endless creations of the last century' (*P*, 3). When his lawyer refers to a curate as a 'gentleman', Sir Walter insists on understanding the word in a sense that was already archaic, correcting him thus:

'Wentworth? Oh! ay,—Mr Wentworth, the curate of Monkford. You misled me by the term *gentleman*. I thought you were speaking of some man of property ...' (*P*, 23)

Unlike Sir Thomas, however, he deals less in abstractions than in the superficialities of appearance and manners, and his speech is correspondingly more concrete. Fashion and complexion are more real to him than moral qualities; thus he dismisses 'a certain Admiral Baldwin' as ' "the most deplorable looking personage you can imagine, his face the colour of mahogany, rough and rugged to the last degree, all lines and wrinkles, nine grey hairs of a side, and nothing but a dab of powder at top" ' *P*, 20). In a long passage of free indirect speech (141–2) his preoccupation with appearance is shown as comically obsessive: '... once, as he had stood in a shop in Bond-street, he had counted eighty-seven women go by, one after another, without there being a tolerable face among them'. Faces, names, pedigrees, liveries, equipages—all these and other external trappings of status wholly occupy his mind, and towards the end of the novel he is dismissed in the single phrase 'heartless elegance' (*P*, 226). It has been suggested that Sir Walter embodies a satirical attack on Chesterfieldian manners and morals, and

specifically on the ideas of Lord Chesterfield's letters to his son.[28]
Certainly the sharpness of the attack on Sir Walter implies scant
respect for Chesterfield as a moralist.

With Lady Catherine de Bourgh we move even further in the
direction of satirical comedy; yet the comedy has a serious
undercurrent, for Lady Catherine is not merely an autocrat who
finds herself verbally outmanoeuvred by a girl of (to her) dubious
social standing, in the process of which we are given some of
Jane Austen's most incisive dialogue—she is also one of those
who, like Sir Walter, mistakes appearances in the form of heredi-
tary and material advantages, for reality. Elizabeth Bennet's
sense of values, on the other hand, is beyond reproach: when she
goes to dine at Rosings,

Elizabeth's courage did not fail her. She had heard nothing of
Lady Catherine that spoke her awful from any extraordinary
talents or miraculous virtue, and the mere stateliness of money and
rank, she thought she could witness without trepidation. (*PP*, 161)

Her assurance is derived from the knowledge that, by any
standards that really matter, she is good enough for Darcy; and
since Lady Catherine puts herself in the position of debating the
issue, Elizabeth's wit and intelligence are given full play in her
speech.

Even before the famous scene in which this debate takes place,
we are given a taste of Lady Catherine's manner. At the Rosings
dinner in Chapter 29, Elizabeth is quickly struck by 'the imper-
tinence of her questions'. Interrogation, point-blank and *de haut
en bas*, is indeed a favourite form of speech with her, often
followed by gratuitous advice or dogmatic assertions of opinion.
She tends to initiate and to terminate topics of conversation, and
expects in return nothing beyond frank and submissive replies to
her inquiries. Her twelve speeches in this short scene include
thirteen questions, and we are given a hint of the later scene in
Elizabeth's reply to the final question:

[28] F. W. Bradbrook, 'Lord Chesterfield and Jane Austen', *Notes and
Queries*, 203 (1958) 80–2.

'Upon my word,' said her Ladyship, 'you give your opinion very decidedly for so young a person.—Pray, what is your age?'

'With three younger sisters grown up,' replied Elizabeth smiling, 'your Ladyship can hardly expect me to own it.' (*PP*, 165–6)

After the direct speech is concluded—this scene, like others, consists of a central passage of dialogue framed by narrative which includes elements of indirect speech—we learn that 'The party then gathered round the fire to hear Lady Catherine determine what weather they were to have on the morrow'. The force of that *determine* is a good example of Jane Austen's uninsistent but effective use of a single well-placed word.

Towards the end of the novel there occurs (Chapter 56) the longer dialogue passage in which Lady Catherine demands to know Elizabeth's intentions with respect to her nephew Darcy. Elizabeth's surprise at learning the nature of her mission gives a serious tone to its opening; but she quickly recovers her equanimity and her wit. Jane Austen contrives to allow her heroine to make all, or nearly all, the debating points in the ensuing contest. Even when Lady Catherine appears to be about to score with her malicious references to Elizabeth's low connections on her mother's side, she ends by losing the point: ' "Whatever my connections may be," said Elizabeth, "if your nephew does not object to them, they can be nothing to *you*".' (*PP*, 356) Yet the points are not made too easily: Lady Catherine is a formidable adversary, and the theme of her attack— Elizabeth's social presumptuousness in thinking of herself as the bride of Darcy—is one that requires answering. Elizabeth succeeds partly by turning upon Lady Catherine her own favourite weapon, the direct question: ' "If Mr Darcy is neither by honour nor inclination confined to his cousin, why is not he to make another choice? And if I am that choice, why may not I accept him?" ' The absurdity of Lady Catherine's arrogant snobbery is underlined by couching *her* most dramatic question in mock-heroic language: ' "Heaven and earth!—of what are you thinking? Are the shades of Pemberley to be thus polluted?" ' With Lady Catherine, however, it is not so much qualities of vocabu-

lary or syntax as the forms in which her utterances are cast—
the question which demands a full and instant reply, the assertion
which brooks no questioning—which creates what Jane Austen
herself refers to as her 'authoritative' tone, and is the linguistic
equivalent of that manner which, we are told, was not 'such as
to make her visitors forget their inferior rank'.

It has been argued in this chapter that Jane Austen not only
displays an impressive versatility in her use of different forms of
speech-presentation, but also offers a wider range of speech-
varieties than has sometimes been suggested. One would not,
perhaps, wish to go quite all the way with one of her earliest
critics, Archbishop Richard Whateley, who wrote that she gives
'a dramatic air to the narrative, by introducing frequent conversations; which she conducts with a regard to character hardly
exceeded even by Shakespeare himself';[29] but his tribute certainly
points in the right direction.

[29] In an unsigned review of the posthumously-published *Northanger
Abbey* and *Persuasion* (*Quarterly Review*, January 1821; reprinted in
B. C. Southam (ed.), *Jane Austen: the Critical Heritage* (1968) 87–105.)

CHAPTER FIVE

THE EPISTOLARY ART

Jane Austen's lifetime belongs more to the eighteenth century than to the nineteenth, and her writing life is divided almost exactly equally between the two centuries. It is not surprising, therefore, that in tracing the development of her literary art we should find at many points, and particularly in the earlier phases, a deep commitment to eighteenth-century conventions of fiction —a commitment that does not, of course, prevent her from ridiculing these conventions on many occasions. On the stylistic level her debt to the eighteenth century has already become clear in the discussions of vocabulary and syntax in earlier chapters. Another aspect, which unites stylistic considerations with others relating to narrative method, is her use of the letter-form. For, whilst none of her novels is, in its final version, an epistolary novel in the sense in which we apply that label to *Clarissa* or *Evelina*, a significant epistolary element can be traced in some of them, often in what appears to be a vestigial state. The epistolary novel had been, especially for women novelists, a very popular form in the second half of the eighteenth century; but by the time that Jane Austen began to read and write fiction, it had already gone a long way towards self-destruction, its melo-dramatic and sentimental excesses (entertainingly chronicled by Miss Tompkins) inevitably making it a less eligible choice of medium for a writer who took the art of fiction seriously and who was possessed of Jane Austen's self-awareness.[1]

[1] Cf. J. M. S. Tompkins, *The Popular Novel in England, 1770–1800* (1932); G. F. Singer, *The Epistolary Novel* (New York, 1933); F. G.

Not that fiction, of course, provided her with the only occasion for letter-writing; and something should first be said about her real-life correspondence. She was a prolific and enthusiastic letter-writer, and such samples as have survived—possibly only a minority of her output, and not necessarily the best or most characteristic—convey a lively sense of the pleasure she found in communicating her day-to-day experiences through this medium. They are primarily letters of information rather than reflection, concerned with personal, family and local news and comment, and scarcely at all with the public issues of the day or with speculations on intellectual questions or the practice of her art. (For this reason her few and mainly casual observations on novel-writing and on her individual books have tended to assume an importance, through frequent quotation, that may be quite out of proportion to what was intended.) For Jane Austen, as for Richardson and Sterne and others, letter-writing is an acceptable substitute for gossip, unpretentious but civilized and highly enjoyable to the parties concerned; and the lively, affectionate, humorous manner of these informal productions served to ensure the continuing vitality of a relationship during the sometimes pro-longed physical separation of the correspondents. To talk on paper was the next best thing to doing so in the flesh. In the absence of the telephone, letters were also capable of suggesting something of the tone of the speaking voice. Jane Austen wrote to her favourite correspondent, her sister Cassandra, on 3 January 1801: 'I have now attained the true art of letter-writing, which we are always told, is to express on paper exactly what one would say to the same person by word of mouth. I have been talking to you almost as fast as I could the whole of this letter.' (*L*, 102) Admittedly, beside the letters of Keats or even Byron, their literary quality often seems slight; yet they have a perceptible relationship to the novels in the acuteness of observation they reveal, and in their frequent and evident delight in impaling a character or episode upon a well-chosen phrase. Perhaps they are

---

Black, *The Epistolary Novel in the Late Eighteenth Century* (Eugene, 1940); N. Wurzbach, *The Novel in Letters* (1969).

M

most closely related to those other largely private documents, the juvenilia, with the same vivacity and outspokenness that found expression there more readily than in the formal utterances of the published novels.

For there are, perhaps predictably, some notable linguistic differences between the letters and the fiction. It has been shown that in the latter considerable importance is attached to decorum of language, and departures from accepted standards serve to indicate moral inadequacies. This should not, however, lead us to suppose that Jane Austen's attitude to language was at all times consistently and unswervingly prim. Although her conversation was not recorded, her letters show her to have been not only acquainted with current colloquialisms, but prepared to use them herself in informal and private contexts. She is capable of using such expressions as 'die of laughter' or 'in the family way' which, in the novels, might well have been used to stigmatize a Mrs Elton or a Lucy Steele. Her vocabulary also contains many words which must still have had the gloss of freshness upon them. Reading the letters with the *OED* at hand shows that many items are recorded as first appearing in print less than fifty years before she used them: *washed out*, *casino*, *chatty*, *bandeau*, *thick* (friendly), *a sad bore* are some examples. Others are even newer: *funny*, in the sense 'odd', which is on record as a colloquial usage from 1806, crops up in a letter of January 1807, and *raffish*, dated 1801, in May of that same year. Indeed, there are several usages which appear to antedate the earliest examples in *OED*. *Boa*, dated 1836 in *OED*, appears in 1808; *transparencies* (1807) in 1800, and *would-be* (1826) in 1813. This suggests the sprightliness of language and tone in many of the letters, but it does not mean that Jane Austen's verbal behaviour as a letter-writer was inconsistent with her practice as a novelist. The conventions of public discourse, like those of public conduct, are not necessarily to be taken as applying *in toto* to private situations. What is implied is that, in the world of the novels, language—including colloquial speech—takes on a heightened significance as an index of human values, and becomes an important element in the conventions of this writer's art.

Another relationship between letters and fiction may be detected in the fact that, even in these intimate writings composed with no thought of a wider audience, she habitually endows social and domestic trivialities with a sense of style. They are retailed in a spirit of fun which both conveys a sense of values—the awareness that this is trivial enough in all conscience, as if the writer were laughing at herself for bothering to mention it—and, at the same time, by its wit and originality, gives gossip an unusual distinction. For example, after several lines describing in detail some new tables, she adds: 'They are both covered with green baize and send their best Love' (*L*, 82). Again, she passes neatly from a discussion of style to a domestic catastrophe: 'Could my Ideas flow as fast as the rain in the Store closet it would be charming' (*L*, 256); and, after relating the purchase of a pair of gloves costing 'only fourshillings', she adds, 'upon hearing which everybody at Chawton will be hoping and predicting that they cannot be good for anything...' (*L*, 306). Another letter ends: 'I have this moment seen Mrs Driver driven up to the Kitchen Door. I cannot close with a grander circumstance or greater wit' (*L*, 335). A favourite device, as in the last example quoted, is to retail trivia in a manner which parodies that activity by the use of language which is deliberately disproportionate to the occasion. In the same way she writes of the 'wondrous happiness' of a trunk arriving safely, and the 'never failing regret' for a dress that has been unsuccessfully dyed (*L*, 190, 215). The quality of style thus gives these passages an interest which transcends that of their subject-matter. A similar spirit may be detected at many points in the juvenilia and in *Northanger Abbey*.

For Jane Austen, then, letter-writing was a way of life as well as a device of art. The juvenilia themselves show how heavily she was indebted to the epistolary mode in fiction. Richardson was one of her favourite authors, but he was only the most celebrated of a very large number of eighteenth-century novelists who favoured this mode of story-telling, which a historian of late-eighteenth-century fiction has described as 'incomparably the most popular up to about 1785'.[2] By that date (or soon after) Jane Austen was already a writer as well as a reader, and quite early in her writing life she must have sensed the capacity of the epistolary novel for dramatic power, vivid immediacy and minute analysis of states of mind. Ian Jack has claimed that 'It was from Richardson and Fanny Burney that she learnt her art',[3] and the importance of the novel-in-letters was pervasive. However, the ease of composition and looseness of structure which attracted so many mediocre authors, combined with its tendency towards repetitiveness and a certain enforced crudity in the handling of point of view, made it ultimately unacceptable as a vehicle for the kind of novel that she, as a maturing and hightly self-conscious artist, wished to write. The history of her relationship with the epistolary mode is, therefore, a record of its early use and gradual abandonment in favour of other narrative techniques, though important traces remain even in the later novels.

One of her earliest writings of any length, *Love and Freindship* (dated 1790), is subtitled 'a novel in a series of Letters', but is in fact little more than a sustained monologue by a single writer, divided into portions of letter-length, since fourteen of the fifteen letters presented are by Laura, thirteen of them to a single recipient. Evidently the conception of a series of letters as a number of simultaneous and parallel dialogues, with the dramatic and contrastive possibilities inherent therein, has not yet been fully grasped. Two years later, *Lesley Castle*, another 'novel in letters' but this time unfinished, contains a genuine exchange of letters between correspondents, with consequently greater variety and contrast. If we designate the five correspondents involved by the first five letters of the alphabet, the pattern is as follows: the first, third, fifth and tenth letters are from A to B, the second, fourth and seventh from B to A, the sixth from

[2] Tompkins, *op. cit.*, 34.

[3] I. Jack, 'The Epistolary Element in Jane Austen', *English Studies Today: Second Series*, ed. G. A. Bonnard (Bern, 1961) 174.

C to B, the eighth from D to E, and the ninth from E to D. That is to say, a 'major' correspondence (between A and B) is supported by one or more 'minor' correspondences—a pattern we shall see repeated on a larger scale in the later *Lady Susan*. This method has the advantage, which Jane Austen had perhaps seen at work in Richardson's *Clarissa* but which is present here in only a rudimentary form, of allowing the presentation of an event from different points of view in succession.

To the same period also belongs the brief *A Collection of Letters*, a series of five epistles with titles parodically reminiscent of Richardson's *Familiar Letters* and other eighteenth-century letter-writing manuals ('From a Young Lady crossed in Love to her Freind', etc.), though their contents quickly make the satiric purpose clear. These are fluent and often racy monologues, ridiculing popular conventions of situation and language. It is worth noting that these early efforts, and notably the *Collection of Letters*, make frequent use of dialogue. Some of it is deliberately non-realistic, as in the following burlesque of dialogue as mere padding:

My Father started—'What noise is that,' (said he.) 'It sounds like a loud rapping at the Door'—(replied by Mother.) 'It does indeed.' (cried I) 'I am of your opinion; (said my Father) it certainly does appear to proceed from some uncommon violence exerted against our unoffending Door.' 'Yes (exclaimed I) I cannot help thinking it must be somebody who knocks for Admittance.' (*MW*, 79)

This is both high-spirited fun and valid criticism of many novels of the period. Elsewhere the dialogue can show an ear already receptive to the rhythms of speech:

She was determined to mortify me, . . . and said loud enough to be heard by half the people in the room, 'Pray Miss Maria in what way of business was your Grand-father? for Miss Mason and I cannot agree whether he was a Grocer or a Bookbinder.' . . . 'Neither Madam; he was a Wine Merchant.' 'Aye, I knew he was in some such low way—He broke did not he?' 'I believe not Ma'am.' 'Did not he abscond?' 'I never heard that he did.' 'At least he died insolvent?' 'I was never told so before.' 'Why was not your *Father* as poor as a Rat?' 'I fancy not.' 'Was not he in the Kings Bench once?' 'I never saw him there.' She gave me *such* a look, and turned away in a great passion ... (MW, 158–9)

We are still closer to *Evelina* than to *Pride and Prejudice*, but such a passage perhaps contains the seeds of Elizabeth Bennet's famous interview with Lady Catherine de Bourgh.

Later in the 1790s, Jane Austen initiated a more ambitious phase of her career with the writing, probably some time before 1796, of the epistolary novel *Elinor and Marianne*. Since this has not survived, we can only conjecture its nature by working backwards from the published novel that represents a radical re-writing of this earlier work, and such conjectures must of necessity be imperfect and incomplete. The abandonment of the epistolary form in *Sense and Sensibility* may be interpreted as an unmistakable symptom of the author's dissatisfaction with it; yet the rejection was not complete, and (as B. C. Southam has pointed out) certain passages of the final novel, and some of its structural and narrative devices, betray the nature of the original design.[4] An examination of the role of letters in this novel will reveal the extent of its relationship to the epistolary method.

Letters make their appearance in *Sense and Sensibility* in a number of ways, ranging from brief allusions to the quotation *verbatim* of an entire letter occupying several pages, and from passing references to letter-writing as an activity to the sending and receipt of letters which play a vital part in the story. A letter can be a useful plot-device, its purpose extending no further than the contrivance of some necessary piece of action; of this kind is the letter received by Mrs Dashwood in the fourth chapter. She is offered a cottage in Devon, and promptly sends her acceptance, after showing the letter she has written to her two daughters. More important than this is the letter which is used to show character and relationships: since a strict code of conventions governed the sending and receiving of letters by

[4] B. C. Southam, *Jane Austen's Literary Manuscripts* (Oxford, 1964) 57.

eligible but unmarried persons of different sexes, the mere possession of a letter became a certificate of intimacy. This convention
is invoked when Lucy Steele shows Elinor the letter she has
received from Edward Ferrars, thereby disclosing her engagement to him. Most important of all, however, is the use of a letter
as the centre of a dramatic situation, and here the most memor-
able of many examples is the scene in which Elinor finds the
prostrate Marianne, 'almost choked with grief', clutching a letter
in her hand and with three others scattered around her—the
cause of this emotional crisis being the receipt of a cold and
formal note from Willoughby.

As one examines the many references to epistolary activity in
this novel, it becomes clear that two main correspondences are
involved, together with a number of minor ones of slighter
interest. One is the partly clandestine correspondence between
Marianne and Willoughby, the other the frequent exchange of
letters between Mrs Dashwood in Devon and her daughters in
London, since the latter are separated from their mother for a
large portion of the action. The first of these begins as soon as
the sisters arrive in London: when Elinor sits down to write to her
mother, Marianne at the same time pens a letter which she
declares is *not* to her mother—whereupon Elinor instantly concludes that it must be to Willoughby, and interprets this as
unequivocal evidence that 'however mysteriously they might
wish to conduct the affair, they must be engaged' (*SS*, 161).
From that point, Marianne is to be found scribbling almost as
often as Richardson's heroines, and when a little later we find
her 'writing as fast as a continual flow of tears would permit her'
(180), we cannot help recalling Pamela's 'O how my eyes run
—Don't wonder to see the paper so blotted'. Marianne is placed
firmly in the eighteenth-century tradition of heroines whose
lachrymose emotions find a partial outlet in letter-writing. A few
pages later (186–8) the reader is enabled to read three of
Marianne's letters; when Willoughby returns them, she puts
them into her sister's hands and the novelist takes the opportunity
of quoting them *verbatim*.

Marianne's correspondence with Willoughby also provides some dramatic scenes which centre on the arrival of the post. When she is anxiously awaiting some word from him, her hopes are raised and then dashed on at least two occasions by the arrival of a letter which turns out to be from someone else. At such moments even a style of handwriting is charged with dramatic and emotional force: just as Lucy Steele had wounded Elinor by her casual reference to the letters she has received from Edward (' "You know his hand, I dare say, a charming one it is!" '), so Marianne is bitterly disappointed to see 'the hand-writing of her mother, never till then unwelcome'.

The other major epistolary element in this novel, the correspondence (largely in the hands of Elinor) between the sisters in London and their mother in Devon, perhaps provides an answer to the problem which has vexed the understanding of the relationship between *Sense and Sensibility* as we have it and its earlier epistolary form: how was a correspondence devised by means of which the story is told in letters, when the principal actors (Elinor and Marianne) are scarcely ever apart? It seems unnecessary to postulate, as M. H. Dodds does, the existence of two confidantes who would have respectively received the letters of the two sisters, but who were jettisoned in the rewritten version.[5] Certainly there are abundant traces of Elinor's letters to her mother, not in letters quoted but in references to that activity. Elinor regards it as her duty to keep her mother informed of developments in the Marianne–Willoughby situation, and to stress its gravity when this is not at first grasped by Mrs Dashwood; and there is a reference to her mother's side of the correspondence:

To give the feelings or the language of Mrs Dashwood on receiving and answering Elinor's letter, would be only to give a repetition of what her daughters had already felt and said; of a disappointment hardly less painful than Marianne's, and an indignation even

[5] M. H. Dodds, 'More Notes on Jane Austen's Novels', *Notes and Queries*, 178 (1940) 405–7.

greater than Elinor's. Long letters from her, quickly succeeding each other, arrived to tell all that she suffered and thought ... (*SS*, 212–13)

Such a passage has a distinct air of having been written to bridge a gap left by the removal of letters which the novelist, on revising her original version, decided to dispense with. (One senses the implication of her sparing the reader Mrs Dashwood's 'long letters'.)

The above discussion has by no means exhausted the catalogue of letters or correspondents in *Sense and Sensibility*. In the penultimate chapter, Elinor, now home again, awaits 'The letters from town', and the communications of Mrs Jennings and Mr Dashwood are given by summary and quotation. Through the greater part of the novel, therefore, letters written, received or awaited play an important part in the development of the action and occupy the stage in a number of episodes. And, to anticipate a point that will be returned to later in this chapter, there is a congruity between letter-writing styles and their authors: Marianne's to Willoughby are 'full of affection and confidence', his is 'impudently cruel', and Lucy Steele's give Mrs Jennings pleasure (' "how prettily she writes!" ') but cause Edward only mortification.

The role of letters in *Sense and Sensibility* can be appreciated by contrasting it in this respect with that other early novel, *Northanger Abbey*, concerning which there is no evidence that it was ever conceived in epistolary terms. Although Catherine Morland, like the Dashwood sisters, is separated from her home for a large part of the action, letter-writing is a much less prominent activity. Some contact is maintained with the parental home—Catherine writes, for instance, to ask permission to visit the Tilneys at Northanger Abbey, and duly receives it; apart from this the only episode of importance is the jilting of James Morland by Isabella Thorpe, which is largely disclosed by means of an exchange of letters: Catherine receives first a letter from her brother (*NA*, 202) and then one from Isabella (216–18), the latter in 'a strain of shallow artifice' which lays bare the writer's true nature; and both are quoted in full. But this virtually exhausts the epistolary element, and an authorial observation in the final chapter refers to the romantic exchange of letters in ironic terms: 'Whether the torments of absence were softened by a clandestine correspondence, let us not inquire'.[6]

The genesis of *Pride and Prejudice* is more problematic: we know that it originally existed as *First Impressions*, but not what kind of a novel the latter (written between October 1796 and August 1797) was, except that it appears to have been considerably longer than the version which, after being several times revised, was eventually published. Southam has suggested that *First Impressions*, like *Elinor and Marianne*, may have been an epistolary novel;[7] and although there is no very convincing external evidence for this hypothesis, there is one fact about the published novel that is, to say the least, very striking—its use of letters, quoted or referred to, as a story-telling device. Whereas there are only nine instances of this use in *Northanger Abbey*, and twenty-one in *Sense and Sensibility*, Southam has counted no less than forty-four in *Pride and Prejudice*. Taken in conjunction with the fact that the later version involved a considerable abridgement (Jane Austen wrote to her sister Cassandra that she had 'lop't and crop't [it] so successfully . . .' (*L*, 298)), which is what one would expect from the transformation of an epistolary novel into a third-person narrative, this strongly suggests an epistolary ancestry. In any case, the importance of letters in this novel is undeniable. They provide both a useful piece of narrative mechanism (their function in this novel has been briefly discussed above, pp. 31–33) and a means of characterization analogous to the dramatic monologue or soliloquy. At the same time as giving insight into the letter-writer's mind and motives, they provide recipients with the opportunity of reacting in ways which reveal their own nature. The novelist is also enabled to introduce ele-

---

[6] This and other passages lead one to suggest that *Northanger Abbey* might be described as an anti-epistolary novel. Compare Henry Tilney's satirical observations on feminine letter-writing and journal-keeping (*NA*, 27–8).

[7] Southam, *op. cit.*, 58.

ments from outside the confines of the society she has elected to represent, without abandoning that society as her setting. It is hardly surprising, then, that in this and other novels the arrival of a letter—which, by its nature, often brings the stimulus of novelty into a stable community in which news is at a premium —is a favourite device.

Jane Austen's last essay in the epistolary novel was *Lady Susan*, written certainly before 1805 and probably much earlier, though not published until 1871. This is a novelette consisting of forty-one letters by a variety of correspondents. Compared with *Love and Freindship*, it represents a considerable advance in the exploitation of the epistolary technique: the form is now used to create genuine dramatic interest, the contrasting natures of the various correspondents being skilfully revealed through their letters. Since the central figure, Lady Susan, is a consummate dissembler, she is apt to give different versions of the truth to different recipients, with appropriate variations in style: some of her letters, therefore, describe the appearances she is at pains to create, others describe the reality behind those appearances. The result is an effective juxtaposition of her letters to reveal the complexity of her personality. Letter 30, for instance, in which she expresses high-flown sentiments in formal prose, is immediately followed by another, this time to her confidante, revealing her true feelings in more direct and colloquial language. The inherent tendency of the epistolary novel towards tedious repetition is avoided by a deft dovetailing of material, notably in Letters 24 and 25. In the former, an incident is recorded by an observer who sees and relates enough to arouse the reader's curiosity but insufficient to satisfy it: Reginald, having announced his intention of leaving the house, visits Lady Susan in her dressing-room and, presumably as a result of her blandishments, is shown on emerging to have changed his mind. We remain, that is to say, firmly outside the centre of action in Letter 24, and are left asking precisely what has transpired inside the room. Letter 25 provides the answer: written by Lady Susan herself, and covering the same space of time as the previous one, it now takes us inside the dressing-room, privileged to hear the conversation that there takes place. Like *Lesley Castle*, the work is built around two main correspondences between pairs of contrasting characters, with the interpolation of subordinate exchanges of letters from time to time. The Lady Susan—Mrs Johnson and Lady de Courcy—Mrs Vernon correspondences account between them for almost three-quarters of the entire series of letters, the four minor correspondences sharing the remaining quarter.

Its brevity prevents *Lady Susan* from being considered as a full-dress attempt at the epistolary form, though it certainly shows a technical skill that is striking in (if we are to accept an early date for the work) a girl of little more than twenty. If we can accept the theory put forward in Q. D. Leavis's well-known essay, it has another claim on our attention as the prototype of *Mansfield Park*.[8] Put briefly, what Mrs Leavis has postulated is a three-tier structure of which *Lady Susan* is the first draft, *Mansfield Park* the final product, and the middle layer—a precursor of the published novel based on *Lady Susan* and written in letter-form—is now lost. In the novel as we have it, not only do letters (quoted or referred to) play an important part, but, Mrs Leavis suggests, a good deal of the narrative writing 'reads like paraphrases of letters'. This may, then, be yet another major indication of the importance of the epistolary element in the early drafts of the novels. It also suggests a genesis for *Mansfield Park* some fifteen years earlier than is generally accepted.

However, although Mrs Leavis's essay is very persuasive, it has not found universal acceptance. Without entering here into a prolonged examination of its arguments, it may be tested by further reference to an episode in the novel which has already been briefly discussed in Chapter 1—Fanny Price's visit to Portsmouth. During this phase of the novel, the heroine is isolated by her physical separation from the other principal characters, and Jane Austen's problem is to prevent the situation from be-

[8] Q. D. Leavis, 'A Critical Theory of Jane Austen's Writings, II: *Lady Susan* into *Mansfield Park*', *Scrutiny*, 10 (1941) 114–42, 272–94.

coming static and to keep open the areas of interest which have
been developed in Fanny's relationships with Edmund, Mary
Crawford, and others. It seems entirely natural that, in these
circumstances, the author should fall back upon epistolary
activity as a substitute for other forms of action. Whereas Q. D.
Leavis maintains that the episode is a survival from an earlier,
epistolary version, in which Fanny was removed from Mansfield
Park in order to render possible an exchange of letters, my own
view would be that the reverse is the case: there are other and
sufficient reasons for Fanny's translation, and, given her isola-
tion, communication by letter is an almost inevitable solution to
the problem thus created. Fanny's disillusion with her own
family, and the lack of sympathy she find in her old home,
mean that the postman is at first eagerly awaited. Eventually news
comes from two directions: from Mary Crawford in London, and
Edmund in Northamptonshire; and as it brings to Fanny knowledge of a situation that is first puzzling and then deeply distressing, she comes to fear what is referred to, in an unusually vivid
phrase, as the postman's 'sickening knock'. Although these
chapters contain a brisk flow of letters, however, Fanny's side of
the correspondence is not given: her role is essentially passive,
as the recipient of the news of others rather than as agent and
communicator. In Chapter 40 a letter arrives from Mary Crawford, followed by another in Chapter 43. Chapter 44 offers a
letter from Edmund and a discussion of Lady Bertram's letter-
writing habits and style, illustrated by a letter from her pen.
Chapter 45 and 46 give, between them, two more letters each
from Edmund and Mary, in which the news of Maria Rushworth's adultery breaks upon Fanny. This double correspondence
gives Jane Austen the opportunity of pointing the contrast between Edmund and Mary; and such a device, it is true, would be
completely at home in an epistolary novel. On balance, however,
there seems no strong reason for regarding the episode as a
survival from a lost early version of *Mansfield Park*: having cut
her heroine off from most of those whose doings were closest to
her heart, it is hard to see that she had any alternative but to

fall back upon these letters as voices from the outside world speaking to Fanny—and the reader—temporarily marooned in Portsmouth.

Letter-writing is less prominent in the later novels, but never disappears entirely. In *Emma*, since most of the action takes place in Highbury, much of the contact with the larger world comes through the post, though few of the letters are actually quoted. The secretive Jane Fairfax is evidently an industrious correspondent as well as a talented stylist, but none of her letters is actually quoted. This has been noted by Ian Jack, who also points out that there are more letters from the minor characters than from the major ones, and further that 'Jane Austen is always less willing to give us a letter which is evidence of a good character than a letter which reveals a bad one'.[9] We have, for example, letters from Isabella Thorpe, Lucy Steele, Mary Crawford, and others; but very few from the heroines—only one each from Fanny Price and Elizabeth Bennet, and none at all from Emma Woodhouse or Anne Elliot. A consideration of two contrasting examples will suggest why this should be so. The interpolation of a letter into the narrative can serve one or both of two quite different purposes. It can advance the plot by reporting action or disclosing information; and it can, no less surely (though usually unconsciously on the part of the letter-writer), reveal character. Where the function of the letter is to narrate, it matters little who writes it, and in fact Jane Austen does give us letters of this kind from her major characters, including Darcy and Edmund Bertram. Where its function is to contribute to characterization, however, there is good reason for preferring the letters of 'bad' characters to those written by the pure in heart, and this reason quickly becomes plain if we recall that a letter may be regarded as a specialized variety of speech—a sustained monologue, much longer than normal dialogue can usually tolerate, but affording the same opportunities for self-revelation through idiosyncrasies of style. When a letter is given from the pen of a character who represents solid virtues, its language and

[9] Jack, *op. cit.*, 181.

sentiments can do little more than to confirm what we already know; the style of such a letter is likely to be neutral or non-idiosyncratic, and its main interest will lie in the information it is designed to convey. Thus, when Fanny receives a long letter from Edmund in Chapter 44 of *Mansfield Park*, it provides her, and the reader, with an insight into his feelings about Mary Crawford, but tells us nothing important about Edmund's nature that we do not already know. His character and motives can survive the prolonged exposure of a detailed and intimate letter without blemish: his language gives us no opportunity for detecting his folly (as with Mr Collins), or his meanness of spirit (as with Lucy Steele), or his hypocrisy (as with Lady Susan). A hero, after all, suffers from the dramatic limitations that he can only be himself. No such handicap afflicts the wicked or selfish or foolish character, however, whose hypocrisies and affectations are often manifested in the letters they write more plainly than in their speech—if not explicitly, then in a falsity of language by which they unconsciously betray themselves. Willoughby's letter to Marianne in Chapter 29 of *Sense and Sensibility* is of this kind. Outwardly proper, even scrupulously 'correct', its formality strikes a hollow note by contrast with the warmth of his earlier speech and behaviour. The salutation 'My dear Madam', the professions of 'sincere acknowledgments' and 'great regret', and the impersonal rigidity of the syntax all imply a calculated cold-ness and a deliberate attempt to terminate his relationship with Marianne, whose own letters, quoted a few pages later, are 'so full of affection and confidence'. Willoughby's capacity for double-dealing makes available to the author the possibility of dramatic surprise or ironic implications in his letter which is not to be found in those of the truthful and consistent Edmund. Its style can also act as a signal of an important change of position; and it is perhaps for reasons like this that Jane Austen seems to have preferred to quote verbatim the letters of the foolish, the deceitful and the wicked, whilst those of the virtuous, even when mentioned, earn no more than a passing reference.

The letters which appear so notably in the final versions of the novels are written in almost as many styles as there are letter-writers. It is true that Jane Austen makes frequent references to the formal conventions of polite letter-writing, sometimes in ironic terms: Lady Bertram, who 'rather shone in the epistolary line', has acquired 'a very creditable, commonplace, amplifying style, so that a very little matter was enough for her' (*MP*, 425), and her letter to Fanny begins in this manner. Under the shock of actually seeing Tom's 'altered appearance', however, her formal style cracks, and the letter is finished 'in the language of real feeling and alarm'. In *Emma*, the letter in which Robert Martin proposes to Harriet Smith is described, though not quoted:

The style of the letter was much above [Emma's] expectation. There were not merely no grammatical errors, but as a composition it would not have disgraced a gentleman; the language, though plain, was strong and unaffected, and the sentiments it conveyed very much to the credit of the writer. (*E*, 50–51)

This tells us something about the canons of epistolary excellence of Emma and her class: not only did Martin satisfy the pre-requisite of grammatical correctness, but he produced a satis-factory 'composition', and the twofold comment which follows, distinguishing between 'sentiments' and 'language' (thought and its garment), is firmly Johnsonian. Revealing, too, is the phrase 'the language, *though plain* ...' Evidently a certain ornateness of diction and syntax was deemed appropriate, especially perhaps in a letter of proposal. Presumably Martin had written from the heart, rather than consulting one of the innumerable manuals of epistolary style of which Richardson's *Familiar Letters* is the most famous example.[10] Jane Austen's own view, however, seems to have leaned towards a less formal and more personal notion of letter-style: as Mr Knightley observes, in an endeavour to be fair to Frank Churchill's long and effusive letter quoted in Chapter

[10] See K. G. Hornbeak, *The Complete Letter-writer in English, 1568–1800* (Northampton, Mass., 1934).

50, ' "One man's style must not be the rule of another's" '
(*E*, 445).

Certainly, the interests of stylistic variety lead her to endow
these letters with highly individual styles. Their language is
carefully differentiated both from the narrative style and, more
subtly, from the dialogue given elsewhere to the letter-writer.[11]
For, though letters bear an obvious relationship to speech, a
character's epistolary style is far from being simply written speech.
The formal style, already referred to, and much more familiar
to Jane Austen's contemporaries than to us (except for a few set
phrases), worked in a direction away from speech, though strong
feelings could on occasion reverse this tendency. Thus Fanny
Price, writing in haste to Mary Crawford, expresses regret that
'her distress had allowed no arrangement', her ideal presumably
being not spontaneity but a decorous formality; and Lady
Bertram, in the passage cited above, switches from such well-
tried phrases as 'this distressing intelligence' and 'the poor
invalid' to the language of maternal feeling: in the latter part of
her letter, the novelist adds, 'she wrote as she might have spoken'
(*MP*, 427). In such instances we see the formal style as an *alternative* to a speech-based style: the writer chooses, or at least
aspires to, a written style remote from the vocabulary and syntax
of the spoken language. More often, however, letters employ a style
which represents an *exaggeration* of the normal mode of expression. Since a letter offers a much more sustained revelation of
an individual manner than dialogue normally provides, it can
also offer a magnified view of an idiosyncratic style, with consequently more humorous or satiric effect—or, in some cases, a
more devastating exposure of weaknesses of character. Two
examples from *Pride and Prejudice* will illustrate this point.

Chapter 13 contains both the letter in which Collins introduces
himself to the Bennet family, and the first sample of his conversation. A better comparison, however, because a more equal one in
point of length, may be made between that letter and his long
speech in Chapter 18 (*PP*, 101–2). His speech has already been

---

[11] Cf. M. Lascelles, *op. cit.*, 101.

N

briefly discussed (see p. 144–45 above); the speech in question is typically pompous and pedantic in its addiction to cliché and pleonasm ('omit an occasion of testifying his respect towards any-body connected with the family', 'attentive and conciliatory manners towards every body'). When one turns to the letter, however, which is less than twice as long as the speech, one finds similar features clustering more densely. The letter-writing formulae ('trespass on your hospitality'), the tired metaphors ('heal the breach', 'the . . olive branch'), and the impressive but empty phrases ('bounty and beneficence', 'promote and establish') are in close relationship to Collins' dialogue style, but represent a kind of distillation of it. Syntactically, too, a letter can permit long and elaborated structures which would be implausible in dialogue: the average sentence-length in this letter is 71.4 words, as against 29 in the speech mentioned. His later letter (296–7) is very similar in style. Lydia Bennet's letter, written after her elopement (291–2), allows us to see her folly and irresponsibility more clearly than her somewhat infrequent and brief speeches have done: ' "What a letter is this, to be written at such a moment" ', comments Elizabeth, and any sympathy the reader may have had for Lydia evaporates in the face of this un-conscious but merciless exposure of her weakness.

Examples like this suggest that, apart from their contribution to the business of the novel, letters could for Jane Austen provide precious opportunities for 'exercises in style', as they had earlier done for Richardson, Smollett, and other novelists. Like Win Jenkins' letters in *Humphry Clinker* (to quote a more extreme case than any to be found in Jane Austen), they permit stylistic variety and experimentation that could not otherwise find a place in the novel, and thus represent a survival of the spirit of parody and pastiche which is so characteristic of her earliest work.

CHAPTER SIX

CONCLUSION

To return for a moment to the elementary fact of chronology cited at the opening of the previous chapter: there is a pleasing aptness in the way in which Jane Austen's working life straddles the eighteenth and the nineteenth centuries, and part of the unusual interest of her role in the development of the English novel—and the question goes far beyond stylistic issues—is her relationship to her predecessors and successors. Ian Watt has seen her as uniting in her work the separate and distinctive achievements of Richardson and Fielding, and at the same time looking forward in her later work, beyond the Victorians, to Henry James and the moderns.[1] Janus-like, in fact, she faces both ways; and no account of her is complete without a recognition of her dual quality as traditionalist and innovator. On the stylistic level, her vocabulary tends to be backward-looking and conservative, whilst her syntax is more obviously experimental and adventurous; but there are, inevitably, qualifications which need to be made to both parts of this statement, for she has an acute ear for lexical novelty, as her dialogue repeatedly illustrates, and she never completely abandons the formal sentence, though it is less in evidence in her later novels. One of the purposes of this study has been to suggest that her prose exhibits a much greater degree of stylistic variety than is sometimes supposed. And if the variations are subtle and small-scale, they are none the less expressive.

[1] I. Watt, *The Rise of the Novel* (1957) 308–11.

Her style has, like that of any great writer, an unmistakable individual quality, the reader detecting behind the prose a 'voice' that is immediately recognizable; and at the same time it has —what is by no means always equally true—a close relationship to a tradition. There is, that is to say, a considerable common element to be found in Jane Austen's novels and in those of many of her contemporaries and immediate predecessors and successors; but, equally undeniably, certain differences exist which lead us to regard Jane Austen as a major novelist and others—Fanny Burney or Maria Edgeworth, say, or (to revive names that now belong to the illustrious obscure) Mrs Inchbald or Charlotte Lennox—as something less. These differences do not, generally speaking, relate to themes or character-types, though her treatment tends to be more restrained in the handling of incident than some of her fellow-novelists: the observation of social differences is more heavily underlined in *Evelina*, for instance, and there is nothing in her work resembling the secret disease of which one of the characters in *Belinda* believes herself to be a victim. The basic material of her novels, superficially regarded, is that of many others of the period: family and social life in the middle and upper reaches of society, the complications of love and the quest for matrimony. And yet the difference is real enough: in practical terms, it is between books which are read and re-read by countless enthusiasts, not all of whom have a professional commitment to literature, and books which enjoy only the life-in-death of the history of literature and the academic thesis. If one had to suggest a single, demonstrable source of this difference, it would be her style: not, of course, style regarded as an autonomous phenomenon or simply as 'surface', a kind of luxury finish only available on goods of superior quality, but style as a function of a writer's intelligence and feelings, manifested through her selection from the linguistic resources of her time. To turn from one of the minor novels of the period, even one which has some claims on the twentieth-century reader's attention, to one of Jane Austen's, is to be immediately conscious of a qualitative difference in the way in which words function: one moves, most

CONCLUSION 189

often, from a low-powered diffuseness to a finely-controlled intensity. Her style shows language used with a density which is evidence of the force and sensitivity of the mind which produced it. Perhaps this contrast is most obvious when the major and minor novels have something in common. A fair example would be Susan Ferrier's *The Inheritance* (1824), which opens in a vein that suggests imitation:

It is a truth universally acknowledged, that there is no passion so deeply rooted in human nature as that of pride.

William Blackwood, the publisher and founder of the famous magazine, said of *The Inheritance* that 'It reminds me of Miss Austen's very best things in every page',[2] but the remark seems curiously unperceptive. One does not have to read very far beyond that opening sentence, with its echo of *Pride and Prejudice*, to feel that there are, on almost every page, 'things' that Jane Austen could under no circumstances have written. Even the opening sentence, quoted above, though it begins with Jane Austen's words, would not have gone on to include the stale metaphor of 'deeply rooted in human nature'. In the paragraphs which follow, there is an occasional phrase which has something like the economical incisiveness of the earlier writer's verdicts on character, as in the description of St Clair: 'a man of weak intellects and indolent habits, with just enough of feeling to wish to screen himself from the poverty and contempt his marriage had brought upon him'. But for the most part the writing is lacking in the precision of vocabulary and the strength and elegance of syntax which one takes for granted in Jane Austen's prose; in place of the freshness and originality of her phrases, one finds only clichés ('time immemorial', 'outraged feelings') and overworked literary allusions ('the . . . ills that flesh is heir to', 'the milk of human kindness'). These last, indeed, betray the weakness of Susan Ferrier's style, which is derivative and second-hand, lacking a direct engagement with a lively intelligence and a constantly vigilant habit of self-criticism.

[2] Quoted by M. Sackville in her introduction to the Holyrood edition of the novel (1929) v.

One further instance from *The Inheritance* will be sufficient. Miss Pratt is a Scots version of Miss Bates, her speech being clearly modelled on the latter; yet, although it has a certain vivacity, it altogether lacks the quality which makes Miss Bates's long monologues at once incoherent and intelligible, irrelevant and informative:

'Just take that back,' said she to the servant, 'with my compliments to Colonel Delmour, and I'll be obliged to him for a wing. Colonel, don't you know it's the fashion now, when you help game or poultry, to ask: "Pray, do you run or fly?" meaning "Do you choose leg or wing?" There was a good scene at Anthony Whyte's. One day fat Lady Puffendorf was there—you know she's so asthmatic she can hardly walk—so when she chose chicken, "Pray, ma'am," says Anthony, "do you run or fly?" Of course a fine titter ran round the company. Lord Rossville, did you hear that? Colonel Delmour, remember I fly.'

Susan Ferrier has given us eccentricity without any of the linguistic originality of Miss Bates's highly individual mode of speech. The interest of such passages as the one quoted lies in the substance of the anecdote itself, rather than in any experimental or unusual quality of style.

What can be said, turning from Jane Austen's contemporaries to her successors, of her contribution to the tradition of fiction in England, and specifically to stylistic traditions? It is more than twenty years since F. R. Leavis gave her one of the very few available places in 'the great tradition',[3] and her status as a novelist has risen steadily since then. Major status in a writer often (though not necessarily) implies a powerful influence on subsequent practitioners; but of *direct* stylistic influence and imitation we cannot expect to find very much beyond her own generation. The reason for this is to be found in the fact that she employed with exceptional sensitiveness an idiom, and especially a vocabulary, that did not long survive her. The words themselves remained, of course; but, as an earlier chapter has tried to show,

[3] F. R. Leavis, *The Great Tradition* (1948) 1.

they quickly lost their force and weight. Jane Austen used an idiom that was certainly not archaic in her time, but which she was probably the last major writer to use; and certainly, in the twenty years between *Persuasion* and *Pickwick*, it changed with extraordinary rapidity. Dickens' first novel both exploits and parodies the formal prose that was evidently still a recognizable style, but had by then become for the most part an absurdly blunt instrument. (Apart from the personal differences between the two writers, these were twenty years of political and social upheaval which went a long way towards transforming English society as well as the English landscape.) We do not find imitators of Jane Austen, therefore, because changes in the language, now more rapid than in earlier, more settled periods, soon made imitation (except as conscious pastiche or parody) impossible.

Nevertheless, an important strand of Victorian and post-Victorian fiction can be seen to owe something to Jane Austen's influence. Most notably in the dialogue given to her characters, whether consciously witty and ironic, or unconsciously self-revealing, she initiates a tradition of sharply-observed domestic comedy in the novel that can be traced through, *inter alia*, Mrs Gaskell and George Eliot to E. M. Forster and Ivy Compton-Burnett. A few examples will suggest that this claim is not an extravagant one. Although, among Mrs Gaskell's novels, it is *Cranford* (1853) which, superficially at least, may seem closest to the Jane Austen world, her last and finest novel, *Wives and Daughters* (1866), also shows this influence. Mrs Gibson, the snobbish and self-centred stepmother of the heroine Molly, is a portrait very much in Jane Austen's characteristic vein of quiet but devastating satire. When she complains of the rigours of night-nursing, we seem to hear the voice of Mary Musgrove in *Persuasion*: '. . . nursing her as I have been, daily, and almost nightly; for I have been wakened, times out of number, by Mr Gibson getting up, and going to see if she had had her medicine properly'.[4] Mrs Gibson is also acutely conscious of social status, and displays an anxious concern for what she imagines to be

[4] L. Lerner quotes this passage, and comments that 'This is pure Jane

'correctness' in speech which is the mark of the socially insecure: she objects to 'such vulgar expressions' as 'Sunday best' and 'the apple of his eye', and tells her daughter that ' "All proverbs are vulgar" '. It is as if Mrs Elton in *Emma* had undergone an increase in linguistic self-awareness. Yet the half-century since Jane Austen's death has wrought a significant change: whereas 'correctness' was in her time still a meaningful concept which could be related to the manners of a reasonably homogeneous social class, by the 1860s it has become 'a matter of convention and appearance rather than of conduct and character',[5] a shallow and artificial 'refinement' having replaced a genuine and disinterested concern for standards. Whereas Mrs Elton's linguistic offences are an accurate index to her character, Mrs Gibson has acquired a delicacy which may deceive the unwary but is only skin-deep; beneath the surface, she is as vulgarly snobbish and selfishly materialistic as Mrs Elton.

George Eliot's debt to the tradition of ironic comedy and character-revelation which Jane Austen was largely instrumental in creating can also be traced most plainly in her dialogue, particularly in the informal conversations between women. A case in point is the scene between Dorothea and Celia Brooke in the opening chapter of *Middlemarch* (1872), in which the sisters reveal their different natures in the process of looking over their dead mother's jewellery. The passage seems to owe something to *Sense and Sensibility* and to the presentation in that novel of two sisters with contrasting temperaments. Dorothea, like Elinor, is serious, even priggish, and somewhat damping towards her more artless and ardent sister; and just as Elinor can respond to Marianne's enthusiasm for the beauties of autumn with the observation that ' "It is not every one . . . who has your passion for dead leaves" ', Dorothea tells Celia, in a tone which carries a

---

Austen', in his introduction to the Penguin English Library edition of *Wives and Daughters* (1969) 8.

    [5] A. Pollard, *Mrs Gaskell, Novelist and Biographer* (Manchester, 1965) 238.

similar assumption of superiority, that ' "Souls have complexions too: what will suit one will not suit another" '.

In the twentieth century, for all the differences in social range and setting, E. M. Forster's novels continue the tradition of realistic and self-revealing dialogue and ironic comment. Forster, like a more recent portrayer of the middle-class English scene, Angus Wilson, made no secret of his admiration for Jane Austen. Ivy Compton-Burnett, writing about a social class which, in Edwardian rather than Regency times, is surprisingly close to that depicted by Jane Austen, offers more obvious parallels. Taking as her province the inherent comedy and drama of family life and personal relationships, she again shows the influence very markedly in the witty and pointed dialogue which has already been referred to in connection with *Pride and Prejudice*.[6]

Most nineteenth-century novelists, however, developed areas of style which Jane Austen did not choose, or was not able, to utilize; and to look at their prose, even at passages which have a superficial affinity with her work in theme and tone, is to become aware of how drastically in some respects the language had changed in a short time. Thackeray's *Vanity Fair* (1848) appeared only a generation after her death, and Thackeray himself is often regarded as having a significant relationship to the eighteenth century, but we are already in a different world of sensibility and, consequently, of style. Its heroine, Becky Sharp, is a 'new woman', ready to make her way in a society *ouverte aux talents* in a way that would have been unthinkable in the still stable and hierarchical world of which Jane Austen writes. The nearest she gets to a character like Becky is perhaps Mary Crawford of *Mansfield Park*, but Mary's unconventionality is not only condemned, it remains unfulfilled: whereas Becky can

[6] D. W. Jefferson points out that Ivy Compton-Burnett inherits Jane Austen's 'tradition of literary and social manners' ('A Note on Ivy Compton-Burnett, *A Review of English Literature*, 1, 2 (1960) 20). M. Pittock analyses the characteristics of a passage of dialogue from *Elders and Betters* in 'Ivy Compton-Burnett's Use of Dialogue', *English Studies* 51 (1970) 43–6.

O

express her scorn for convention and decorum in acts of defiance, Mary has to satisfy herself in speaking and letter-writing. Or, to evoke another comparison, *Vanity Fair* might have borne some resemblance to *Emma* if the heroine of the latter had been a much cleverer and more unscrupulous Harriet Smith. The curious thing, of course, is that Thackeray is writing a historical novel set in Jane Austen's own period: 'While the present century was in its teens . . .' are its opening words. Yet while she was writing about a rural squirearchy which had long endured but whose days were numbered, Thackeray, using a largely metropolitan setting, is picturing the new era which was emerging even during her lifetime. While she emphasizes stability, he is concerned with describing the effects of change; and the difference has certain obvious stylistic correlates.

The following passage from early in the novel (Chapter 3) is not by any means remote from Jane Austen in subject-matter, but it could not have been written by her. This much is evident on stylistic grounds, and it is worth inquiring why this should be so:

If Miss Rebecca Sharp had determined in her heart upon making the conquest of this big beau, I don't think, ladies, we have any right to blame her; for though the task of husband-hunting is generally, and with becoming modesty, entrusted by young persons to their mammas, recollect that Miss Sharp had no kind parent to arrange these delicate matters for her, and that if she did not get a husband for herself, there was no one else in the wide world who would take the trouble off her hands. What causes young people to 'come *out*', but the noble ambition of matrimony? What sends them trooping to watering-places? What keeps them dancing till five o'clock in the morning through a whole mortal season? What causes them to labour at pianoforte sonatas, and to learn four songs from a fashionable master at a guinea a lesson, and to play the harp if they have handsome arms and neat elbows, and to wear Lincoln Green toxophilite hats and feathers, but that they may bring down some 'desirable' young man with those killing bows and arrows of theirs? What causes respectable parents to take up their carpets, set their houses topsy-turvy, and spend a fifth of their year's income in ball suppers and iced champagne? Is it sheer love of

their species, and an unadulterated wish to see young people happy
and dancing? Psha! they want to marry their daughters . . .

One's first impression on reading such a passage may well be that
Thackeray has, compared with Jane Austen, a wider range
of lexical resources with a consequently greater possibility of
stylistic variety and inventiveness. On closer inspection, however,
it becomes apparent that, while making a point of satirizing
fashionable jargon (as in 'some "desirable" young man', with
its intrusive and over-insistent quotation marks), Thackeray himself has a fatal addiction to cliché, of which such phrases as
'the wide world', 'the whole mortal season' and 'love of their
species' are some of the most obvious examples. The occasional
striking phrase, represented here by 'Lincoln Green toxophilite
hats', seems intended to serve as a corrective to the triteness of
much of the prose, but is likely to suggest only affectation and a
somewhat desperate striving after originality. In the same way,
the celebrated Thackerayan irony takes the form of an almost
automatic use of words—*modesty*, *delicate*, *noble*—in contexts
where their normal significance is diminished almost to vanishing-
point. The disadvantage of such a device is that it disqualifies this
important area of vocabulary, the language of moral and ethical
judgement, from being used for serious purposes elsewhere.
The rhetorical questions, and the colloquial exclamations and
apostrophes, similarly seek to inject vigour, flexibility and variety
into a style which is deadened by the weight of cliché and the
mechanical ironic devices. They seem an inadequate compensa-
tion for the loss of that precision and control which are evident in
every paragraph that Jane Austen wrote.

By such contrasts one perceives the remarkable distinction of
her style. How can it be defined more positively? Nearly ninety
years ago, Mary Augusta Ward suggested that two of the
potential qualities of great works of literature are 'expansion'
and 'condensation'.[7] The former involves ambitious conceptions

[7] M. A. W(ard), 'Style and Miss Austen', *Macmillan's Magazine*, 51
(December 1884) 89–91.

executed on a large scale with energy and elaboration: it is the art
of Tolstoy and Balzac, and in the English novel it is perhaps
Dickens, with his panoramic visions of society, his stylistic versatility, and his passion for detail, who best exemplifies this quality.
In Jane Austen, according to Mrs Ward, it is not to be found:
'she is a small, thin classic'. One of her supreme merits, however,
is 'condensation', an economical, self-restrained quality of construction and expression in which there are no superfluities or
digressions, no padding or diffuseness, but in which every chapter
and paragraph, even every word and phrase, makes a calculated
contribution to the total meaning. The modern reader is not
likely to be prepared to endorse this nineteenth-century view of
Jane Austen without making some important qualifications, and
without claiming a place for her much higher than that assigned
by Mrs Ward. Her main contention, however, is acceptable and,
in relation to Jane Austen's style, helpful. In a 'condensed' style
language is likely to take on a density of meaning, a heightened
expressiveness; special effects such as humour or irony can be
created by only minute departures from a serious or literal norm.
Thus, whereas Dickens ensures that his intentions reach their
destination by emphasis and repetition (anaphora being one of
his favourite rhetorical devices), and Thackeray finds it necessary
to underline his ironies in a manner which deprives them of all
subtlety, Jane Austen often needs no more than an unexpected
phrase, an unfamiliar word-order, or a single word out of key
with its context, to signal her purpose. Such an expressive use of
variations implies a high degree of consistency in the style which
serves as their background, and herein lies the source of a twofold
possibility of misunderstanding. The danger with a consistent
style is that, superficially regarded, it can easily appear to lack
distinction and individuality; and delicately-manipulated devices
of variation can be overlooked on account of their very un-
obtrusiveness. To this the frequent failure of her style to win
adequate recognition must be attributed. Certainly, if style is
regarded as worthy of close attention only when it is markedly
eccentric or overtly experimental, like the prose of Pater or

Sir Thomas Browne, James Joyce or Virginia Woolf, then Jane
Austen is unlikely to make any very insistent claim for special
treatment. What her novels display is a consistently scrupulous
attention to verbal values, a sensitiveness to nuances of vocabulary and phrasing, and a flexibility of approach to syntax which
can combine the strengths of an inherited tradition with a
readiness for innovation. Furthermore, her achievements in the
writing of fictional dialogue go beyond anything that preceded
her in the English novel and are in themselves a major claim to
the attention of the student of style. All in all, by any definition
of style that is not unreasonably exclusive, these qualities are surely
sufficient to require us to regard her prose (that 'ordinary correct
English' of Chapman's phrase) as of unusual interest and distinction.

BIBLIOGRAPHY

What follows is in no sense a Jane Austen bibliography, nor are all the works listed directly related to her writings. I have confined myself to books and articles which bear on the topic of this study and have contributed to my own thinking about it. Works to which reference is made only incidentally in the foregoing pages have not been included. The best recent bibliography of Jane Austen is by B. C. Southam, in *The New Cambridge Bibliography of English Literature*, Volume III (1800–1900), ed. G. Watson (Cambridge, 1969) 692–700.

Works by Jane Austen
The Novels of Jane Austen, ed. R. W. Chapman, 5 vols., Third Edition (1932–34).
Minor Works, ed. R. W. Chapman (1954).
Jane Austen's Letters to her Sister Cassandra and Others, ed. R. W. Chapman, Second Edition (1952).

Books and Articles on Jane Austen
(i) *General*
J. E. Austen-Leigh, *A Memoir of Jane Austen* (1870).
W. & R. A. Austen-Leigh, *Jane Austen: Her Life and Letters* (1913).
H. S. Babb, *Jane Austen's Novels: the Fabric of Dialogue* (Ohio, 1962).
F. W. Bradbrook, 'Dr Johnson and Jane Austen', *Notes and Queries*, 205 (1960) 108–12.

Jane Austen and her Predecessors (Cambridge, 1966).

— 'Lord Chesterfield and Jane Austen', *Notes and Queries*, 203 (1958) 80–2.

— 'Style and Judgment in Jane Austen's Novels', *Cambridge Journal*, 4 (1951) 515–37.

— 'The Letters of Jane Austen', *Cambridge Journal*, 7 (1954) 259–76.

L. W. Brown, 'The Comic Conclusion in Jane Austen's Novels', *Publications of the Modern Language Association*, 84 (1969) 1582–7.

J. Cady & I. Watt, 'Jane Austen's Critics', *Critical Quarterly*, 5 (1963) 49–63.

R. W. Chapman, *Jane Austen: a Critical Bibliography*, Second Edition (Oxford, 1955).

— *Jane Austen: Facts and Problems* (Oxford, 1948).

— 'Jane Austen's Methods', *Times Literary Supplement*, no. 1047, 9 February 1922, 81–2.

D. J. Greene, 'Jane Austen and the Peerage', *Publications of the Modern Language Association*, 68 (1953) 1017–31.

C. Griffin, 'The Development of Realism in Jane Austen's Early Novels', *English Literary History*, 30 (1963) 36–52.

H. ten Harmsel, *Jane Austen: a Study in Fictional Conventions* (The Hague, 1964).

C. B. Hogan, 'Jane Austen and her Early Public', *Review of English Studies*, 1 (1950) 39–54.

A. B. Hopkins, 'Jane Austen the Critic', *Publications of the Modern Language Association*, 40 (1925) 398–425.

G. Hough, 'Narrative and Dialogue in Jane Austen', *Critical Quarterly*, 12 (1970) 201–29.

I. Jack, 'The Epistolary Element in Jane Austen', *English Studies Today*, Second Series, ed. G. A. Bonnard (Berne, 1961) 173–186.

M. Lascelles, *Jane Austen and her Art* (Oxford, 1939).

Q. D. Leavis, 'A Critical Theory of Jane Austen's Writings', *Scrutiny*, 10 (1941–2), 61–87, 114–42, 272–94; 12 (1944) 104–119.

L. Lerner, *The Truthtellers: Jane Austen, George Eliot, D. H. Lawrence* (1967).

C. S. Lewis, 'A Note on Jane Austen', *Essays in Criticism*, 4 (1954) 359–71.

A. W. Litz, *Jane Austen: a Study of her Artistic Development* (New York, 1965).

— '*The Loiterer*: a Reflection of Jane Austen's Early Environment', *Review of English Studies*, 12 (1961) 251–61.

M. Lochhead, 'Jane Austen and the Seven Deadly Sins', *Quarterly Review*, 305 (1967) 429–36.

N. Page, 'Jane Austen and "The Best Chosen Language" ', *Wascana Review*, 4, 2 (1969) 67–76.

— 'Standards of Excellence: Jane Austen's Language', *Review of English Literature*, 7 (1966) 91–8.

E. W. Parks, 'Jane Austen's Lure of the Next Chapter', *Nineteenth Century Fiction*, 7 (1952) 56–60.

G. Ryle, 'Jane Austen and the Moralists', *Oxford Review*, 1 (1966) 5–18.

M. Schorer, 'Fiction and the "Matrix of Analogy",' *Kenyon Review*, 11 (1949) 539–60.

N. Sherry, *Jane Austen* (1966).

B. C. Southam, 'Jane Austen and *Clarissa*', *Notes and Queries*, 208 (1963) 191–2 (see also a reply by E. E. Duncan-Jones, 350).

— *Jane Austen's Literary Manuscripts* (Oxford, 1964).

— (ed.), *Jane Austen: the Critical Heritage* (1968).

L. Trilling, 'A Portrait of Western Man', *Listener*, 49 (1953) 969–74.

[A. B. Walkley], 'Discoloured Words', *The Times*, 28 December 1921, 6.

M. A. W. (Mary Augusta Ward), 'Style and Miss Austen', *Macmillan's Magazine*, 51 (December 1884) 84–91.

I. Watt, *The Rise of the Novel* (1957).

— (ed.), *Jane Austen: a Collection of Critical Essays* (Englewood Cliffs, 1963).

A. H. Wright, *Jane Austen's Novels: a Study in Structure* (1953).

(ii) Individual Novels
Northanger Abbey
C. S. Emden, '*Northanger Abbey* Re-dated?', *Notes and Queries*, 195. (1950), 407–10.
J. K. Mathison, '*Northanger Abbey* and Jane Austen's Conception of the Value of Fiction', *English Literary History*, 24 (1957) 138–52.
C. J. Rawson, ' "Nice" and "Sentimental" ': a parallel between *Northanger Abbey* and Richardson's Correspondence', *Notes and Queries*, 209 (1964) 180.
K. Sørensen, 'Johnsonese in *Northanger Abbey*', *English Studies*, 50 (1969) 390–97.

Sense and Sensibility
C. Gillie, '*Sense and Sensibility*: an Assessment', *Essays in Criticism*, 9 (1959) 1–9.
Q. D. Leavis, Introduction to MacDonald Illustrated Classics edition of the novel (1958).
A. D. McKillop, 'The Context of *Sense and Sensibility*', *Rice Institute Pamphlets*, 44 (1957) 65–78.
K. C. Phillipps, 'Lucy Steele's English', *English Studies* (1969) lv–lxi.
J. M. S. Tompkins, '*Elinor and Marianne*', *Review of English Studies*, 16 (1940) 33–43.
I. Watt, Afterword to Harper's Modern Classics edition of the novel (New York, 1961).

Pride and Prejudice
R. A. Brower, 'Light, and Bright, and Sparkling: Irony and Fiction in *Pride and Prejudice*', in *The Fields of Light* (New York, 1951) 164–81.
S. Kliger, 'Jane Austen's *Pride and Prejudice* in the Eighteenth Century Mode', *University of Toronto Quarterly*, 16 (1947) 357–70.
M. Laski, 'Some Words from *Pride and Prejudice*', *Notes and Queries*, 205 (1960) 312.
E. E. Phare, 'Lydia Languish, Lydia Bennet, and Dr Fordyce's

Sermons', *Notes and Queries*, 209 (1964) 182–3 (see also reply by F. W. Bradbrook, 421–3).

D. Van Ghent, *The English Novel: Form and Function* (New York, 1953), 99–111.

Mansfield Park

F. W. Bradbrook, 'Sources of Jane Austen's Ideas about Nature in *Mansfield Park*', *Notes and Queries*, 206 (1961) 222–4.

Q. D. Leavis, Introduction to MacDonald Illustrated Classics edition of the novel (1957).

D. Lodge, 'The Vocabulary of *Mansfield Park*', *Language of Fiction* (1966) 94–113.

W. Reitzel, '*Mansfield Park* and *Lovers' Vows*', *Review of English Studies*, 9 (1933) 451–6.

S. Rosenfeld, 'Jane Austen and Private Theatricals', *Essays and Studies*, 15 (1962) 40–51.

L. Trilling, '*Mansfield Park*', *The Opposing Self* (New York, 1959) 206–30.

Emma

W. C. Booth, *The Rhetoric of Fiction* (Chicago, 1961) 243–65.

F. W. Bradbrook, *Jane Austen: Emma* (1961).

M. Bradbury, 'Jane Austen's *Emma*', *Critical Quarterly*, 4 (1962) 335–46.

J. F. Burrows, *Jane Austen's 'Emma'*, (Sydney, 1968).

W. J. Harvey, 'The Plot of *Emma*', *Essays in Criticism*, 17 (1967) 48–63.

E. N. Hayes, '*Emma*: a Dissenting Opinion', *Nineteenth Century Fiction*, 4 (1949) 1–20.

A. Kettle, *An Introduction to the English Novel* (1951), I, 86–98.

E. F. Shannon, Jr, '*Emma*: Character and Construction', *Publications of the Modern Language Association*, 71 (1956) 637–50.

L. Trilling, '*Emma*', *Encounter*, 8 (June 1957) 49–59.

Persuasion
A. Gomme, 'On Not Being Persuaded', *Essays in Criticism*, 16 (1966) 170–84.
N. Page, 'Categories of Speech in *Persuasion*', *Modern Language Review*, 64 (1969) 734–41.

Works on language, style, and literary history
B. H. Bronson, 'Personification Reconsidered', *English Literary History*, 14 (1947) 163–77.
J. Copley, *Shift of Meaning* (1961).
D. Crystal & D. Davy, *Investigating English Style* (1969).
D. Davie, *Purity of Diction in English Verse* (1952).
L. Glauser, *Die Erlebte Rede in Englischen Roman des 19. Jahrhunderts* (Bern, 1948).
I. A. Gordon, *The Movement of English Prose* (1966).
K. G. Hornbeak, *The Complete Letter-writer in English, 1568–1800* (Northampton, Mass., 1934).
S. A. Leonard, *The Doctrine of Correctness in English Usage, 1700–1800* (Madison, 1929).
C. S. Lewis, *Studies in Words* (1960).
D. Lodge, *Language of Fiction* (1966).
W. Matthews, 'Polite Speech in the Eighteenth Century', *English*, 1 (1937), 493–511.
— 'Some Eighteenth-Century Vulgarisms', *Review of English Studies*, 13 (1937) 307–25.
J. H. Neumann, 'Chesterfield and the Standard of Usage in English', *Modern Language Quarterly*, 7 (1946) 463–75.
E. Partridge, *Slang Today and Yesterday*, Third Edition (1950).
J. Platt, 'The Development of the English Colloquial idiom during the Eighteenth Century', *Review of English Studies*, 2 (1926) 70–81, 189–96.
R. Quirk, *The Use of English* (1962).
W. V. Reynolds, 'Johnson's Opinions on Prose Style', *Review of English Studies*, 9 (1933) 433–46.

— 'The Reception of Johnson's Prose Style', ibid., 11 (1935) 145–62.

J. Spencer (ed.), *Linguistics and Style* (1964).

J. Sutherland (ed.), *The Oxford Book of English Talk* (1953).

J. M. S. Tompkins, *The Popular Novel in England, 1770–1800* (1932).

S. Tucker, *Protean Shape: a Study in Eighteenth-century Vocabulary and Usage* (1967).

S. Ullmann, *Language and Style* (Oxford, 1964).

— 'Style and Personality', *Review of English Literature*, 6, 2 (1965) 21–31.

E. R. Wasserman, 'The Inherent Values of Eighteenth-century Personification', *Publications of the Modern Language Association*, 65 (1950) 435–63.

G. Watson (ed.), *Literary English since Shakespeare* (1970).

W. K. Wimsatt, Jr, *Philosophic Words: a Study of Style and Meaning in the Rambler and Dictionary of Samuel Johnson* (New Haven, 1948).

— *The Prose Style of Samuel Johnson* (New Haven, 1941).

H. C. Wyld, *A History of Modern Colloquial English*, Third Edition (Oxford, 1936).

INDEX

Addison, Joseph, 63, 107
Andrews, W. T., 86*n*
Austen, Cassandra, 3, 83, 169, 178
Austen, James, 83, 139
Austen, Jane, Works of:
  (1) NOVELS:
    Emma: 3, 7, 32, 35, 42–8, 49,
57–8, 59–60, 64–5, 66, 67, 68, 69,
70–1, 74, 75, 80, 82, 89, 90, 97,
99, 104–5, 107–9, 114, 117, 122,
124–5, 130, 136–8, 141–3, 151–3,
156, 157–8, 160, 161, 182, 184–5,
194
    Mansfield Park: 3, 34–42, 47,
64, 69, 74, 75, 76, 80–1, 88, 89,
90, 96–7, 99, 105–6, 109–10, 112–
113, 125–6, 139, 143–4, 150–1,
157, 158–61, 162–3, 180–82, 183,
184, 185, 193–4
    Northanger Abbey: 15–20, 30,
42, 47, 54, 59, 69, 77–8, 82, 92–4,
109*n*, 112, 118, 120–1, 124, 138,
140–1, 150, 153–4, 156–7, 171,
177–8
    Persuasion: 11–12, 48–53, 62,
69, 74, 75, 84–5, 90, 97, 99–102,
109, 125, 127–36, 138, 140–1,
163–5
    Pride and Prejudice: 24–34,
35–6, 38, 48, 66, 67, 72, 75, 80,
87, 88, 90, 103–4, 115, 118–19,
120, 121, 125, 144–45, 165–7, 174,
178, 185–6
    Sense and Sensibility: 20–4,
46, 47, 62, 64, 67–8, 69, 70, 71,
72, 73, 74–5, 76, 79–80, 94–6, 97,
106–7, 109–12, 119, 122–3, 138,

141, 145–7, 154–5, 158, 174–7,
178, 183
  (2) OTHER WRITINGS:
    Collections of Letters, A: 173
    Elinor and Marianne: 174, 178
    First Impressions: 178
    Lady Susan: 3, 109–10, 139,
173, 179–80
    Lesley Castle: 172–3, 180
    Letters: 34, 47, 59, 64, 75, 77,
114, 120, 169–71
    Love and Freindship: 13, 76,
92, 172, 179
    To the Memory of Mrs Lefroy:
54*n*
    Volume the First: 13, 64
    Watsons, The: 3
  (3) TOPICS DISCUSSED:
    alliteration, comic, 14
    ambiguity, use of, 15–19, 48
    chiasmus, 95
    chronology of writings, 3–5, 90
    clichés, 144, 155
    colloquialisms, 14, 149, 154,
170
    dialogue, 25–31, 33, 36, Chapter 4 *passim*
    dialogue, avoidance of, 33–4,
137–8
    direct speech, 27, 107, 120–1,
131
    dramatic elements, 25–8, 34,
117–18
    erlebte Rede: *see* free indirect
speech
    figurative language, 46, 152
    foreign phrases, 152

(3) TOPICS DISCUSSED–*Cont.*
 forms of address, 152
 free indirect speech, 107, 123–136
 French expressions, 14, 152
 indirect speech, 27, 121–2
 inner speech, 36–7, 131–3
 interior monologue: *see* inner speech
 key-words, 39–42, 54*n*, Chapter 2 *passim*
 letter-writing in the novels, 31–33, 52–3, Chapter 5 *passim*
 nonce-word, 47
 occupational dialects, 140–1
 oratio trimembris, 93, 99, 104, 109–11
 oxymoron, 29
 proverbial expressions, 29, 155–156
 punctuation, 50, 98, 120, 124, 126
 puns, 14, 46–7
 regional dialects, 141
 reported speech: *see* indirect speech
 similes, comic, 14
 slang, 149
 social dialects, 147–67
 'strong language', 46, 79
 style indirect libre: see free indirect speech
 syntax, 9, 14, 44, 49–52, 53, Chapter 3 *passim*, 134, 135, 187, 197
 vulgarisms, 148–9, 151
 zeugma, 14, 29
Austen-Leigh, J. E., 51, 54*n*

Babb, H. S., 2–3
Beattie, James, 149
Belinda, 82, 153*n*, 188
Bickerton, Derek, 86*n*
Black, F. G., 168*n*
Blackwood, William, 189
Blair, Hugh, 150
Bleak House, 73, 89, 163

Boswell, James, 63, 142
Bradbrook, Frank W., 15, 149*n*, 165*n*
British Critic, The, 115–16
Bronson, B. H., 56
Brontë, Charlotte, 84, 116
Brontë, Emily, 84, 100, 102
Brower, R. A., 25
Browne, Sir Thomas, 74
Bühler, W., 123*n*
Bulwer, Edward, 117
Burney, Fanny, 10, 82, 124, 128–9, 172, 174, 188
Byron, Lord, 88, 169

Cady, Joseph, 8*n*
Cecilia, 82
Chapin, C. F., 87*n*
Chapman, R. W., 3, 10, 51, 72, 152*n*, 197
Charade, 43
Chesterfield, Lord, 73*n*, 148*n*, 154, 155, 164–5
Clarissa, 107, 145*n*
Coleridge, S. T., 11, 12
Compton-Burnett, Ivy, 29, 191, 193
Conversation, 25–6
Corneille, Pierre, 55
Cowper, William, 81–2, 96
Crabb, G., 79
Craik, Wendy, 127*n*
Cranford, 191
Crystal, David, 117*n*

Davie, Donald, 87*n*
Davy, Derek, 117*n*
Dickens, Charles, 28, 57–8, 73, 84, 89, 100, 119, 124, 140, 145, 163, 191
Dodds, M. H., 176
Dombey and Son, 57–8, 140
Don Juan, 114
Draper, R. P., 86*n*

Edgeworth, Maria, 10, 82, 153, 188
Eliot, George, 57, 141, 191, 192–3
Emden, C. S., 3

Evelina, 82, 128–9, 174, 188

Familiar Letters, 173, 184
Ferrier, Susan, 189–90
Fielding, Henry, 55, 89, 120, 124, 141, 187
Forster, E. M., 191, 193
Freud, Sigmund, 8

Gaskell, Mrs., 191–2
Glauser, Lisa, 123n
Goldsmith, Oliver, 63
Gothic fiction, 16, 19, 92
Gray, Thomas, 63
Greene, D. J., 145n
Gregory, M. J., 119n, 123
Grose, Francis, 149

Harding, D. W., 8
Hardy, Thomas, 57, 141
Hayter, Alethea, 12
Heart of Midlothian, The, 28
Hemingway, Ernest, 98, 101, 107
Hogan, C. B., 8n, 116n
Hornbeak, K. G., 184n
Hough, Graham, 1
Hughes, L., 27n
Humphry Clinker, 186

Idler, The, 36, 60
Inchbald, Mrs., 10, 188
Inheritance, The, 189–90

Jack, Ian, 172, 182
James, Henry, 51, 54, 187
Jane Eyre, 116
Jefferson, D. W., 193n
Johnson, Samuel, 14, 15, 19, 52, 63, 67, 72, 74, 75, 81, 91, 92–4, 96–7, 100, 107, 142, 149, 184
Joseph Andrews, 89

Kafka, Franz, 8
Keats, John, 169
Kemble, Fanny, 116
Kettle, Arnold, 60, 65
Kipling, Rudyard, 8

Lascelles, Mary, 2, 46n, 140, 149
Lawrence, D. H., 8, 85–6, 160
Leavis, F. R., 9, 190
Leavis, Q. D., 3, 35n, 38–9, 180–1
Lennox, Charlotte, 188
Leonard, S. A., 150n
Lerner, Laurence, 50, 88, 191n
Leslie, James, 78
Lewes, G. H., 90
Lewis, C. S., 60, 81
Life of Johnson, 142
Little Dorrit, 100
Litz, A. Walton, 12, 83n
Lodge, David, 39
Loiterer, The, 83, 139

Macaulay, Lord, 140
Marx, Karl, 8
Middlemarch, 192–3
Milton, John, 63, 80
Monthly Review, The, 114
Mudrick, Marvin, 8
Murray, Lindley, 150
Mysteries of Udolpho, The, 77

Neumann, J. H., 155
Newman, John Henry, 8

Oaths, 153n
Our Mutual Friend, 28
Oxford Book of English Talk, The, 116
Oxford English Dictionary, The, 23, 68, 70, 72, 73, 74, 77, 141, 154, 170

Pamela, 175
Partridge, Eric, 149n
Pegge, Samuel, 149
Perkin, H., 147
personification, 54n, 56
Phillipps, K. C., 2, 150
Pickwick Papers, The, 124, 191
'picturesque, the', 23
Piozzi, Mrs., 78
Pittock, M., 193n
Platt, J., 154–5

Pollard, Arthur, 192n
Pope, Alexander, 72
Poppleton, G. H., 78

Quirk, Randolph, 117n, 123n

Radcliffe, Mrs., 10, 92
Rambler, The, 60, 96
Rawson, C. J., 77n
Read, Herbert, 102
Richardson, Samuel, 27n, 52, 77n, 92, 107n, 115, 119, 141, 145n, 169, 171–2, 173, 175, 184, 186, 187
Roderick Random, 140
Roget, P., 79
Romantic poetry, 11, 79, 80, 87
Rosenfeld, Sybil, 114n

Sackville, M., 189n
Saintsbury, George, 7–8, 84
Scott, Sir Walter, 11, 28, 60, 141
Shakespeare, William, 62, 145, 167
Sherburn, George, 27n
Siddons, Mrs., 114
Simpson, Richard, 8
Singer, G. F., 168n
Sir Charles Grandison, 107
Smith, A. H., 117n
Smollett, Tobias, 140, 186
Sons and Lovers, 85–6
Sørensen, K., 109n
Southam, B. C., 3, 8n, 63n, 114n, 145n, 174, 178
Sterne, Laurence, 50, 101, 169

Sutherland, James, 116
Synonymy, 78–9

Tanner, Tony, 98
Taylor, William, 79
Thackeray, W. M., 84, 193–5
Thompson, F. M. L., 89
Tompkins, J. M. S., 138, 168, 172n
Trilling, Lionel, 34, 35n
Trusler, J., 39, 78
Tucker, Susie, 72, 73, 75n
Twain, Mark, 8

Ullmann, Stephen, 55, 123n, 131

Vanity Fair, 193–5

Ward, M. A., 195–6
Watt, Ian, 1, 8n, 87n, 187
Waugh, Evelyn, 153
Westminster Review, 90
Whateley, Richard, 167
Wilson, Angus, 193
Wilson, Edmund, 61
Wilson, F. P., 62
Wimsatt, W. K., 91
Wives and Daughters, 191–2
Woolf, Virginia, 48–9, 91, 107
Wordsworth, William, 11, 68, 76, 88
Wright, Andrew H., 136
Wurzbach, Natalie, 168n
Wuthering Heights, 100, 102
Wyld, H. C., 116

Yule, G. U., 56